Advertising, Commercial Spaces and the Urban

Consumption and Public Life

Series Editors: Frank Trentmann and Richard Wilk

Titles include:

Mark Bevir and Frank Trentmann (*editors*)
GOVERNANCE, CITIZENS AND CONSUMERS
Agency and Resistance in Contemporary Politics

Magnus Boström and Mikael Klintman
ECO-STANDARDS, PRODUCT LABELLING AND GREEN CONSUMERISM

Jacqueline Botterill
CONSUMER CULTURE AND PERSONAL FINANCE
Money Goes to Market

Daniel Thomas Cook (*editor*)
LIVED EXPERIENCES OF PUBLIC CONSUMPTION
Encounters with Value in Marketplaces on Five Continents

Nick Couldry, Sonia Livingstone and Tim Markham
MEDIA CONSUMPTION AND PUBLIC ENGAGEMENT
Beyond the Presumption of Attention

Anne M. Cronin
ADVERTISING, COMMERCIAL SPACES AND THE URBAN

Amy E. Randall
THE SOVIET DREAM WORLD OF RETAIL TRADE AND
CONSUMPTION IN THE 1930s

Kate Soper, Martin Ryle and Lyn Thomas (*editors*)
THE POLITICS AND PLEASURES OF SHOPPING DIFFERENTLY
Better than Shopping

Kate Soper and Frank Trentman (*editors*)
CITIZENSHIP AND CONSUMPTION

Harold Wilhite
CONSUMPTION AND THE TRANSFORMATION OF EVERYDAY LIFE
A View from South India

Forthcoming:

Roberta Sassatelli
FITNESS CULTURE
Gyms and the Commercialisation of Discipline and Fun

Consumption and Public Life
Series Standing Order ISBN 978–1–4039–9983–2 Hardback
978–1–4039–9984–9 Paperback
(outside North America only)

You can receive future titles in this series as they are published by placing a standing order. Please contact your bookseller or, in case of difficulty, write to us at the address below with your name and address, the title of the series and the ISBN quoted above.

Customer Services Department, Macmillan Distribution Ltd, Houndmills, Basingstoke, Hampshire RG21 6XS, England.

Advertising, Commercial Spaces and the Urban

Anne M. Cronin
Lancaster University, UK

First published 2010 by
PALGRAVE MACMILLAN

Palgrave Macmillan in the UK is an imprint of Macmillan Publishers Limited, registered in England, company number 785998, of Houndmills, Basingstoke, Hampshire RG21 6XS.

Palgrave Macmillan in the US is a division of St Martin's Press LLC, 175 Fifth Avenue, New York, NY 10010.

Palgrave Macmillan is the global academic imprint of the above companies and has companies and representatives throughout the world.

Palgrave® and Macmillan® are registered trademarks in the United States, the United Kingdom, Europe and other countries.

ISBN: 978–0–230–21680–8 hardback

This book is printed on paper suitable for recycling and made from fully managed and sustained forest sources. Logging, pulping and manufacturing processes are expected to conform to the environmental regulations of the country of origin.

A catalogue record for this book is available from the British Library.

A catalog record for this book is available from the Library of Congress.

10 9 8 7 6 5 4 3 2 1
19 18 17 16 15 14 13 12 11 10

Printed and bound in Great Britain by
CPI Antony Rowe, Chippenham and Eastbourne

Contents

Illustrations

Acknowledgements

I would like to thank many people at Lancaster University and else-where who have offered various kinds of support and have read drafts of chapters. My thanks in particular to Becky Coleman, Tim Dant, Monica Degen, Anne-Marie Fortier, Bob Jessop, John Law, Adrian Mackenzie, Maureen McNeil, Paul Newnham, Celia Roberts, Andrew Sayer, Lucy Suchman, Elaine Swann and John Urry. The research that formed the basis of this book was supported by ESRC grant number RES 000221744.

Chapters 2, 3 and 4 were originally published as: Cronin (2008) 'Calculative spaces: cities, market relations and the commercial vital-ism of the advertising industry', *Environment and Planning A*, 40 (11): 2734–2750 (courtesy of Pion Limited, London); Cronin (2008) 'Mobility and market research: outdoor advertising and the commercial ontol-ogy of the city', *Mobilities*, 3 (1): 95–115 (courtesy of Taylor & Francis); Cronin (2006) 'Advertising and the metabolism of the city: urban spaces, commodity rhythms', *Environment and Planning D: Society and Space*, 24 (4): 615–632 (courtesy of Pion Limited, London). They appear here in revised, expanded form.

1
Introducing Commercial Spaces

Any encounter with television, the internet, or urban streetscapes would suggest that we are living in the age of advertising. But the ubiquity of advertising in the west has been the focus of comment for centuries and many have claimed theirs as the ultimate era of advertising. In 1758, Samuel Johnson reputedly said that 'ads are now so numerous that they are negligently perused', and that 'the trade of advertising is now so near to perfection that it is not easy to propose any improvement' (cited in Williams 1980: 172). Notwithstanding the hyperbole surrounding its power and scope certain characteristics of advertising can be identified, one of which is its long association with cities (see Wischermann and Shore 2000). Lewis Mumford (1945: 228) noted the significance of the growth of bureaucracy for urban development such that 'a new trinity dominated the metropolitan scene: finance, insurance, advertising'. Indeed, cities have been understood as agglomerations of people and commerce, and as sites of the centralisation of power as Mumford describes. But urban life was also thought to offer up city populations to the devices of the mass media, of which advertising was considered the most pernicious. Wirth (1964) describes how the changes to community wrought by urban capitalism resulted in the increasing significance of the media: 'it follows, too, that the masses of men in the city are subject to manipulation by symbols and stereotypes managed by individuals working from afar or operating invisibly behind the scenes through their control of the instruments of communication' (Wirth 1964: 82).

In parallel to such claims about advertising and its urban foothold, many argue that today is the age of commercialisation. But how should commercialisation be defined? Some have focused on privatisation, arguing that we are witnessing the emergence of a new spatial order

1

in which public and private interests are becoming blurred (Zukin 1991, 1995). Another related focus is the growth of entrepreneurialism and the birth of the neo-liberal 'entrepreneurial city' with its stress on competitiveness, public–private partnerships and the development of local economics based on service industries such as tourism and leisure (Harvey 1989). One element of this is place marketing, or the promotion of cities, but this in itself is not a new phenomenon. Mumford (1945: 230) remarked on the significance of 'the metropolis as advertisement' which aims 'to give the stamp of authenticity and value to the style of life that emanates from the metropolis'. But in a new context of neo-liberal entrepreneurialism, cities must compete with one another for investment and tourist revenue (Hall and Hubbard 1998; Judd and Fainstein 1999; Kearns and Philo 1993). Western cities have become more centred on leisure and consumption (Miles and Miles 2004; Stevenson 2003), and branding and architecture interface to produce 'brandscapes' (Klingmann 2007).

In the context of these debates, advertising's economic and ideological role comes into sharp focus and, equally, the visual aspect of cities takes on a new significance (Cronin and Hetherington 2008). Seen as one of the 'creative industries', advertising plays an important role in global, national, and urban economies (Hartley 2005; Lash and Urry 1994; Scott 2000). It is understood to be part of the 'knowledge economy', and as an economic, social, and spatial form it is seen as part of the clustering of assets, knowledge base, sources of innovation and cultural production that together form the contemporary western city (Amin 2000).

This book offers a micro-study of one aspect of the commercial character of contemporary cities: the outdoor advertising industry and the impact of its products on urban space. Drawing on an ethnographic study of the industry and photographic studies of advertising in cities in the UK and the USA, this book explores the nature of 'the commercial'. It analyses the relationship between commercial practices in the industry, especially research and promotion practices, and the production of urban space. And it explores the interface between the visual, the material, the spatial and the temporal, and reconceptualises advertising's role of mediation.

Advertising and the city

Several important studies have explored the history of outdoor advertising, some of which focus on its relationship to nineteenth century urban space. Accounts analyse how Euro-American cities have long been centres for consumption, discourses around commodities, and ideologies of the market. In eighteenth-century Europe, trade cards, shops signs and a more general emphasis on commodity display functioned as important forerunners of outdoor advertising (Berg and Clifford 1998; Coquery 2004; Scott 2004). And in the nineteenth century, outdoor advertising became a significant factor in creating a public space built around words and images (Henkin 1998). With the development of new printing technologies in the nineteenth century, advertising posters could be mass-produced at little cost, and by 1885, 522 billposter firms were operating in 447 British towns (Fraser 1981).

Advertising posters covered much of the available space in cities and new posters were pasted directly over the old ones creating a thick layer of peeling adverts on the sides of buildings (Fraser 1981). Indeed, outdoor urban advertising was a site for developing new promotional techniques for the industry as a whole, with London and Paris seen as the models for advertising innovation (Haas 2000). In Paris, large illuminated billboards were placed on top of buildings, generating much fascinated commentary at the time. In 1920s' Germany there was a commercial struggle for the distribution of illuminated city advertising space in which competing advertising companies carried out 'lightfests' at night consisting of grand displays of illuminated advertising (Segal 2000). This illumination of city space at night was an interesting new organisation of space and time, lighting up the evening sky with symbols of daytime consumption.[1]

But advertising also organised city space in other, more mundane ways. In nineteenth-century Paris, advertising subsidised public facilities, for example, companies constructed public urinals which were liberally covered in advertisements (Segal 2000). Buses were plastered in adverts and the streets were teeming with sandwich-board men and people distributing handbills. Advertisements were even projected onto public buildings by magic lanterns (Elliott 1962; Nevett 1982). Thus, for many years advertising has played a key role in the urban economy and in orienting the visual aspect of Euro-American cities. And despite major technological developments in many areas of the media and promotion during the twentieth and twenty-first centuries, advertising posters still remain central to outdoor advertising's repertoire of formats.

But this interest in the relationship between nineteenth-century outdoor advertising and urban space has not been carried through into studies of contemporary cities. The urban studies literature on today's cities takes account of consumption, but little work focuses on advertising. More generally, there appears to be a division in the urban literature between those studies which explore the political economy of cities and those which explore the representational aspects. Political and political economy studies focus on various forms of governance, globalisation, and international divisions of labour (e.g. Harvey 2001; Sassen 2001, 2006). And those studies which make any reference to advertising do so as part of a wider analysis of the economic impact of the culture or creative industries (Hartley 2005; Scott 2000).

Advertising's relationship to cities has more often been addressed in representational or cultural accounts, although most studies offer only a passing reference to it or subsume it within a general account of the visual culture of urban space. Walter Benjamin, for instance, remarks only briefly on the architectural quality and striking scale of urban advertising billboards, 'where toothpaste and cosmetics lie handy for giants' (1979: 89). In more recent urban studies, the visual aspect of cities has been the focus of considerable attention. Kevin Lynch's (1960) classic study highlighted the significance of individuals' mental imaging of urban space in their orientation around cities. This account of 'the image of the city' did not address the significance of advertising but placed an emphasis on visuality that was echoed in later studies, most notably that of Venturi, Scott Brown and Izenour (1972). This account encouraged architects and urban theorists alike to learn from the architecture of the commercial and to appreciate the complex interplay between the architecture of shops, hotels and casinos, and the illuminated signs and advertising billboards which lined the routes to and around these sites. The aim was to understand Las Vegas as 'a communication system' in which signs and symbols interface with buildings such that 'the graphic sign in space has become the architecture of this landscape' (Venturi et al. 1972: 9). In this new understanding of commercial urban spaces, illuminated signs and advertising billboards create the very fabric of place: 'if you take the signs away, there is no place' (Venturi et al. 1972: 12).

Later studies developed these insights into 'urban semiotics' with the aim of creating understandings of city spaces as sign systems (e.g. Gottdiener and Lagopoulos 1986). Like de Certeau's (1998) readings of cities and spaces, such accounts frame the urban as a kind of text which can be decoded or excavated to reveal the character of the city: 'the metropolis therefore lends itself to serve in textual terms as an object of research. It constitutes a series of spatial images – hieroglyphics – which can be deciphered in order to provide access to deeper underlying questions about society' (Leach 2002: 2). In this mode, some accounts developed Venturi et al.'s (1972) approach to buildings *as* advertisements (e.g. Crilley 1993). Here, architecture functions as a material–symbolic form oriented towards promoting particular policy strategies around private funding, aiding cities in their attempts to attract inward investment. In this context, 'buildings themselves are designed to "read" as gigantic outdoor advertisements' (Crilley 1993: 236).

Other accounts reject a strictly textual account in which the city dweller or, more often, the social analyst can interpret the city by reading its signs. Studies explore how 'the urban' intertwines with cultural forms such as cinema, producing particular ways of seeing and thinking (e.g. AlSayyad 2006; Clarke 1997; Donald 1999). Others attend to the visuality of urban spaces through the medium of photography, exploring how space is produced and is always in process (Liggett 2003). Some accounts explore how cities are constituted by flows of desires, dreams, ideas and advertising texts which form the material for the urban dream-work in which people engage (Pile 2005). In many of these analyses there is surprisingly little focus on outdoor advertising in cities. And when advertising is addressed, its impact tends to be seen as negative, or it is associated with the less wholesome aspects of cities. Borden, for instance, casts billboards as an urban scourge: 'not really buildings, not really here, they are simply a temporary covering, a mask across the face of the city at its most leprous. They hide a multitude of sins' (2000: 104). More generally, accounts of the representational or cultural aspects of the city attempt to link the sensory and the imaginative to the material; there is an insistence on the importance of the figuration of the urban in shaping people's material experience of cities (see Highmore 2005).

The analytic division of labour enacted by representational and political economy accounts of the city is not absolute. Sharon Zukin's analyses of cities attempt to draw together a political economy approach with an attention to the symbolic, the visual and the representational. Zukin (1991, 1995) argues that western cities now capitalise on culture in unprecedented ways using it explicitly as an economic base. In this trend, the 'symbolic economy' plays a significant role alongside the 'political economy' (centred on land, labour and capital). The symbolic economy is divided into two parallel productions systems: (1) the production of space ('with its synergy of capital investment and cultural meanings') and (2) the production of symbols (which 'constructs both a currency of commercial exchange and a language of social identity') (Zukin 1995: 24). Zukin's studies show how cities can foster and channel cultural and symbolic resources in order to create more robust urban

economies. But she also notes how that the visual or symbolic is significant in terms other than the strictly economic. She argues that cities
form 'a visual repertoire of culture' which she sees as a 'public language'
or vernacular (1995: 264). This is a suggestive point, but Zukin does not
develop it fully or explore the specificities of different aspects of such
a public language. She also seems to imply a distinction between the
economic co-option of the visual (where urban cultural resources are
mined for economic gain) and the public, civic function of an urban
visual culture (through which people make sense of urban life).

✳   My analysis will explore the ways in which the commercial, economic
aspects of advertising and cities are not distinct from the production of
visual vernaculars. I will argue that 'the commercial' and 'the representational' are far more nuanced and their interface far more complex
and open-ended than most urban analyses suggest. Equally, I argue that
advertising can be seen as a medium or as a mediator only if we expand
the scope of what such mediation may mean. Some studies analyse the
form and function of advertising in a particular medium – such as television or cinema – and assess advertising's impact on the development of
that medium (Gurevitch 2008; Williams 2003). More often, advertising
itself is understood as a medium that acts to translate and disseminate
capitalist ideals. In this mode, advertising is seen as active and ideo-
logically powerful (Goldman 1992; Goldman and Papson 1996, 2006).
It is imagined to mediate social ideals through a commercial lens, offering 'solutions' to the very 'problems' it sets up (Williamson 2000). Or it
is seen as a medium that creates its own (powerful) public language, an
'institutionalised system of commercial information' which constitutes
a 'major form of social communication' (Williams 1980: 170, 185).

In terms of form and economic impact, advertising appears to stand
between the commercial or economic (as a commercial stimulation of
consumption) and the cultural (as a producer of images, ideas, dreams).
Advertising might thus be imagined to mediate between 'culture' and
'economy'. But the analysis of my ethnographic material suggests no
simple categorical separation between the cultural and the economic.
Nor does it suggest a straightforward mingling of distinct 'cultural' and
'economic' aspects (see Amin and Thrift 2004). If we are to argue that
advertising affects forms of mediation, more care needs to be taken in
identifying such mediations and assessing their significance.

One way into exploring these diverse aspects of advertising practice
and form is a close attention to the *stories* that are involved in advertising production and advertising products. One such line of analysis
sees advertising as a mode of social communication (see Leiss, Kline,

Jhally and Botterill 2005; Williams 1980). Describing advertising, Sut Jhally argues that, 'this commercial discourse is the *ground* on which we live, the *space* in which we learn to think, the *lens* through which we come to understand the world that surrounds us' (2009: 418, emphasis in the original). Jhally argues that we must focus on the cultural role of advertising, paying attention to the values it shapes and the stories it tells. Analysing advertising's stories will tell us much about society: 'if human beings are essentially a story-telling species, then to study advertising is to examine the central story-telling mechanism of our society' (Jhally 2009: 218). The story-making character of advertising has been explored elsewhere, for instance in my analysis of how understandings of advertising, and advertising texts themselves, animate the relationship between people and things (Cronin 2004a).

But stories are complicated formations and their relationship to fiction and truth is not straightforward. In his 1963 analysis of the image culture of America, Daniel Boorstin cautioned against a simplistic denunciation of advertising as false and manipulative. Boorstin argued that advertising embodied a wider trend in US culture which placed the emphasis on 'credibility' rather than 'truth'. Advertising was the 'art of invention' which created neither seductive lies nor truth, but *verisimilitude*. Boorstin understood both advertising practitioners' and the general public's approach to advertising as 'less interested in whether something is a fact than in whether it is convenient that it should be believed' (1963: 215). Following this logic, Boorstin argued, we should redirect our attention from what people see as the 'peculiar lies' of advertising to its true power – the 'peculiar truths' that it circulates (Boorstin 1963: 216). These are stories about the shape of society and our relationship to goods and services – a strand of analysis taken up by Schudson (1993) in his account of advertising as 'capitalist realism' which trains people in the art of living in a capitalist mode.

This focus on story-telling reframes questions about advertising. It does not ask if advertisements truthfully represent society or consumer goods. An emphasis on story-making considers representation not as a (successful or deceptive) mirroring, but as a production, a process, and an ordering. Making a story involves creating a narrative order. But as John Law argues, 'representations are not just a necessary part of ordering. Rather, they are *ordering processes in their own right*' (1994: 26, emphasis in the original). This expanded sense of representation points to how advertising, and its relationship to urban space, might be said to represent (a particular moment in) capitalism. But advertising does not straightforwardly represent or signify the ideological power of capitalism; advertising is not a set of signs from which capitalism's form and trajectory can be 'read off'. Advertising represents capitalism in the sense that it is part of the wider processes of ordering, articulation, story-making and money-making. Together these constitute capitalism not as a structure, but a network of practices in which 'capitalism is "instantiated"' (Thrift 2005: 1).

As a story-making and representational practice, advertising performs one aspect of the market relations that in turn helps to form capitalism. These performances rework relationships, facilitate modes of articulation or visibility, and construct possibilities. I discuss how industry practitioners also tell stories about advertising, about their research practices, about target markets and urban spaces, and about research data. These are representations that order their commercial world – they act to structure and stabilise market relations between media owners, media agencies and clients and in this way facilitate profitable relationships. These stories are neither empirically verifiable nor simple fictions; they are 'peculiar truths' that open up the commercial world in surprising ways (see Chapters 2–4). I also examine the forms of story-making that advertising and its spatiality make available to people through perceptual practices and 'fabulation' (see Chapters 5–7). This is a form of embodied, practical, perceptual engagement that sees 'life', animation and openness in the social and natural world. It is a kind of representational activity, but one which extends beyond conventional understandings of textuality or signification. It creates an urban visual vernacular but not in the sense of a shared language.

These stories and story-making practices are now taking on a new significance with shifts in the form of capitalism and market relations. Markets are increasingly being understood as performed or practised rather than as given structures within which practices take place (Callon 1998; MacKenzie 2006; MacKenzie and Millo 2003; MacKenzie, Muniesa and Siu 2007). And flows or exchanges of knowledge are thought to organise these performative processes (Knorr Cetina and Bruegger 2002b). There is a parallel interest in examining how constituent elements of those markets are also practised or performed: analyses of financial markets explore 'how "abstract" or "virtual" assets are brought into being and made tradable' (MacKenzie 2007: 357).

These developments should be seen in the context of a new 'soft capitalism' (Thrift 2005: 11). This is a capitalism based on circulation, especially of forms of knowledge (LiPuma and Lee 2004). The circulation of these knowledges acts in a performative way to conjure capitalism into existence (Thrift 2005). It is a form of capitalism that involves 'a continual struggle to release new forms of representation that can capture how the world is...and new forms of surface that can define how space and time should turn up in that world' (Thrift 2005: 13). This capitalism is contingent and adaptive, and corporations need to 'surf the right side of the constant change that results' or risk failure (Thrift 2005: 3). The global financial crisis of 2007 onward shows the vulnerability of financial and market performances to radical meltdown. In the recent literature, markets and market relations are considered to be multilayered, flexible and fragile. And while market exchange can be said to be centrally important in capitalist societies, no one society is entirely organised around one form of that market exchange (Slater and Tonkiss 2001). Indeed, the nature and significance of markets is not self-evident: 'even if markets in some sense dominate, they do not themselves represent a single and homogeneous principle' (Slater and Tonkiss 2001: 199). What is being exchanged, and the nature of this exchange, may be shifting.

The story-making character of the circulation of knowledges in soft capitalism has implications for space and cities. There are important consonances between the characterisation of both this new capitalism and spatiality. Doreen Massey (2005) argues that space is processual, the product of interrelations and of heterogeneity. Space is the 'dimension of multiple trajectories, a simultaneity of stories-so-far' (Massey 2005: 24). In this context, new ways of apprehending and producing spatialities are emerging. Thrift (2004b: 584) argues that an intensification and proliferation of modes of thinking involving calculation, including the exercise of qualitative judgements and 'working with ambiguity', produces new forms of spaces. This calculativity may form a 'space-time background through an array of new co-ordinate systems' which may allow new forms of movement (Thrift 2004b: 596). These metrics and ways of mobilising them may create a new '"movement-space" which is relative rather than absolute – but which...relies on an absolute space for its existence' (Thrift 2004b: 597).

I explore how the metrics and practices of the outdoor advertising industry are meshed together into shifting story-making processes that perform market relationships. They hold those relationships together through time as a (fairly) stable, (partially) predictable and (often) profitable web of commercial relations. But these practices also perform urban spaces and I analyse what forms of spatiality, or 'stories-so-far', this enables. If the advertising industry and its textual products can be seen as ideological forms that shape ideas, dreams and spaces, then they do so in this expanded sense of representation and in the new context of soft capitalism.

Researching the outdoor advertising industry and urban space

A more detailed outline of the UK advertising industry is presented in Chapter 2. My concern here is to introduce some of the industry's key characteristics and reflect upon my processes of researching the industry's relationship to urban space. Outdoor or 'out of home' advertising chiefly comprises roadside billboards, panels in pedestrian zones, advertisements on buses, in train and underground stations, and on taxis (taxis covered in 'liveries', or 'wrapped' taxis, and on panels inside taxis). Such advertising sites are all oriented towards speaking to the largest number of potential consumers possible. And as the greatest density of people can be found in cities, this is where the vast majority of advertising panels are located.

As part of the 'knowledge economy', the outdoor advertising industry trades in spaces, ideas, research metrics, signs and images. The industry's key actors comprise media owning companies[2] (such as JCDecaux which owns advertising structures and rents out space on them), media agencies (which mediate between media owners and clients), and clients who wish to advertise. In order to sell advertising space, media owners research potential consumers (their spending power, consumption profiles, patterns of movement around cities) and city spaces (density of people, visually prominent locations, flows of movement). Media owners use this data to pitch their particular company's portfolio of sites to potential clients and also to promote outdoor as an advertising sector (which is in competition with larger sectors such as television). So while advertisements attempt to sell products and services to consumers, outdoor advertising companies attempt to sell urban spaces, routes and knowledge about potential consumers to companies wishing to advertise.

There are many forms of publicity in cities that do not originate from the mainstream advertising industry but nevertheless form part of the visual cityscape. Figure 1.1 shows an 'artisanal' ad for a music release that is created from plastic bags tied to railings.

This is a free form of advertising which uses the principles of 'buzz' marketing – creating word-of-mouth publicity and excitement – and whose cryptic text can be followed up on the internet. The same strategies may sometimes be used by the mainstream advertising industry to

Figure 1.1   An 'artisanal' street advertisement in London (author's photograph)

create an edgy, 'street' feel to particular advertising campaigns. I elected to research the products and practices of the industry rather than these marginal forms as I wished to explore ethnographically the industry's commercial and spatial practices in the context of shifts in capitalism. But non-standard advertisements and graffitied or 're-purposed' advertisements on billboards did form part of the context in which I explored outdoor adverts in the photographic element of the project.

The project comprised two parts: an ethnographic exploration of the UK outdoor advertising industry and a photographic study of two cities, Manchester (UK) and Detroit (USA). The ethnographic section involved spending time at the London central office of a major media owner specialising in transport advertising (on buses and in the London Underground) as well as special promotional events (e.g. promotional activities in parks). During this phase of the research I was given excellent access to the company's activities and I observed a wide range of everyday practices. These included: directors' strategy meetings (planning the next month's activities and considering challenges from competitors); group staff meetings to outline weekly activity plans; staff training sessions (e.g. training in how to present research data to media agencies and clients); meetings of a specialist research strategy team; meetings and discussions of the marketing team; brainstorming sessions of teams working on 'pitches' derived from briefs sent by potential clients; production of promotional pitches (for media agencies and for clients); accompanying direct sales representatives 'cold calling' on potential clients; accompanying media sales representatives pitching to media agencies; attending pitches from media agencies and research companies. In addition to observation, I conducted a range of in-depth, semi-structured interviews of 45–90 minutes with members of staff at the main ethnographic site. These interviews followed up on themes I saw emerging from my observation, such as the relationship between media agencies and clients. I also collected a large amount of electronic and print material from the company, particularly from its 'Knowledge Bank'. This included results of commissioned research projects and was used by practitioners as a resource when they put together pitches.

Alongside this detailed focus on one media owning company, I conducted a range of interviews with several other rival media owning companies. I also collected data and conducted in-depth interviews at media agencies, specialist poster companies, research companies that were used by the key media owning company in my study, and industry trade bodies. These industry bodies were the Outdoor Advertising Association, the Institute for Practitioners in Advertising (with a specialist Outdoor section), the Advertising Standards Authority (the regulatory body) and POSTAR (an industry body that produces data on the number of people passing every advertising panel in the country, and which grades the visibility of those panels according to a range of criteria). This range of ethnographic practices produced rich data. It enabled me to track the circulation of industry research data and analyse how the relationships between the different organisations impacted upon the production of understandings of space and potential consumers.

The photographic section of the project comprised studies of Manchester and Detroit which explored the visual and material character of advertising texts and their physical structures (e.g. billboard panels, advertising kiosks). I paid attention to how advertisements and their structures interfaced with their urban surroundings. I attempted to cover all areas of the city where advertisements appeared but did not want to restrict myself to a rigid mapping of space. Instead, I remained open to what I found and adjusted my analytic emphasis as the photographic studies progressed. During this process, I noticed that I was taking, and later using, the photographs in a range of ways. They acted as documentary evidence – *this* advertisement, on *this* type of panel, appeared in *this* location. The shots I selected also functioned as exemplars – of a particular theme, of specific locations, of certain structures. Sometimes the shots focused on a specific textual content, sometimes on striking juxtapositions of advertising text, location or material form. Sometimes my practices were oriented more by a creative urge to capture a 'great shot' with striking aesthetics that I thought spoke of advertising or of the city in particular ways. I saw this as my own conversation with urban space as I was coming to understand it.

As the project progressed I gradually became aware of the interdependence of these different photographic practices. The photographic process and my analysis of the resulting archive of photographs became a way of representing advertising and representing the city – I used my photographic practices to do the work of connecting, relating, and performing meanings. In her photographic study of urban spaces, Helen Liggett suggests that 'when used to make connections to the city, the camera is not an instrument of representation; it is a way of making space and attracting meanings' (2003: 120). This active, processual character of engaging with and performing spaces was certainly evident in my own practices. But my study also aimed to connect and articulate the photographic element with the ethnographic data about the industry. The process of thinking these different elements and producing academic narratives about them was far from neat. The writer Georges Perec describes his thinking and writing process as one of classification, but a form of classification that refuses to stabilise or 'make sense' in any coherent way:

> My problem with classifications is that they don't last; hardly have I finished putting things into an order before that order is obsolete.... The outcome of all this leads to some truly strange categories. A folder full of miscellaneous papers, for example, on which is written 'to be classified'; or a drawer labelled 'Urgent 1' with nothing in it (in the drawer labelled 'Urgent 2' there are a few old photographs, in 'Urgent 3' some new exercise-books). In short, I muddle along. (Perec 1999: 196)

This may offer an accurate view of the sense-making activities of many a qualitative research project, although the contingent character of these practices is generally rendered invisible in the final narrative. Perec's account also offers insights into the *material* practices of thinking and writing, and points to how ordering is a central, if fluid, part of these processes.

In the practices of analysing my various forms of material there emerged a range of stories. What also emerged was the significance of representation and story-making practices in the industry and in advertising's relationship to the urban. These were spatial practices that oriented around an expanded sense of 'representation'. I came to understand how the industry's commercial practices of research and promotion folded data about 'consumers' and spatial practices back into the location of advertising panels and the text of advertisements. As I describe in the chapter outline below, this shifted the analysis away from a strictly 'textual' assessment of the content of advertisements to an analysis that paid attention to relationalities, connections, tensions and performances.

The structure of the book

The first half of the book explores the commercial practices of the outdoor advertising industry in the UK, drawing on the data gathered in my ethnographic research. Chapter 2 situates the industry's commercial knowledge production and marketing practices within debates about the 'new knowledge economy'. This is understood as design-intensive, centring on the production of signs and the trade in information (Lash and Urry 1994; Leadbetter 1999). Creativity, commodities and innovation are central to this knowledge economy, or what Thrift calls 'the cultural circuit of capitalism' (2005: 6). The chapter uses these debates on the performative nature of contemporary capitalism to frame my analysis of how cities are calculated and performed by commercial knowledge practices. These practices not only map but actively enact city spaces while marking them with images, brands and material structures. I analyse how practitioners imagine their research practices, the resultant research data, and market relationships between media owners, media agencies and clients as flexible and full of 'commercial energy'. These vital, calculative understandings are folded back into practices of locating and selling advertising space, and act to animate urban space. These spatialities are temporalised in complex ways as the industry attempts to work into and capture commercial futures.

Chapter 3 expands this emphasis on knowledge practices by examining a key focus the industry's research – mobility (of people, transport systems, and of urban spaces themselves). It begins by outlining the long-standing academic interest in movement, mobility and city space. This includes classic analyses such as those of Simmel (1995), Benjamin (1979, 1999), Park, Burgess and McKenzie (1968 [1925]), and more recent analyses such as those of Sennett (1992, 1994), Appleyard, Lynch and Myer (1966), and Venturi, Scott Brown and Izenour (1977). The chapter contrasts these academic understandings with the forms of understanding produced by the industry's market research. These conceive urban space *as movement*. They do not imagine the city as a bounded geographic entity, but as moments of potential visual encounter between consumers and advertising sites. Companies' research project design emphasizes mobility as a 'new segmentation' that supplements conventional marketing classifications such as socio-economic class. Some projects conceive of an urban 'mobile mindset' which predisposes people to search out new products and be open to spontaneous purchasing; in other projects people's movement in urban space is refined to an idea of *mobility as attention*. These conceptualisations are used as promotional tools to persuade potential clients to use outdoor rather than broadcast or press advertising. They operate in performative feedback loops, folding ideas back into practices and spaces. This creates a commercial ontology of the city based on mobility, as well as a commercial aesthetics of mobility that orients the size and style of advertising structures and their textual content.

In Chapters 2 and 3, therefore, the commercial relationships between elements of the industry are analysed in relation to their research practices. But these relationships have some unexpected outcomes: the industry's knowledge practices create possibilities for those who move through urban space to know that space differently. Chapter 4 further explores both the generative power of industry practices and the unintended possibilities they open up. It focuses on a particular set of urban movements that are created by the industry's practices – commercial or commodity rhythms. There has been a recent intensification of interest in Henri Lefebvre's (1991, 1992) concept of urban rhythms and what accounts of cities a 'rhythmanalysis' can offer. But no attention has been paid to the commercial rhythms of outdoor advertising that mark urban space in subtle and ambiguous ways. The chapter analyses the multiple ways in which advertising institutes urban rhythms. It assesses how the practices of posting new advertising in standard 2-week cycles creates commercial rhythms that naturalise consumer capitalism's cycle of innovation and promotion. I explore how a 'commercial rhythmanalysis' can offer a novel framework for analysing the visual and commercial economies of cities. I analyse how the industry establishes a time–space of 'commodity rhythms' that attunes people to the rhythms of commercial innovation and promotion, and links peoples' embodied, biographical movements in the city with the 'biographies' of commodities. This highlights how advertising's impact on cities goes beyond the potential commercial effects of individual campaigns, whether they are promoting specific commodities, brands or events. It also points to how advertising's significance extends beyond the textual content of specific advertisements.

So Chapters 2–4 explore how advertising sites, advertising sights, and industry research data link places. They do not merely map them, but actively perform them. Marketing knowledge practices effect a temporary holding together of people–space–movement that is accomplished by various creative interventions and is shaped by promotional imperatives. In these practices, the city is a 'commercial object' that is called into being. In parallel, media owning and research companies imagine society as a market and their market research effects certain commercial realities and spatialities. But spatiality is not passive. Multiple and sometimes conflicting spatial demands exert influence on the industry: media owning companies compete to dominate spaces but must ensure that the visual impact of their products does not overly antagonize the public or urban planners. The industry aims to populate all manner of city spaces, but this very ubiquity risks turning outdoor advertising into an unnoticed or disregarded 'urban wallpaper'. And in performing research practices, marketing practices, and maintaining commercial relationships, the industry finds that the urban is produced as open, flexible, and not necessarily amenable to its calculative and promotional practices.

The second half of the book explores my photographic studies in relation to material outlined above. These chapters take insights from debates in geography and elsewhere about non-representational theories, or what Lorimer (2005: 83) calls the 'more-than-representational'. As Dewsbury notes,

> the nonrepresentational argument comes into its own in asking us to revisit the performative space of representation in a manner that is more attuned to its fragile constitution … the project of nonrepresentational theory then, is to excavate the empty space between the lines of representational meaning in order to see what is also possible. (2003: 1911)

This more expansive account of the non/post/more-than-representational offers intriguing possibilities for *thinking together* the commercial practices of the industry and the photographic studies.

Chapter 5 further pursues the question of how urban space is mediated by outdoor advertising. The entry point in this chapter is a focus on the body and embodied perception. Many argue that urban space is experienced through the body (Lefebvre 1991; Sennett 1994) and that people's visual experience of cities is complex, situated, and sensorially multi-modal (Degen, DeSilvey and Rose 2008). So how should we understand people's experience of outdoor advertising? This chapter develops the theme of practice by conceiving perception as practice – a practice that in turn informs how spaces are performed. Using Henri Bergson's (2004, 2006) work on perception and fabulation, I reconceptualise advertising's work of mediation of urban space. I examine how this mediation is bodily and perceptual; I analyse how mediation operates materially (in bodily terms but also in terms of objects, structures and spatialities); I argue that such mediation is fundamentally temporal (it involves the processual quality of commercial practices and the temporalities of the city); and finally I argue that mediation is political (it articulates a politics of the possible and the imaginable). This approach emphasises how the reception or decoding of advertising texts is not the only, nor indeed the primary, significance of outdoor advertising. The material and spatial qualities of advertising structures are an important element in organising the urban perceptual field (see Figure 1.2). Here, I discuss how the relationship between the architecture of advertising and perceptual practices is spatially and temporally active and transformative.

Chapter 6 draws on the conceptual framework developed in Chapter 5 and presents an account of outdoor advertisements in Manchester (UK) and Detroit (USA). The aim is not to offer a direct comparative analysis, but rather to explore how the different socio-economic situations of cities are expressed in the spatio-temporality of outdoor advertising. Outdoor advertising companies can most easily secure permission to erect advertising panels in areas of cities that are either undergoing regeneration work, or that are derelict and unsightly. In these cases, advertising is considered to perform a useful function of screening the building work or zones of urban decay. By populating these areas, advertising performs a material, visual enactment of specific urban rhythms of regeneration and urban dereliction. In Figure 1.3, for instance, certain urban processes are made tangible in the visual consonance between the boarded-up, run-down building and the 'backstage' view of billboard.

In my account of Manchester and Detroit I explore the different ways in which advertising's presence, its structures, and its texts articulate spatio-temporalities of the urban. In Manchester, the advertising structures express a sense of economic buoyancy and positive momentum, whereas in Detroit the advertising structures express a sense of economic and social stagnation. Extending the previous chapters' work on perception and fabulation, Chapter 6 examines how these different

Figure 1.2 The spatial architecture of advertising (author's photograph)

enactments of space and time produce forms of urban vernacular. These visual vernaculars are embodied and *felt*; they provide the syntax for imagining cities both in the present tense and in potential futures.

Chapter 7 draws together the analyses of the book and reconsiders them through the prism of public space, commercialisation, the creation

Figure 1.3   The 'backstage' view of the urban (author's photograph)

of 'publics', and forms of public address. I explore Ash Amin's (2008: 8) argument that urban space holds (modest) collective promise, but that this promise is located in 'the entanglement between people and the material and visual culture of public space, rather than solely in the quality of social interaction between strangers'. Extending Zukin's (1995) comments on how visual cityscapes can function as a public language or vernacular, I engage with Amin's suggestive, if loose, account and offer an analysis of a particular commercial form of vernacular. I analyse how the outdoor industry's research and commercial practices interface with the production of advertising structures, spatialities and texts, and with people's perceptual, fabulatory practices. I explore how these elements interact to produce forms of 'publicness' such as public address, 'the public/s', and public spaces. One result of this is the production of an embodied form of visual, urban vernacular through which people make sense of their environment but which also offers people ways of comprehending and acting upon wider social forces and processes. It acts to open up 'the political' in an everyday, vernacular register.

2
The Industry and the City: Knowledge Practices as Commercial Experiments

This chapter explores the practices of the UK outdoor advertising industry and its relationship to urban space. Using my ethnographic material, I analyse how practitioners in the industry actively produce and maintain commercial relationships between media owners, media agencies and clients. The practices and circulation of marketing knowledges are centrally important in this nexus: commercial knowledge practices form a 'horizon of expectation that is itself constitutive' (Amin and Thrift 2004: xv). These knowledge practices are woven into spatial practices, for the industry works with, and aims to shape, urban spaces and people moving through those spaces. The resulting amalgam is performative, calculative and future-oriented.

In framing his analysis of the production of space, Henri Lefebvre remarks that scientific understandings of the material world have posited that energy, time and space must be neither conflated nor separated. But these understandings of materiality and physical energies that were developed in physics and astronomy, he argues, must not exclude 'social energies' by maintaining a distinction between ' "human" and physical fields of force' (1991: 14). In effect, 'space considered in isolation is an empty abstraction; likewise energy and time' (1991: 12). My concern in this chapter is to explore this relationship of energy–time–space in relation to the city and the market practices of the UK outdoor advertising industry using my ethnographic material. I argue that in this nexus of relationships, the energy that is held in a productive tension with time and space has a particular commercial character – or what I call a 'commercial vitalism' – that is closely linked to forms of calculation.

Many years ago Simmel noted the growing significance of calculation, particularly in relation to the metropolis, the seat of the money
economy:

> Modern mind [sic] has become more and more calculating. The cal-
> culative exactness of practical life which the money economy has
> brought about corresponds to the ideal of natural science: to trans-
> form the world into an arithmetic problem, to fix every part of the
> world by mathematical formulas. Only money economy has filled
> the days of so many people with weighing, calculating, with numer-
> ical determinations, with a reduction of qualitative values to quan-
> titative ones... the conditions of metropolitan life are at once cause
> and effect of this trait. (Simmel 1997: 177)

But more recently, calculation and measurement in relation to market
research and space have been understood rather more narrowly, predominantly in terms of the practices of classifying groups of people or
spaces using various geodemographic apparatuses. Such studies tend
to emphasise the apparent reach, power and ambition of marketing
and its associated knowledge practices. Goss, for instance, argues that
the spatial marketing technique of geodemographics aims to order
and manage diversity and is based on 'an instrumental rationality
that desires to bring the processes of consumption further under the
control of the regime of production' (1995: 172). In parallel, Gandy
(1993: 2) sees the contemporary emphasis on various forms of data
collection and ordering as a 'panoptic sort' which classifies people
according to their economic value and functions as 'an extension of
technical rationalization into the social realm of the consumer and
political behavior'. For Elmer (2004: 49), the 'everyday data economy'
is a powerful calculative formation in which geographical data are
used to create maps that simulate space–time relations which are
then deployed to govern consumption. Many accounts emphasise the
drive to classify, or what Lyon (2002: 3) calls the 'phenetic fix', and
attribute great power and scope to such classificatory practices and
technologies.

Such analyses broadly follow Weber's (1967) understanding of bureaucracy and rationalisation in which the generation of multiform
measurements, calculations and representations facilitates central control and order. Other accounts take a more Foucaultian approach to
spatiality, focusing on how various mappings have *produced* cities, their
early 'paper rationality' imagining cities as collectives entities (Joyce

2003: 55) and subjecting them to forms of governance (Osborne and Rose 1999). In such understandings,

> numbers and other 'inscription devices', actually constitute the domains they appear to represent; they render them representable in a docile form – a form amenable to the application of calculation and deliberation. (Rose 1999: 198)

The stress on the role of classification, and particularly marketing data, in producing and maintaining a social order is in part shaped by the fact that most accounts analyse the archives and technologies of production (databases etc.), and their products (maps, classificatory tables etc.). It is perhaps unsurprising that readings of these objects of research might emphasise their omniscience and power, mirroring the claims generated by the technologies' producers. But if we look at the articulation and performance of such ideals, technologies and products in the actual practices of marketing research we can see a more complex picture in which the status of that data is more ambiguous. As John Law reminds us, there are no orders but *orderings* and these are 'more or less precarious accomplishments that may be overturned' (1994: 1–2). Such orderings and classificatory schemes tend to take the form of representations such as maps but, as Bowker and Star (1999) note, they can take material as well as symbolic form and are embedded in a range of physical entities such as paper forms and software instructions encoded in silicon.

Yet such schemes, alongside a form of calculative drive, are also embedded in the commercial relationships between various actors in the field. Indeed, some accounts propose a more expansive view of calculation including processes of the classification (or 'qualification') of products and these practices' role in actively constituting markets (Callon, 1998). In my ethnographic work, there was ample evidence of commercial calculation in relation to the classification of people and products in the industry's market research practices. But what also emerged was a broader range of calculative actions – or 'commercial experiments' – that performed or enacted market relations between the various actors in the field. As the industry's product is, in effect, space – space on advertising billboards and panels – the performance of such practices is spatialised in ways that have yet to be fully examined in studies of the city. Recent accounts have sought to understand the constitution of cities by flows and rhythms of information (Castells 2000), of capital (Harvey 1989), of social relations (Lefebvre 1991), of emotions and affect (Pile 2005), of ruination and memories (Edensor 2005), of technologies (Thrift 2005), of images (Liggett 2003), and of networks of infrastructures (Graham and Marvin 2001). But far less attention has been directed at the production of urban space by the practices of marketing.[1] It is this nexus of commercial energy–time–space that forms the focus of this chapter.

After describing the nature of the UK's outdoor advertising industry, the first section of this chapter explores the industry's conceptualisation of urban space and its relation to the media owners' products (space on outdoor advertising sites). The second section examines the nature of the commercial experiments that enact the field of the outdoor advertising industry. The chapter then goes on to explore the calculative energies or apparent commercial vitalism in the market research practices of the industry. I conclude by arguing that these market research practices produce not only demographic classifications of people and spaces (or more precisely, taxonomies of 'people-and-space') and actively constitute a specific set of market relationships, but also perform the city as 'calculative space'.

The industry and the city

A specialist sub-field of advertising, the outdoor advertising industry trades in producing and selling spaces on which to advertise outdoors (or 'out of home'). The categories of outdoor advertising outlined in the first chapter accounted for only 5.5% of all advertising spend in the UK in 2008.[2] But their commercial impact is arguably disproportionately large in relation to this figure. An advertising practitioner described the standard industry view on this:

> Basically, if you want to build a brand, posters are the strongest medium. They can be seen everywhere, they're impactful, they make you look big. People might miss a TV ad, but if they're driving in [to a city] on the same arterial routes every day, they won't miss a poster. And you can do it quite cheaply. You can just take six arterial routes and have a poster on each of them and everyone thinks that they've seen the biggest brand around. (director, advertising agency)[3]

Indeed, media owners of outdoor advertising sites promote it as one of the few ways to reach a mass market in today's context of the fragmentation of media and audiences.

Media owners such as JCDecaux, Clear Channel Outdoor, CBS Outdoor (formerly Viacom), Titan and Primesight construct and maintain poster sites. The sites for outdoor advertising panels and billboards are classified according to a range of criteria, valued and then sold in stretches of time to clients wishing to advertise (usually via advertising agencies). The category known as 'outdoor advertising' comprises primarily billboards (e.g. roadside) and posters (e.g. on panels at bus shelters, or on free-standing panels in pedestrian or shopping zones). Other cognate categories are 'transport advertising' (including advertisements on the side of buses and taxis, next to train lines and inside trains) and 'ambient advertising' (including advertisements on telephone kiosks, beer mats, petrol pump nozzles, in public toilets and on the floor of shops).

Media owners also have contracts with local councils whereby they construct and maintain bus shelters or other amenities in return for the right to sell advertising space on them. They sell space to clients via the intermediaries of media agencies or specialist poster companies such as Posterscope and Kinetic which assess the client's needs and buy a suitable package of advertising space from the media owners. Market research companies are commissioned by media owners to produce data to use as a pitch to help them sell space or to assess a campaign's impact after it has been posted.

Research and calculation play a central role in this nexus of relationships between media owners, media agencies and clients. To promote their assets, media owners commission market research companies to produce data on the benefits of the types of sites they hold and the people or 'target markets' likely to view those sites. As I will explore, the data produced by these research projects are not necessarily viewed by its practitioners as accurate or 'true'. Instead, the generation and circulation of marketing data forms an agreed currency: media owners continually generate 'pitches' in PowerPoint presentation form containing various types of market research data. These are presented to representatives of media agencies or specialist poster agencies (or, more rarely, directly to client firms) in face-to-face meetings. These pitches aim to persuade potential clients that outdoor advertising is an excellent promotional medium or that a media owner's particular portfolio of sites – perhaps the London Underground train system or large poster sites in petrol station forecourts – are best placed to target a particular audience. Media agencies take the PowerPoint presentations with their data-rich content and segment and reconstruct them, and then use them to pitch to clients who may wish to advertise. Indeed, all project findings are presented by the industry in ways which integrate a pitch – they are all oriented towards persuading media agencies and clients of the value of using a particular company's services.

These pitches' statements about the effectiveness of advertising and the flows of potential consumers moving into and around cities may be heavily criticised in terms of methodological rigour and validity. Indeed, the generation of these knowledge-claims must be seen as part of a self-promotional imperative in a highly competitive arena (Cronin 2004 b, c; Grabher 2002; Lury and Warde 1997; Miller 1997; Nixon 2003; Schudson 1993; Slater 1989; Tunstall 1964). Outdoor advertising companies must first persuade potential clients that advertising is the best way to spend their marketing budget. Then they must compete with other outdoor companies by claiming that they own the best-placed sites and deploy the most efficient measuring and targeting strategies.

But although the validity and reliability of these research practices and resulting data are viewed even within the industry as suspect, they function efficiently as an industry currency. They play a key role in producing and maintaining commercial relationships between media owners, media agencies and clients. And data can be used as a decision-support technology, a post-rationalisation, or an alibi for commercial decisions. As all parties in the industry agree to the system, this use of data 'stitches together' these market relationships enabling them to function smoothly (see Cronin 2004 b, c). As I go on to argue, the specific character of this market is produced and reproduced by the performances of commercial relationships between these actors. In doing so, they enact both these market relations and a set of conceptualisations of urban space.

Odih and Knights (2000: 79) have argued that marketing knowledges have 'an unproblematic allegiance to positivist methods within an empiricist epistemology' and that,

> It is axiomatic to this form of epistemology that 'time' and 'space' should be ascribed the characteristics of abstract, quantifiable, singular units... 'Time' and 'space' are conceptualised as existing externally to the individual, in fixed rationally co-ordinated spheres. (Odih and Knights 2000: 79)

While this view may be represent academic marketing discourses, this description jars with what I observed of the outdoor advertising industry's calculative knowledge practices. Despite the nature of their product – outdoor advertising sites that are almost exclusively situated in or on key approaches to cities – 'the city' as a conceptual zone does not exist in the industry's repertoire of understandings. As an industry spokesman explained to me, 'there is no interest in [the city as an] environment whatsoever. They're interested in the numbers of people. The fact is that the numbers of people [just happen to be] in places called cities.'

This loose conceptualisation of spatiality was illustrated in the study time and again. Cities were understood not as fixed arrangements of specific locations but as spaces and times of *density* – densities of people which could be translated by market research's classificatory practices into 'target markets'. The busy urban road, the pedestrian shopping zone, the sides of buildings, buses moving along commuter routes, all figure in the industry's understandings and mapping techniques but not as cartographically determinate sites in a city. They are framed and quantified as time–spaces through a standard industry taxonomy which includes the metrics of 'Opportunity to See' and 'Visibility Adjusted Contacts'. This taxonomy frames the classification of each advertising site according to the number of people who may see it (the density of visual contacts). The field of orientation used by the industry focuses on core themes: centrality (the density of flows of people in and around a city centre will generate an intensity of 'hits'); positioning in relation to flows of people (busy commuter routes will deliver large numbers of hits); scale (size is understood to translate into 'impactful' advertising and generates a range of its own classifications such as 'super-sides' and 'mega-rears' in advertising on buses); contingent proximities (high street shops often advertise on the sides of buses which operate as mobile billboards travelling through commercial centres).

This is not a classic planners' view of city space as a range of discrete sites located in determinate grids and networks. Space is understood only as the support surface or medium for moments of visual contact with potential consumers. Urban spaces come to exist as commercial realities only in the form of flexible resources, that is, as quantifiable moments of encounter with potential consumers moving in that space. These are translated and sold as opportunities for 'conversations' with consumers about products and services, or as chances for brands to inhabit people's lives by sharing their everyday space. In these senses, 'the city' as understood by social scientists is clearly the context for the industry's activities. These activities contribute in turn to producing urban space by impacting upon the imagescapes of cities, marking routes of densities of people and modes of transport, and producing and circulating market research about such spaces. But the nature of 'the city', a question so intensely debated in academia, does not feature as a point of reference for the industry. Only when prompted will industry practitioners even mention the city and then only as a category that is not relevant to their commercial practices. As a director of research explained,

> I've got panels at 450 of their supermarkets and a third of the UK population visit them, and one of Tesco's stores is 100,000 sq ft, it's a quarter of a mile long and it's got an iPod department store within it. Is that a city? (practitioner, media owning company)

So while much recent social theory has posited space as a product of social relations rather than as a neutral, empty container, this has for many years been a practical truism for the outdoor advertising industry. It understands space only and insofar as it relates to people inhabiting, moving in and acting upon it. Central to practitioner's understandings is the role of calculation. But space is not just where commercial calculation happens (the space of the organisation; the space of urban centres of the advertising industry) or the product of their marketing activities. It constitutes a productive nexus of energy–time–space, similar to Lefebvre's formation: 'though a *product* to be used, to be consumed, [social space] is also a *means of production*; networks of exchange and flows of raw materials and energy fashion space and are determined by it' (1991: 85, emphasis in the original). Space is understood and enacted in the industry as fluid, lived, contingent; what would be conventionally considered a city or urban space is understood and worked upon as a complex of energy–time–space. As I explore in the following section, this is enacted in the form of 'commercial experiments'.

Commercial experiments

In this section I draw on Thrift's understanding of performance as that which 'holds organizations together and pushes them on' and involves 'an ability to act convincingly into the situation that presents itself by taking whatever propensity for dynamism may be offered that is also a practical ethic of discovery and invention' (2006: 144). Within this broad framework of performances, I identify 'commercial experiments' in the advertising industry as a specific set of performances that are linked to calculation. Below I examine how practices of calculation – about the characteristics of potential consumers, about numbers of these consumers that can be reached and about fruitful commercial relationships between actors in the field – are experimental in a twofold fashion. Firstly, for media owners they constitute a continual process of trial and error to identify what forms of classification or which promotional pitches will have traction with particular clients at particular times. Such experiments are thus oriented towards making efficacious market relationships. These experiments are framed by the central issue of advertising's effects (although not, as we shall see, by a simple calculation of whether certain advertising will sell goods or services). Secondly, these performances are experimental in that they alter the elements involved in the calculative process as well as altering the process itself; they are alchemies of commercial spaces, times and energies. These are modes of production of space, in Lefebvre's terms, that enact complex relationships and produce some surprising results.

Market relationships between media owners, media agencies, research companies and client firms are continually performed and the maintenance of these relationships is carefully tended. For instance, despite having no immediate interest in a particular sales pitch, media owners will attend presentations by research companies which are promoting their new ideas, research data or targeting strategies. They do so in order to maintain the relationship for future collaborations. And in commercial relationships deemed productive, this courtesy is of course reciprocated. In the performance of market relations in my study, the marketing data and creative pitches that are continually produced and circulated function primarily to structure and maintain particular commercial relationships. Constituting more than a mere competition within a market, marketing is here a competition over the very structure of markets and the nature of market relations (see Slater 2002b). This performance of commercial relationships and its calculative nature revealed itself to be subtle and complex. It involved a currency of commercial knowledges in which classification and calculation (of potential consumers, of spaces they move in and of useful commercial relationships) formed an 'economy of qualities' (Callon, Méadel and Rabeharisoa 2002: 202) or nexus of continually shifting orderings.

The commercial relationships in the advertising industry are framed by the thorny issue of cause and effect, or the impact of advertising on sales. This is one of the key factors that gives a specific character and orientation to the industry's commercial experiments. It is recognised both in the industry itself and in academic studies that advertising's impact on sales is a highly ambiguous area that is performed by claim and counter-claim in a highly competitive arena (Alvesson 1994; Kover and Goldberg 1995; Lury and Warde 1997; Miller 1997; Schudson 1993,

Tunstall 1964). The majority of actors in my recent and previous stud-ies (Cronin 2004a, b, c) believe that it is impossible to prove a direct, unequivocal causal link between advertising campaigns and sales of goods or services. They cite the problems of distinguishing the effects of advertising from other promotional activities (e.g. pricing, packaging, promotional events) and extraneous factors including consumer trends and even the impact of the weather (for instance, on sales of summer clothing). This ambiguity is a central feature of the industry in which, Cochoy argues, marketing's 'performances are hard to describe, com-plex to evaluate, and difficult to measure empirically'(1998: 217).

This appreciation of advertising's ambiguous impact is distributed among the various actors in the sector. Research companies specialising in both qualitative and quantitative research reported that producers of goods and services who commissioned them were themselves rather vague about advertising's effect on 'sales uplift'. This weak impact is mirrored in the industry's research findings of people's recall of specific advertise-ments. Research companies fairly consistently find in post-campaign research that the numbers of people who recall a client's advertising are generally small. For instance, in a bespoke post-campaign research pro-ject on plasma screen advertising for an internet company in London Underground train stations, a research company in my study found that only 4 per cent of people questioned recalled any advertising at all in the tube station in which they were interviewed. And it is generally recog-nised that even accurate recall of a brand or advertising message does not straightforwardly translate into increased sales. The research director of an outdoor specialist firm noted with regard to advertising's effects on sales, 'we're slightly in the dark with a lot of this'. One marketing commu-nications agency, Young and Rubicam, commissioned research on adver-tising effects which employed econometrics, a modelling technique often used by clients to assess the impact of various factors on sales figures:

> We actually hired a proper econometrician to try to look at the input of advertising, and unfortunately what we found was some-thing we didn't really want to know which was that the variance that you could directly attribute to the input of advertising wasn't large enough to be statistically relevant. Whoops! (POSTAR spokesperson, previously employed by Young and Rubicam)

Following this inconvenient finding, industry practitioners strategically altered the model so that they could attribute more impact to various forms of communication such as PR and advertising.

The industry's ambiguity about advertising's direct commercial effects is mirrored in a sceptical view of the validity of research practices and the data produced. A practitioner at a quantitative research firm that is often employed by the industry describes this in relation to TGI, a research database:

> The great thing about that is it's a single source database on media and product service consumption. So you can cross analyse the two areas and that's like the holy grail to the media world – single source data. Everybody knows TGI is a little bit ropey round the edges but it's the best we've got. So it works on that basis and it is like a currency so that a media buyer will have a look at people who are interested in buying CDs for instance or, I don't know, people who have widescreen TVs... and then they'll go and check their media habits and they'll find that they index greater than a hundred on outdoor. So they think 'lovely, we'll pile into outdoor for this campaign'. But the numbers will be pretty damn ropey because once you get down to that level of detail even the huge samples the TGI reckons it gets you're into difficult areas. But it is used as currency because it's available, it's there, it's the best they've got, so they use it. (practitioner, quantitative research company)

Not only is the reliability of the data seen as questionable, the 'shelf life' of the data produced from a particular research project will be fairly short. This is partly because research projects are set up for short-term tactical reasons rather than for longer-term strategy. And the data produced from them will often be used as a lure for other potential advertisers:

> A lot of it will turn over extremely quickly because it's been done for a tactical reason but [media owning companies] will then try and hold information on specific product categories so that they can go to... they've got something about Renault, they'll then want to go to Peugeot and talk to them about look how good it was for these guys, you're doing something similar, how about thinking about a similar thing? They have no compunction about showing off the research they've done for client X and go and speak to prospective client Y in the same product category. In fact half the time, that's what they want the case study for, so they can get more advertisers from that product category in. For instance, we're doing work on FMCG [Fast Moving Consumer Goods] clients on radio because there

aren't enough of them. We know that that sort of work, if you get a good case study out of it, it will be touted around for some time to come. (practitioner, quantitative research company)

In the industry, then, this ambiguity translates into a flexible and nuanced understanding of cause and effect and the validity of research data. Market research data and figures about advertising's direct impact on sales are viewed as less than accurate, but this does not mean that they are seen as failing or invalid. With a particular focus on account-ancy and its practices of producing calculable spaces, Peter Miller argues that 'economic calculation is a congenitally "failing" operation' in that the technologies of specific fields such as accountancy – and, we might add, marketing – 'often intersect poorly with the specifics of "the real"' (1994: 257). But this failure, he argues, does not constitute a problem for commerce: highlighting the inadequacies of one calculative model or technology facilitates the task of consultants in selling new ones to clients as there is a deeply rooted sense that commercial problems can be solved if only firms had the appropriate calculative tools.

For Miller, it appears that certain calculative models' 'failings' and their replacement with newer models merely serve to illustrate the structuring efficiency of the over-arching framework of the market which seeks out and exploits gaps for innovation and hence opportun-ities to generate profit. But what other avenues for research are opened if, as in Burrows and Gane's (2006) study, we ask not if geodemographic techniques of research and classification are *accurate*, but what work they do in the industry. What if these calculative 'failings' identified by Miller are part not of a pre-set 'logic' of the market (as an abstract, over-arching or framing entity), but of a range of commercial experiments that continually perform market relations? What commercial realities do they enact? The issue of cause and effect in the industry is not, then, simply a 'problem' which constantly risks sliding into 'failure': flexible understandings of cause and effect, or the impact of advertising on sales, hold a central role in performing this set of market relations.

In these performances, this loose coupling of cause and effect pro-duces a flexible relation to data and the calculative nature of commer-cial experiments. There is a continual production of classifications which are understood to be not referentially accurate but are seen to be commercially useful. For example, a 2005 survey was commissioned by a large media owner of advertising space in the London Underground and on buses. It aimed to explore the lifestyles of various social groups, their spending habits and their movement and travel patterns. This material was then used by the media owner to pitch itself to clients by promoting its capacity to understand and efficiently target potential consumers. The study was based on just over one thousand internet-based interviews of adults aged 16–55 living or working in London. It identifies, and classifies, its respondents as 60 per cent ABC1 and 40 per cent C2DE and then more precisely as:

> *'culture fashionistas'* (88% aged 16–34; 41% AB – cool jobs, high status; probably work in media related jobs; client-facing business people who entertain on an expenses account; very well groomed with a keen interest in toiletries and cosmetics; very tech savvy – they are hi-fi and audio connoisseurs, with a good looking mobile phone in their pocket); *'Bonkies – big bonus, no kids'* (68% ABC1, 35% social grade AB – good jobs; square mile glamour couples with a double income; streetwise high flyers; they believe their choice of car says a lot about them; they embrace new technology and gadgetry, particularly computers and hi-fi & audio); *'Fair trade creatives'* (72% aged 16–34; 74% ABC1 – okay jobs; very politically aware – look to Europe in terms of a social model; strong consideration for their own emotions and feelings – and probably other people's too; more of an emphasis on comfort – less formal more leisure orientated dress; their fashion sense is probably more influenced by music – wearing the likes of Camper shoes, anti-fit jeans and Puma); *'Backbone of London'* (55% C1C2 – hardworking mid-market; traditional gender roles; know who they are and what's important – they stick to their principles and values; probably shop at major high street chains – Next and Debenhams); *'Goldie lookin tool kit'* [sic] (62% aged 16–34; 70% male; 70% C1C2DE; sport – both playing and watching is a key focus in their lives; their C1C2 SEG means they probably work in skilled manual trades; they have a keen interest in cars); *'Domestic goddesses'* (57% ABC1; 69% women; 49% married; 59% have children; shopping is both a necessity and a pleasure – particularly window shopping); *'The Royle Family'* (57% C2DE; 25% unemployed or homemaker; little or no disposable income; very 'stay-at-home' – they rarely travel out of their house or local area).

These classifications will change from project to project and will reflect the commercial imperatives of the moment, such as the targeting of a particular set of new clients, rather than accurately mirroring some external reality (in the manner of an 'academic study', as the industry understands such a distinction). But it is crucial that such data have commercial traction in that they must facilitate an efficient performance of commercial relationships. As a senior industry practitioner commented,

> In advertising and marketing services people use data in the most amazing ways, and it will not necessarily stand up to scrutiny. You know, hey, maybe that's not what anyone in the marketing services industry wants.... They want to be roughly right rather than precisely wrong. (spokesperson, advertising trade association)

To be 'roughly right' here translates as 'sufficiently valid', that is, capable of contributing to the performances of commercial relationships in ways which benefit all parties. We can see this dynamic operating clearly in the use of research data as a decision-support technology. The currency of market research data organises and stabilises the exchanges between media owners, media agencies and specialist agencies, and client companies in a range of complex ways including as a decision-support technology. I observed many instances of media owners creating pitches to present to clients on the basis of 'gut feeling' or intuition – about what direction a brand should go; the most appropriate format for outdoor advertisements to complement television campaigns; selecting the most 'impactful' format for the campaign, such as bus advertising or sponsoring an event; finding a creative 'hook' to appeal to both clients and their consumers.

Often it is only at this stage that practitioners will search various industry databases such as TGI or NVision for specific quantitative or qualitative data to support their approach – 'nugget-hunting' as one practitioner at a research company called it, a tendency noted to be prevalent in marketing (see Hackley 2001). As one senior industry practitioner describes, 'most of the decisions in advertising are made by intuition. So they want a bit of data to support their pre-formed prejudices'. This intuition is based on their commercial experience, ideas circulating in the trade press or in the practitioner accounts published by the 'great men' of advertising (e.g. Bullmore 1991; Fletcher 1999; Ogilvy 1964, 1983), companies' archives of previous campaigns, practitioners' own experience as consumers, and a more general notion of 'creative insight'. The sourcing of data is thus an eclectic process with an emphasis on novelty, as the Research Director at a specialist media agency put it, 'we pull it from all sources.... I suppose it's like the magpie effect, really. We take anything that's shiny, anything that's shiny and new we'll take.' Indeed, media owners use a diverse range of sources such as standard marketing databases, Google and online news sites to provide details to support their gut feeling or to post-rationalise a particular pitch.

This decision-support function also works at the level of the client. As a research company worker explained, practitioners at the client firm may require qualitative research on a particular advertising campaign which assesses not so much impact on sales as the general tone of the campaign: 'it's reassurance and testing that you've got it right'. And on all levels – within media owner firms, media agencies and brand managers at client firms – practitioners are oriented by personal interests, most notably their fear of losing their job due to inadequate performance. Research data can thus be used as an alibi for decisions made. The spokesperson of POSTAR, an industry body that monitors the numbers of people passing poster sites, explained that with the use of official industry figures, 'at the very least you won't lose your job because I'm going to provide you with statistical data that says, you know, "not me, guv – the figures said it was ok"'. Thus figures are often used not to direct but to support decisions on a range of levels, such as to post-rationalise a client pitch or to provide a statistical alibi for brand managers at client firms should a campaign appear to not have the intended effect on sales.

This performance of specific market relationships, and the example of the use of data as a decision-support technology, is an explicit and accepted characteristic of the industry – indeed, one company providing market research software is called 'Decisions Made Easy'. Research data is seen as a malleable resource and its reference to 'the real world' is understood as flexible and strategic. For instance, the research director at a specialist agency commented that he often held back from investigating data too closely as clients do not really want you to 'mess with' their established understanding of outdoor advertising.[4] These modes of calculation, measurement and the presentation of data are thus best seen as commercial experiments. Their defining characteristic is not their 'failure' to capture the world, for instance, in the ambiguous impact of advertising on sales; the small numbers of people recalling ads; the sketchy marketing classifications of people or certain spaces or routes in those spaces. Certainly, this dynamic enables media owners, media agencies and research companies to offer new solutions to clients as Miller (1994) suggests. But these experiments or calculations do more than this. They continually act to constitute market relationships on a micro level: instead of failing, they are productive of a functional network of commercial relationships that cohere sufficiently across time to enable that company to make money.[5]

Commercial vitalism and creative insight

But the commercial experiments of the industry do not operate solely on the level of decision-support or post-rationalisation – they have a strategic orientation to the future. In effect, they are experiments with time that are fundamentally spatialised and involve forms of calculative energy. How the various actors in the industry understand their calculative practices is highly significant. As I describe below, they conceptualise their practices of calculation, alongside the performance of their commercial relationships, as a kind of commercial vitalism. These reflexive understandings impact upon the industry because they come to be recursively incorporated into the form of their commercial practices and in turn into the performance of urban spaces as calculative spaces.

Vitalism as a non-humanistic life force or energy has a long genealogy associated with the work of Bergson, Simmel and Deleuze amongst others (see Lash 2006). And in contemporary analyses it has gained renewed prominence. As Whatmore notes, recent work in cultural geography, 'puts the onus on "livingness" as a modality of connection between bodies (including human bodies) and (geo-physical) worlds' (2006: 603). Characterising understandings of this new vitalism, Fraser, Kember and Lury (2005) emphasise process and becoming over being, in which process is seen as a radical relationality through which entities are constituted. The significance of relationality in thinking about (and through) process is that,

> it acts as a 'lure for life', an enticement to move beyond the conflation of life with the (life) sciences, to conceive life as not confined to living organisms, but as movement, a radical becoming. (Fraser, Kember and Lury 2005: 3)

The outdoor advertising industry produces and feeds off an understanding of its own practices as a form of commercial vitalism (or a creative enlivening of their market practices and market relationships). In doing so, the industry enacts and exploits an energy–time–space that is made up of knowledges, practices, city space and commercial ideals of 'target markets' that are all oriented to the future. It comes to imagine and inhabit commercial futures as they are performed spatially through the vital processes and radical relationality of its own practices. I am not suggesting that there is an ontology of the market (based on a commercial vitalism or other characteristic). Rather, I am arguing that the industry's own *understandings* of its practices and market relationships *as a* form of commercial vitalism have a significant impact on how market relations are made and remade, and on the production of urban space.[6]

To ensure its on-going financial viability, the industry has to be adept at understanding the economic and cultural moment in order to respond to it. The advertising industry is thus part of a capitalism that is 'a means of crafting the moment' (Thrift 1998: 164). Here, firms are as 'uncertain about the future as we all are because the future unfolds as a virtuality – it is continually creating temporary actualizations out of new questions – not a known quantity' (Thrift 2005: 4). The 'moment' that is being crafted is multiform and indeterminate, and as various commentators have noted, is marked by complexity and non-linear manifestations of change (Bauman 2000; Urry 2000b). In such a context the understandings of the temporality of consequences are altered such that,

> the decision-making process becomes dominated by the expectation of unexpected side-effects. When this goes so far as to reverse the sequence of decision-making – when the expectation of unexpected consequences precedes the decision itself – then, in the language of economics, externalities have been internalized.... The result is that the more we know, the more our facts, decisions and objects become dominated by the unexpected consequences that are now an integral part of them. (Beck, Bonss and Lau 2003: 21)

In the outdoor advertising industry, the unexpected or indeterminate has long been a key factor that organises its internal market relations, particularly in the form of the ambiguous relationship of advertising to sales discussed above. But more than this, the data gathered in my study suggests that the industry reflexively aims to become part of these virtual futures by asking new questions. Industry practitioners try to become part of the *performing* of those futures by trying to harness what they see as the creative, commercial energies or vitalism produced in that performance (which in turns shapes the performances of the industry's own market relationships). The industry's practical rationality is not purely limited to short-term, easily defined benefits, but has an orientation to the future and its yet unknown potential. Thus, the industry reflexively engages with the performative nature of capitalism and in doing so, the knowledge practices of the industry attempt to bring the future into the present. The commissioned research projects and practitioners' redeployment of marketing data in the industry's databases is a continual iteration of the multiple and contradictory nature of people, places and consumption: an ever-more refined classification of demographics; redefinitions of types or families of commodities and services; social trends in travel, work and leisure patterns; market share of advertising by television, the internet and the press. Projects and data are continually updated, recycled, redeployed, their usefulness defined not in terms of precision or referential accuracy but as technologies of crafting the moment, of organising knowledge and resources to most profitably inhabit that moment and be best placed to ask the next set of questions which perform temporary actualisations.

For the outdoor advertising industry, such experiments involve engaging the industry's actors in performing a certain set of commercial futures – on one level, media owners, media agencies and specialist agencies, research companies and client companies align their actions to ensure optimum performance and reward. These performances act to constitute a market or economic field. For instance the trade body, The Institute of Practitioners in Advertising (IPA), has recently attempted to produce a common currency of research data and consumer classifications, or 'single source survey and multi-channel planning system', called 'Touchpoints' based on a survey of 5,000 adults in the UK. The subjects were given PDA (Personal Digital Assistant) diaries for 7 days to record their daily practices including a focus on lifestyle, media consumption, travel patterns and time spent outdoors. This initiative was designed to formulate and stabilise the field of advertising relationships, but it constitutes a finely balanced dynamic in which the stabilisation of the field of the market is set in a productive tension with the drive for internal competition. Thus, there are continual attempts to destabilise or reinterpret market relations by companies which aim to achieve a 'point of difference' or competitive advantage by claiming new market research techniques, new technological advances in outdoor sites (e.g. Bluetooth-enabled posters for consumer interaction), or a monopoly on product types such as a contract to sell advertising space on the Underground train system in London.[7] One practitioner describes this dynamic:

> Proprietary thinking, proprietary tools, proprietary insight from industry systems that exist, that's important because it creates individuality and point of difference and it's what generates business and why you are more successful or less successful than your competitors. (research director, specialist media agency)

The production of difference both as a taxonomic currency of potential consumers and spaces and as competitive leverage is central to the market. But while Lyon's (2002: 3) phrase, the 'phenetic fix', elegantly captures this drive to classify and materialise those classifications as commercial realities, it fails to encompass the way in which the industry orients itself towards commercial futures in a manner which exceeds often loosely conceived ideas of 'innovation'. Indeed, for many accounts of market research's classificatory practices such as Elmer's (2004: 134), 'to profile is to attempt to account for the unknown'. But capturing the unknown is only part of the story. Based on the constant production of market research data and commercial mappings, these performances of market relations should be seen not merely as attempts to exploit the present: they are open-ended, reflexive attempts to be part of performing the horizon of commercial reality that acts to bring market relations into being.

This sense was articulated by practitioners most often as 'creative insight', a galvanising concept that organised their everyday practices. Although creativity is a staple concept in the whole advertising sector, it has less traction amongst media owners, that is, the group which formed the focus of my study. Trading space and market research on that space constitutes the core of their activities. And while it is true that intensified competition in the industry has recently forced media owners to engage in more 'creative' work (e.g. mocking up posters to sell the concept of outdoor advertising to specific clients), creativity is generally seen as the remit of 'creative agencies' (those that generate the textual content of advertisements). In the media owners' sector of the industry, 'creative insight' is used in a broad sense to indicate forms of knowing that are flexible, not rooted in conventional interpretations of data, and are not strictly referential – they are seen as 'vital knowledges' in which 'creativity' acts as the vital energy that drives them.

This was most clearly evident in my study in the prevalence of brainstorming sessions. One particular session focused on a pitch for a large contract for a soft drink and was oriented towards capturing the intangible in two key ways. Firstly, the session aimed to develop understandings of the product's 'brand personality' ('radical', 'extreme', 'challenging', 'fun') by throwing around key words and associations and drawing on advertising folk knowledges, practitioners' own experiences, and previous advertising campaigns for the product. The lack of detail or data they received in the brief from the company did not restrict these calculations. Secondly, it attempted to establish competitive advantage by concluding that the product's brand personality did not tally with the target market for the product and by tying their particular portfolio of advertising sites to a potential campaign (e.g. special campaigns in parks). These calculations were framed by the standard industry practice of competitively pitching for contracts. In effect, the dynamism of the market relationships between media owners, media agencies and clients is performative. It animates the search for, and circulation of, forms of (vital) knowledges which in turn animate the field and, in their performative action, enact commercial futures.

Of course, on a mundane level companies are strategic about the futures they release. I observed how in commissioning research from research companies – for instance, on a particular poster campaign's impact on viewers – media owners were very careful about producing the frame of reference or the terms of the questionnaire used. As a practitioner at a media owning company noted: 'I would say that a lot of people orchestrate the questions around the answers [they want to get] ... . We don't want to ask questions if they are going to get us negative answers ... if the information that comes through does provide negative information, we have to provide that, we have to disclose it.'

But in more general terms, companies are very open to more diffuse commercial experiments as they are seen as a highly productive means of inhabiting the moment and performing futures. On one level, this involves predicting trends in the commercial field, for example, up or downturns in clients' overall advertising spend, or potential changes to planning laws which may impact upon companies' ability to secure new sites for advertising panels. But more radically, through a flexible approach to producing and processing commercial knowledges, the industry attempts to capture the creative energy that it considers is produced in the collective performance of its own commercial relationships. The spokesperson of the Institute for Practitioners in Advertising, a key trade association, describes the tension in the industry between the impulse to measure and classify, and the more diffuse benefits of maintaining an open stance to the unknown:

> There's a tremendous desire to measure everything and for everything to be accountable because it's only by knowing something that you can accurately develop it – [that] would be the argument. The problem is that the more you record, the more you are beholden to what you record and it's almost always [a] proxy of reality [as] it's very, very difficult to really, truly model the world we live in ... I mean, it's fantastically complex so attempting to extract a handful of strands and then saying that, 'there you go, that's why that happened' is incredibly difficult ... And if all your decisions are based on what you can measure, there is still a world that you can't measure that has potential value and if you approach it cleverly ... you can derive far

more benefit from it than you could have imagined just because you have difficulty with measuring it. (spokesperson, IPA)

This encapsulates the industry perception that I observed many times – that formal quantitative calculation and measurement can be unduly restrictive. On one level, this corresponds to Callon and Muniesa's (2005) observation that there is no longer a strict division in calculative practices between (qualitative) judgement and quantitative (or numeric) calculation. But the practices I observed suggest something more – an awareness among practitioners that the referentiality of their classifications and calculation to 'the real world' is mutable and flexible, and that the commercial energy or vitalism which is performed in these market practices and relationships can be tapped for their benefit.

Massey argues that space is 'a simultaneity of stories-so-far' (2005: 9), but times and spaces are here folded together with an eye to the future and we also need to understand the product of this folding as a temporal and spatial simultaneity of *stories-to-come*. Some of these stories are: the openness of people's engagement or disengagement with advertising or with the visual field of cities in general; new ways of competitively inhabiting positions in the nexus of commercial relationships such as offering new services to clients that dispense with the need for media agencies as intermediaries; shifting trends such as 'green' consumption; and new questions whose very form has yet to be imagined. One unforeseen consequence of the intensification of the circulation of marketing data in the industry's practices is the production of the city as calculative space.

Calculative spaces

Drawing on Lefebvre's (1991) conceptualisation of energy–time–space, I have argued that the outdoor advertising industry understands the performance of its market relationships as generating a kind of commercial vitalism which can be tapped for the industry's benefit. This understanding, and the ways in which the industry acts upon it, animates the specific market relations of the field and is in turn animated by them. Within the nexus of energy, time and space, the recursive performance of marketing knowledges and practices effect a temporary holding together of urban space and people in that space. The loose coupling of advertising and effects on sales, in parallel with flexibly referential understandings of space and people, orients the advertising industry and allows the play of creative insight. Space and market relations are, in effect, in a performative relationship. Clearly, this is not an abstract, Cartesian map-ping of space: the industry understands people and space as articulated in a self-constitutive relationship which is dynamic, unpredictable and overlaid with multiple realities. This is a practical, commercial under-standing which has parallels with recent academic understandings of urban space as 'an enormous confluence of relationships without fixed sites' (Amin and Thrift 2002: 123). In effect, the classificatory and map-ping practices of the industry, together with the performance of its com-mercial relationships, produce *calculative spaces*.

Most accounts of calculation and space frame their analysis in terms of governance: in order to render them manageable, spaces are crafted by various representational strategies to be calculable, thus delivering them up to technologies of governance (e.g. Miller 1994; Osborne and Rose 1999). In parallel, some accounts suggest that such technologies produce calculative subjects (Rose 1999). In my study, practitioners were clearly reflexive agents who practise various forms of calculation and measurement, but their status as calculative subjects is rather dimmed by a fact I continually encountered – almost none of the practition-ers fully understood how the databases, metrics or research systems worked, thus restricting their manipulation of them (although they could produce a limited range of outputs through various conventions of use). This level of ignorance was voiced by the spokesperson of the IPA who said of econometrics, 'it's a bit of a dark art and it's something I have only a vague understanding of'.

Thus, the calculative dynamics clearly present in the industry do not originate only from the practitioners. As Callon and Muniesa (2005) have argued, economic calculation is distributed among human actors and material devices. Here, this includes various marketing databases (standard marketing sources such as TGI as well as more general sources such as that of the Office for National Statistics) and paper-based distributions (client briefs, flipchart notes from brain-storming sessions, creative pitches). But market relationships between media owners, media agencies, research companies and clients also constitute a calculative nexus. As I have outlined, the practice and circulation associated with research data performs market relation-ships and here produces them as a calculative formation – calculation of market position, financial gain and potential consumers is central to this formation. But more than this, an orientation towards calcula-tion and facilitation of calculative functions becomes fundamentally embedded in these market relations through the recursive nature of such performances.

The confluence of multiple commercial factors creates a new support surface for market relations – a calculative space. It is clear that the outdoor advertising industry has a range of appreciable effects on urban space. Advertising on panels, billboards, buses and taxis all directly impact upon the making of spaces. Advertising adds its semantic content to the rich textual mix of city space, helps shape the affective geographies of urban space, and introduces new visual technologies into public space (moving image billboards, interactive bus shelters etc.). Advertising constantly reiterates the *commercial* nature of supposedly public urban space in a hyper-visible way, and also finances urban infrastructures such as the London Underground through the large contract fee required from the media owner of tube advertising sites.

But alongside these more immediately evident features is the production of the city as calculative space. As space is a product of social relations, these practices or commercial experiments go towards forming the nature and potential of that space. The calculative nature of such space is performed through a recursive, shifting relationship between the various elements I have outlined above: the use of intuition or gut feeling in producing creative insight; the strategic deployment of various market research techniques and technologies; the production and reformation of various data through the circulation of PowerPoint presentations; the loose coupling of commercial cause and effect allowing flexible new modes of understanding data and commercial relationships; and a 'light touch' with regard to data in order to preserve an orientation to the future that unleashes its unforeseen potential. These factors are combined with a core understanding of space as a pliable resource and of its fluid relationship with people, and these understandings are folded inextricably into the production of specific market relationships.

This produces a calculative space which is an admixture of space, people, calculation techniques, calculation technologies and an orientation towards the potential of creative insight. For the industry, it makes no sense to try to separate these elements: they constitute a set of experiments that produces a commercial reality which can be channelled for profit. One result is that a calculative quality, characteristic or orientation comes to be interwoven into the creative process of producing the city as a fluid, flexible entity. It is an understanding of space as 'folded and animate'; one result of a shift to a world of 'qualculation' characterised by continual calculation facilitated by machines which constitutes a means of 'making qualitative judgments and working with ambiguity' (Thrift 2004b: 584). This should be understood as *process* and radical relationality: forces of commercial calculation, times and spaces are continually disaggregated and reconstituted.

We can only begin to speculate on the impact of this. The recursive incorporation of the industry's understanding of its performances as a form of commercial vitalism may animate the city in new ways. As the city comes alive through commercial experiments, this process may afford alternative ways of knowing that exceed the conventional modes of reading the city through meanings, messages, signs and symbols. It is less that the city is *speaking* in a new language of calculation and commercial vitalism than *processing* new understandings of itself. The calculative energy of such spaces allows for commercial innovations in market performances, for instance, alternative understandings generated by possible connections between standard marketing metrics and creative insight. Indeed, if government is 'animated by a spatial diagram of its objects, its problems and its means of action' as Osborne and Rose (1999: 738) suggest, calculative spaces will engender shifting modes of governance or perhaps fresh ways of imagining governance. But this produces not a homogenised city space subjected to and governed by commercial knowledge-producing activities, but multiple, co-existing time-spaces of the urban which are animated by a calculative energy.

3
Mobility, Market Research and Commercial Aesthetics

Based on ethnographic research on the outdoor advertising industry in the UK, this chapter explores the industry's conceptualisation of mobility in its market research and graphic design practices. While much of the recent work on mobility and space has explored social change (such as in migration or tourism), technological change (e.g. mobile phones), or travel policy, there has been much less emphasis on commercial and marketing understandings of mobility. This is a significant omission as commerce and commercial knowledge-producing activities are central to shaping what the city is and can be – that is, they play a key role in producing a commercial ontology of the city.

As the industry's assets are based in outdoor urban environments, including transport environments, it is unsurprising that questions of how and why people move around these spaces should be a focus of the industry's research. Perhaps more surprising is the relationship that has developed between these market research practices, the design of outdoor advertisements and the visual reception of the advertisements by people in these spaces. The first section of the chapter examines the literature on mobility and cities, and notes the paucity of analysis on contemporary outdoor advertising. The following sections explore the industry's market research practices and their focus on mobility, and these practices' relationship with the development of what I call 'a commercial aesthetics of mobility' in the graphic design of outdoor advertisements. The final sections of the chapter analyse how movement is framed by the industry as *attention* or a kind of 'mobile reception'. I then go on to explore how the interaction of these market and graphic design practices creates for the city's inhabitants alternative modes of seeing and knowing urban space.

Thinking the city through mobility

There is a well-established academic interest in movement, bodies and cities, and several studies have sought to understand cities *through* the conceptualisation of movement. Sennett notes that the discovery of the circulation of blood in the body influenced eighteenth-century under-standings of the ideal design of urban space: 'planners sought to make the city a place in which people could move and breathe freely, a city of flowing arteries and veins through which people streamed like healthy blood corpuscles' (Sennett 1994: 256). Social relations in modernity also came to be viewed through the lens of movement. Simmel argued that analysis had for too long focused on the static configuration of place, for 'humanity in general only gains the existence that we know through mobility' (1997: 160). Benjamin (2003: 65), too, proposed that with modernity came 'the advent of new mobilities, which gave life an altered rhythm' and 'new tempo' which he saw in the urban speed and rhythm of traffic but also in the cycle of fashion and the temporality of news-reporting. Park, Burgess and McKenzie's (1968 [1925]) classic study, *The City*, placed mobility at the centre of its understanding of the morphology of the modern metropolis:

> Transportation and communication, tramways and telephones, newspapers and advertising, steel construction and elevators – all things, in fact, which tend to bring about at once a greater mobility and a greater concentration of the urban populations – are primary factors in the ecological organization of the city. (Park, Burgess and McKenzie 1968: 2)

For them mobility was 'the pulse of the community' from which one could read off social change (Park, Burgess and McKenzie 1968: 59).

The significance of advertising, flagged but not fully analysed by Park, Burgess and McKenzie, received some attention in the 1960s and 1970s from studies of road systems and their relation to the sign systems of outdoor advertising. Kevin Lynch's (1960: 2) important analysis, *The Image of the City*, focused on people's mental image of urban space and argued that 'moving elements in a city, and in particular the people and their activities, are as important as the stationary physical parts'. Appleyard, Lynch and Myer's (1966: 63) later study of American highways proposed that 'the experience of the city is basically a moving view' and focused on the visual sequencing of various elements of roadway infrastructure such as bridges in relation to moving observers.

In both these studies outdoor advertising was cited as part of the visual landscape but received only cursory analysis. It was only with Venturi, Scott Brown and Izenour's study of Las Vegas' 'commercial vernacular architecture' of shop fronts and billboards as a 'communication system' that outdoor advertising came to be analysed in any detail (1972: 119, 8). For them, highway signs and advertising billboards formed the 'mega-texture of the commercial landscape' through which cars moved, forming a 'brutal automobile landscape of great distances and high speeds' (Venturi, Scott Brown and Izenour 1972: 119). Movement was not merely incidental to their analysis – it took a central place: 'the Las Vegas Strip is not a chaotic sprawl but a set of activities whose pattern, as with other cities, depends on the technology of movement and communication and the economic value of land' (Venturi et al. 1972: 76).

The relationship between outdoor advertising, movement and urban space that Venturi et al. explored is far from new. Nineteenth-century English cities were nightly replastered in advertising posters by 'external paper hangers', and the streets thronged with 'sandwich-men' carrying advertising boards and people distributing handbills (Elliott 1962: Fraser 1981; Nevett 1982; Wischermann and Shore 2000). Advertisers exploited cities' densities as efficient means of communicating with large numbers of people but also enlisted mobile means of circulating their advertising 'puffs'. Turner quotes a nineteenth-century commentator's description of one such mobile device:

> An indescribable column mounted like the tower of Juggernaut upon the body of a [carriage] – a hybrid between an Egyptian obelisk and the ball-surmounted column of an English country gentleman's estate. It bore the inscription of 'washable wigs'. (cited in Turner 1965: 74)

In another of Turner's examples of mobile commercials, a hatter in the Strand 'mounts a huge lath and plaster Hat, seven-feet high, upon wheels; sends a man to drive it through the streets' (Turner 1965: 75). Indeed, the expansion of outdoor advertising in public space – visible to all members of society – caused considerable consternation. This was directed primarily at its perceived effects on public morality and decency, and on the impact outdoor advertising was having upon the aesthetics of the countryside and cities. In 1893, the National Society for Checking Abuses of Public Advertising (SCAPA) was set up to attempt to curb the impact of advertising on such spaces (Fraser 1981) to the derision of the United Bill Posters Association which described it as the 'Society of Busybodies' (Turner 1965: 107). Mobile forms of advertising were seen as particularly invidious as they encroached on public space in all manner of ways. In 1894, a leading pill company offered a free mainsail bearing the company's advertising slogan to every boatsman and fisherman in the country, to which Eastbourne Council responded by prosecuting a local fisherman who had taken up the offer on the charge that he was 'disfiguring the foreshore' (Turner 1965: 109). This historically rooted emphasis on advertising's effects on the aesthetics of space has been taken up in contemporary times by the Campaign to Protect Rural England which seeks further restrictions on advertising such as that on trailers parked in fields next to motorways. More general concerns about decency, as well as honesty in advertising, are dealt with by the Advertising Standards Authority which is the conduit of a complex range of social critique (see Cronin 2004a).

There were clearly few limits to the ingenuity of advertisers and their exploitation of the circulation of people and vehicles in nineteenth-century cities. The visual landscape was cluttered with a variety of forms of promotion and the result was, as Henkin (1998) argues, that outdoor advertising came to play a significant role in helping build a public space formed through words and images. Advertisers were coming to appreciate the significance of people's mobility and were seeing them as mobile target markets: in 1927 one promoter bragged of Times Square in New York, 'more people were passing through [the district] than any other spot, creating a concentrated purchasing power of potential customers' (cited in Leach 1996: 236). And by the 1920s, America's outdoor advertising industry was exploiting an understanding that 'the road now comprised a boundless marketplace "millions of miles long"…. The highway had become the "buyway"' (Gudis 2004: 1). Writing from the perspective of an advertising practitioner in 1930s' America, Agnew (1938: 149) noted how the outdoor advertising industry came to understand and exploit this new mobile market of 'people on wheels':

> The increased mobility of the people, due principally to the automobile and the new highways, has greatly extended the boundaries of retail trading areas…. This moving population is 'the outdoor market' which is reached only by advertising outdoors. (Agnew 1938: 93)

The outdoor advertising industry had taken mobility seriously and had understood what Simmel called 'the miracle of the road' which succeeds in 'freezing movement into a solid structure that commences from it and in which it terminates' (Simmel 1997: 171). It is therefore surprising that following the 1960s and 1970s studies of commercial architecture and highways, there have been very few detailed analyses of contemporary outdoor advertising. More attention has focused on market research knowledges of space but such studies tend to emphasise residential location and identity (especially socio-economic group) over mobility (Burrows and Gane 2006; Gandy 1993; Goss 1995). Monmonier (2002: 140), for instance, argues that for market researchers, 'knowing where we live is nearly as useful as knowing what we might buy'. And in her study of television in public spaces, McCarthy (2001: 110) argues that such place-based media present their value to potential advertisers in terms of 'an ability to guarantee correlations between space and identity'. She notes that those selling advertising space on out-of-home television target wealthy *mobile* groups, for instance in airports. But she places less emphasis on how companies attempt to understand and target consumers while they are *on the move*.

Recent work in social theory, however, has taken up Simmel's call for a focus on movement, understanding mobility as 'socially produced motion' (Cresswell 2006: 3). This new 'mobilities paradigm' aims to go beyond 'terrains' as spatially fixed geographies (Sheller and Urry 2006). But while there is growing interest in data gathering in sites of mobility such as airports (Adey 2004; Curry 2004), there is still little work focusing how market research conceives of mobility. The following section addresses this absence and focuses on the market research of the outdoor advertising industry, examining the particular significance that the industry places on mobility.

Market research and mobility

In his classic work, *The Production of Space*, Lefebvre plays with understandings of energy, time and space that have been developed by the disciplines of physics and astronomy to comprehend the material world. These conceptualisations, he suggests, offer interesting avenues for analysis should we include social as well as physical energies in the conceptual framework:

> When we evoke 'energy', we must immediately note that energy has to be deployed with a space. When we evoke 'space', we must immediately indicate what occupies that space and how it does so: the deployment of energy in relation to 'points' and within a time frame. When we evoke 'time', we must immediately say what it is that moves or changes therein. (Lefebvre 1991: 12)

In Chapter 2, I explored the production of the city through this nexus of energy–time–space by focusing on the outdoor advertising industry's calculative practices of measuring and classifying people and spaces. There I identified a particular form of energy – a calculative energy that forms what the industry understands as a 'commercial vitalism'. Here, I am supplementing that analysis with a focus on energy as *mobility* and I examine how the industry attempts to understand and exploit the productive nexus of mobility–time–space.

In producing understandings of urban space, the practitioners of the outdoor advertising industry place some emphasis on specificity of location with the aim of targeting particular groups of potential consumers. For instance, 'Personicx Geo' is a market research tool used by the industry which is promoted as a 'segmentation and GIS solution'. It classifies domestic postcodes into 60 'predictive clusters' based on lifestyle, lifestage, income and attitudes. For example, the 'Social Explorers' cluster is defined in these terms:

> These households enjoy an income of £25,000 to £29,000 from their job in middle management. That income allows them to indulge in the hobbies they enjoy such as gourmet foods and wines and going to the pub. They like going skiing and taking holidays in the sun in the Caribbean and Asia. They are generous with their money and donate to animal welfare, wildlife and human rights charities. They make good use of their digital and satellite televisions, using them for betting, home finance, home shopping and internet access. These people also own premium products and services which may be unconventional.

But while the emphasis on locale – here refined to postcode area – and specificities of topography are important for some of the industry's clients, the industry places far greater stress on people's mobility and understands space through *movement* rather than location. On one level, the industry recognises that panels facing moving traffic will 'hit' large numbers of viewers and it can sell this capacity to potential clients. A practitioner at a media owner specialising in mega-posters described a poster site on a major arterial road:

> If...you've got your A class site there, it's head on to 5 lanes of traffic. It's big, it's 600 square metres, it's at the entrance to the city and you call it 'city gateway'. It's got massive amounts of traffic flow, it's

completely head on, it's near loads of rich people, loads of financial institutions and it's also fairly near the retail environment and surprise, surprise, it's our number one selling site. (Director of media owning company)

But the space itself needs to be sold in ways which capture the clients' attention. This is usually framed as 'delivering an audience'. When asked about what precisely his company is selling, the same practitioner responded:

I suppose internally we're selling space because we're selling city gateway. That space is 600 square metres, and if you're looking to persuade someone to buy it, then space is just a product, it's just a feature, it's just not interesting, it's not very persuasive. We need to be talking about audience delivery because that's what [clients] are buying. They're looking to buy an audience in order to communicate with that audience, in order to engage with that audience, and if we're not delivering an audience in an engaging manner, they're not buying. (Director of media owning company)

In order to facilitate media owners' task of selling outdoor space, or delivering audiences, industry bodies produce data on those potential (mobile) audiences. For instance, I described in Chapter 2 how The Institute for Practitioners in Advertising (IPA) has produced 'Touchpoints'. This is a marketing database which aims to provide an industry standard for marketing data and classifications. It was based on a research project conducted by a major market research company, TNS, and studied 7 days in the life of 5,000 people in the UK in late 2005. Research subjects filled in PDA (Personal Digital Assistant) diaries every 30 minutes for 7 days. The main findings of the project emphasised increasing time spent outdoors (or 'out-of-home'), a focus clearly of interest to an industry selling outdoor advertising space in competition with broadcast and press media. The findings were presented in such a way as to stress a broad segmentation of 'The Outsiders' and 'The Insiders' – 'The Outsiders': 19 million adults; 41 per cent of the population; more important to them to be outside the home than at home; spend at least 7.5 hours a day OOH [out-of-home]; mean hours out of home 9.6 per day. 'The Insiders': nearly 17 million adults; 35 per cent of adults; spend 5 hours out of home or less per day; they spend an average 12 hours a day awake and at home. The findings were used by media owners in their pitches to potential clients to claim 'mobility as a new segmentation':

- There is a structural shift in time in-home/time out-of-home
- We spend 6.5 hrs a day OOH, but this is much higher for valuable groups
- 19 million adults – The Outsiders – spending 9.6 hours or more OOH per day
- Younger, upscale, affluent, active
- Traditional in-home media exposure is more and more polarised to Insiders – spend 12 hours in-home
- The growing car commute is impacting on availability to read – Outsiders penetration and engagement time much reduced
- Outsiders are early adopters of new technology
- Their communication channels are increasingly Outdoor, Internet and Radio and converging mobile technology[1]

These companies are increasingly using ideas about mobility as a marketing taxonomy, supplementing conventional marketing segmentations of socio-economic class. The research director at a major outdoor advertising company described this group of highly mobile people: 'they're not all young people, they're not all old; they're a broad spectrum. They're not all ABC1, they're not all C2DE. The definition of them is their mobility, either the amount of travel or the amount of time that they spend outside of their home.'

Another company commissioned a study they called 'The Mobile Pound' which aimed to understand people's movement in cities and then pitch it as a sales point to clients who might be persuaded to use outdoor advertising. Part of their pitch was that people on the move had a 'mobile mindset' which predisposed them to search out new products and be open to spontaneous purchasing. As one practitioner in the company described,

> The more mobile you are the more you are actively looking for new products and new things to try, and it's not to do with how much money you have or what type of person you are...it's the mindset...you are out and about more, you do more things, you're more spontaneous, you're actually looking for new brands.... On the high street [people] tend to be awake, they tend to be alert.... Obviously they're doing something, they're trying to avoid some of the people around them, they're actually looking for shops, looking in shop windows.... The mindset is open to opening a dialogue

with them when they're on the high street…. And the more mobile people are, the more likely [they] are to be exposed to outdoor advertising in this receptive state. (practitioner, media owning company)

This company translated these understandings into claims about 'consumers on the move' that would be attractive to their potential clients:

- 75% of purchase *decisions are made* out-of-home
- 61% of adults agree they are *more interested in* things to buy when they're 'out and about' as opposed to sitting at home
- 54% of people have *bought things on impulse* that they have seen advertised when 'out and about'[2]

Here, the mobility of people in urban space is not defined solely in abstract terms through their movement; it is understood by the industry as a social practice situated in specific contexts. Thus, the movements of travel are interspersed with moments of stasis that the industry calls 'dwell time' or 'captive message time'. This time waiting on tube platforms, in train stations, at bus stops and in airports is highly valuable and is carefully researched and quantified. The average time spent waiting on a tube platform, for instance, was found to be 3 minutes, a fact that was much played upon in the industry's promotional strategies.

New technologies are deployed within the industry to tap into the perceived benefits of people's mobility and their dwell time. As well as more established techniques such as viral marketing or experiential marketing,[3] various companies in my study were starting to deploy technologies such as Bluetooth-enabled posters (e.g. from which a passer-by could download a short video or electronic coupon), interactive advertising at bus shelters (in which people can press a button to hear a promotional music or film clip), and roadside digital poster sites which can be updated in real time and sold according to time of day (known as 'day part') for time-sensitive advertising such as lunch offers. Some such panels show five advertisements per minute interspersed with travel information such as news on traffic jams. But it is easy to overstate the ubiquity and power of such new technologies in outdoor advertising. Almost all of these technological innovations are restricted to advertising sites in London and, due to cost, there are still very few of them. Media owners are concerned about 'ROI' (return on investment) and it has not been easy to sell space on some of the new sites. For instance, advertising space on new digital panels on tube escalators sold rapidly when the technology was being launched – many companies want to achieve a 'media first', that is, the extra promotional benefit of being featured in trade press accounts of a new advertising form, technique or technology.[4] But after its much-heralded inception, the media owner has found it hard to sell that space. Industry practitioners speculate that this is because the brand managers in the client firms tend to be conservative about their choice of media (the 'safe', default choice is television advertising). So while the new technologies attempt to tap into and benefit from people's mobility, it is less clear that these technological innovations amount to a rapidly spreading, ever-more sophisticated exploitation of people on the move. The picture seems rather more uneven and complicated.

From my research, then, it became clear that the industry's conceptualisation of the city as energy–time–space was based primarily on mobility. Equally, it emerged that the impact of the industry on the city is not restricted to its visual effect on the city's image-scape or its economic input (in subsidising transport systems, for instance). The outdoor advertising industry plays a key part in forming the commercial ontology of the city through its production of marketing knowledges about people and space. By continually generating measurements and calculations of people *moving* in urban space, the industry represents the city in quantitative figures (e.g. the numbers of people passing every panel is assessed and collated by the industry body POSTAR) and qualitative accounts (e.g. the 'mobile mindset').

Understandings of spatiality, bodies and movement have been the subject of numerous academic analyses (e.g. Deleuze and Guattari 2004; Goffman 1972; Merleau-Ponty 1962). But it seems clear that commercial knowledges of these same themes have more immediate, tangible impacts on the world as it is apprehended and lived by most people. Such marketing representations do not mirror or distort the reality of spaces; they function actively to make or perform spaces. This can be understood through the concept of retroduction. For Massumi, this is more than a retrospection or an incorporation of elements learnt from previous interactions. Retroduction is a performance which is 'a production, by feedback, of new movements. A dynamic unity has been retrospectively captured and qualitatively converted' (Massumi 2002: 10). This is a recursive feedback relationship in which understandings and practices performatively loop back on one another. In this conceptualisation, 'space itself is a retroduction, by means of the standardization of measurement' (Massumi 2002: 10). My focus in the following section is how such marketing practices of measurement and classification form a retroductive production in which spaces come to be constituted and understood *as movement*. By feeding back marketing understandings of mobility into the practices of targeting 'mobile' people, the industry creates for city space a commercial ontology of mobility. One element of this can be tracked in the production of a commercial aesthetics of mobility.

The commercial aesthetics of mobility

> When nothing arrests our gaze, it carries a very long way. But if it meets with nothing, it sees nothing, it sees only what it meets. Space is what arrests our gaze, what our sight stumbles over: the obstacle, bricks, an angle, a vanishing point. Space is when it makes an angle, when it stops, when we have to turn for it to start off again. There's nothing ectoplasmic about space; it has edges, it doesn't go off in all directions, it does all that needs to be done for railway lines to meet well short of infinity. (Perec 1999: 81)

Outdoor advertising forms part of what our sight 'stumbles over' in the busy visual clutter of contemporary cities. As part of a broader sensory regime, space and sight articulate to produce the lived city, and it is this relationship that is both influenced by, and acts to constitute, advertising's commercial aesthetics of mobility. Companies' appreciation of the mobility of potential consumers in urban spaces impacts upon the graphic style and textual content of ads. It shapes the structural design of advertising panels, such as the size of billboards which aim to capture the attention of people in cars. But it is a common complaint within the industry that creative advertising agencies – the agencies which produce the textual content of advertisements – misunderstand outdoor formats and tend to produce inappropriate content which makes little visual impact in the specific outdoor environment, for instance, on a bus travelling along a high street or on a billboard by a busy road. This is of concern to the industry as poor graphic design of advertisements reflects badly on the outdoor advertising sector as a whole – such advertisements are less likely to generate positive responses from people in post-campaign research when they are asked to recall specific campaigns. This has led one company to produce material to coach creative agencies in the most appropriate design of outdoor advertisements centred on an understanding of mobility and reception whilst mobile. 'Project Leonardo' aimed to provide a benchmark for graphic design on bus advertising:

What makes a top campaign?

- Contrasting colour schemes
- Noticeable ad colours
- Fewer rather than more words
- Clear, concise branding
- A simple proposition
- Some degree of familiarity with product or advert

Now we know great bus ads have ...

- Around 7 words
- Clear branding
- Large text
- Primary colours /b/w for backgrounds[5]

These rules of graphic design, linked to an understanding of the mobility of the target viewers, are well established in the practices of the industry. In 1938, Agnew outlined the principles of good poster advertising emphasising bold lettering, brevity of message and appealing clear-cut images. These graphic techniques 'that may be absorbed quickly and from a distance are effective for displays showing to automobile and fast-moving mass traffic on the important streets, highways and boulevards' (Agnew 1938: 220). Unlike the urban environment that they will inhabit with its rich semiotic 'noise', advertisements must be uncluttered and unambiguous. Contemporary practitioner-oriented accounts emphasise these same rules of legibility, colour and simplicity, all designed to attract and hold the attention of the moving urban target market:

> The poster has been called the pictorial equivalent of a shout. Today we might replace shout with sound bite.... Today the outdoor ad is a SITE BITE, ideally an integration of image and message – simple but not simplistic. (Bernstein 1997: 212–213)

The 'site bite' of the poster, however, orients itself less to the static audience understood in terms of location, than to the mobile audience that sees on the move. Gudis (2004: 94) proposes that roadside advertising embodies 'an aesthetics of speed'. In her analysis of the growth of automobile culture, highways and roadside billboards in America, this is an appropriate way of conceiving the graphic design of posters which were designed to be seen at a distance and at speed. But once you include an analysis of other outdoor advertising formats that are typically found in UK cities, such as panels in pedestrian areas, building 'wraps' in urban centres, advertising on buses and taxis, bus shelter advertising, advertising in underground train stations, the more appropriate phrase would seem to be 'an aesthetics of mobility'. In the UK travel landscape, quite distinct from the wide open spaces and super-extensive highways of America, imagining an aesthetics of mobility rather than speed takes account of the rhythms of movement and stasis (or 'dwell time') typical of UK travel practices. It also flags a particular way of seeing oriented by those practices.

This concern with movement and mediation is part of a long-standing academic interest in the 'ways of seeing' that various forms of mobility elicit. Schivelbusch (1980) famously noted how the blurring of the foreground view on railway journeys shifted emphasis to the distant or panoramic view thus instituting the panorama as the new norm for apprehending and appreciating the landscape. Cinema studies have also sought to understand the relationship between moving bodies and moving images. Several accounts emphasise not merely the abundance of images of the city in film, but the co-informing relationship of film and the city. City life with its speeds and stimulations produced particular modalities of vision – fragmented, saccadic, saturated with signification – and films offered ways of understanding and inhabiting the constantly moving and evolving city (AlSayyad 2006; Clarke 1997; Donald 1999). Others have suggested that driving in the city resonates with the experience of viewing film sequences. Robertson draws on the visual sequencing work of Appleyard, Lynch and Myer (1966) to suggest the cinematic quality of automobility: 'the melting of one scene into another, one view disappearing before another is set up, echoes and hints of past and future views, sudden transitions and connecting links' (Robertson 2007: 86).

Advertisements certainly aim to conform to a distinctive commercial aesthetic in which their graphic design is bold, simple and striking. But people's visual engagement with them is also influenced by other urban ways of seeing generated by various transport technologies and cultural forms such as cinema and photography. Moreover, the visual engagement with urban texts may be influenced by other sensory inputs such as smell or hearing. In individuals' mediated urban journeys, for instance, static advertising texts may become animated by their car's internal soundtrack creating 'a sonic envelope', as Bull (2005: 247) puts it, in which sound and vision meld to form a sensory amalgam. 'Mobile reception' of stationary advertisements, integrated with other sensory inputs, creates an ambiguity about what is moving and what is not, a paradox summed up by de Certeau's observations of a railway journey as, 'a travelling incarceration. Immobile inside the train, seeing immobile things slip by. What is happening? Nothing is moving inside or outside the train' (1998: 111). The impression produced by the retroduction of marketing understandings of 'mobile people' and the commercial aesthetics of mobility is that the city itself is moving – its buildings, its inhabitants, its ways of knowing and being known – creating a commercial ontology of mobility. This fluid sense of movement creates interesting research problems for the industry which responds by focusing on perception as a form of attention.

Mobility as attention

The recursive feedback relationship, or retroduction, of commercial aesthetics, marketing understandings of 'mobile consumers', and the experience of mobility in urban space is particularly evident in the example of car advertisements. As an advertising format, the outdoor sector is especially popular with clients advertising products associated with mobility such as mobile phones and cars. The UK telecommunications industry spent £102,468,775 on outdoor advertising in 2006, while the motor industry and the travel and transport industries spent £57,856,745 and £53,606,272 respectively. It is the mobile nature of the urban experience, the outdoor use of mobile phones, and the opportunity to advertise on mobile billboards such as buses and taxis, that make outdoor advertising attractive for such industries. The telecommunications firm T-Mobile, for instance, 'wrapped' 450 taxis in London and 160 in Birmingham for a year in branded 'liveries'. Whereas mobile phones are a recent arrival on the outdoor advertising scene, cars have long been advertised in this way.

While there is some work on the textual content of car advertisements (Dery 2006; Shukin 2006; Wernick 1991), less attention has been directed at car advertising's role in the performative production of space and mobile reception. This occurs through the interaction of several elements: (1) a commercial aesthetics of mobility; (2) marketing knowledge practices; and (3) the perceptual experience of moving in urban space. Within the industry, cars have come to be understood as 'the new mobile living room', as the MD of a media owning company put it. This parallels academic understandings of 'dwelling in the car'

(Urry 2006: 22) which may involve a range of leisure activities but may also include office work (Laurier 2005). But the industry is interested less in what people may do in cars than the amount of time they spend en route where they will come into visual contact with a range of advertising sites such as billboards.

Car advertisements speak in an affective register offering pleasure, pride, glamour and status, and try to tap into the range of emotions that cars elicit in their owners, such as attachment or feelings of independence (see Sheller 2005). At home in their urban environment, car advertisements on roadside billboards are thought to speak in direct ways to 'consumers on the move'. But what is involved in this communication? The industry has found that people moving in urban space register the brand names and advertising messages in advertisements far less often than the industry would like (see Chapter 2). So although the advertisements are created with an ideal target market – or receiver of the message – in mind, the communication is rather more of a diffuse and often unheeded monologue than a direct dialogue. This is a mediation with lacunae, misunderstandings and often indifference or hostility on the part of the viewer.

But there are other forms of mediation taking place. Thrift (2004a: 51) notes that with the development of sound and video systems, climate control, sound insulation and ergonomically designed interiors, the car has come to function as a monad which 'refers to the world outside itself via heavily intermediated representations'. But in their status as commodity, cars also refer to the world via the measurement and calculation practices of market research. As a retroduction, cars engage in dialogue with urban space via the feedback loops of the measurement systems of an industry body called POSTAR. This body produces vehicular and pedestrian counts by estimating the traffic that flows past each of the 100,000 roadside advertising panels in the UK, and then classifies each site according to a broad range of criteria including 'panel orientation' (angle of panel to incoming traffic), 'set backs' (distance from the kerb to the panel), 'eccentricity' (the angle a driver would have to turn their head to see a panel).[6] These classifications emphasise the visual accessibility of panels to a moving 'consumer' or 'target market'. The data they help produce frames an understanding of space as densities of target markets and, more precisely, as the mobility of these targets. This is then fed back into the more qualitative practices of how marketing practitioners classify consumers.

In effect, practitioners' understandings of the mobile modes through which people may engage with advertisements impacts upon how those practitioners imagine specific target markets of consumers. In crude terms, outdoor advertising companies' assets are based on people moving around urban space (especially in cars) and some of the spaces they sell, for instance, on buses and taxis, themselves move around that space. The mobility of people as 'consumers' or 'target markets' is emphasised in their promotional pitches, as is their disposable income that their mobility purportedly makes them predisposed to spend (as we saw in the 'mobile mindset' example discussed earlier). In another example of this recursive effect, a research project carried out for the London Underground to explore potential advertising opportunities produced a classification of tube users as:

> interesting people e.g. experiences, hobbies/interests; independent mindset; appreciate and thrive on the buzz, diversity and opportunities of London; outgoing, energetic and enthusiastic personalities; social people who enjoy going out and having fun.[7]

I have argued that the industry understands urban space primarily in terms of mobility, but what is most striking in the industry's identification and classification of potential consumers is the conceptualisation of mobility *as attention* or a kind of mobile perception. While academic research tends to cast modes of attention in urban spaces in terms of distraction (Benjamin 1999) or the 'blasé attitude' of inattention and reserve (Simmel 1991: 24), for evident commercial reasons the industry promotes an ideal of visual attentiveness as the epitome of urban modes of mobility. Research commissioned by the Outdoor Advertising Association described the visual attention to digital escalator panels in the London Underground in these terms:

- An escalator ride is a classic 'empty moment'
- 'Up' and 'down' trips take about 60 secs – passengers actively seek distraction or stimulation
- People look once or twice per minute – around 4–9 secs duration
- Screens act as one – cumulatively can elicit long duration glances (46 secs longest recorded)
- Eyes pass progressively from screen to screen – linear media
- Lots of creative potential – not a TV showroom window but linear content

This form of 'mobile reception' or attention is framed as an active seeking of stimulation to fill the 'empty moments' of mobility and as a temporally extended set of visual engagements. This understanding is fed back into the production of advertisements on escalator panels to form a narrative sequence. To return to the example of car advertising, mobile reception is understood and implemented in the textual production of ads as a kind of mimesis: the car-in-motion on the road is re-presented in the form of a static, textual car-on-billboard. The graphic design or commercial aesthetics – itself defined by the textual 'rules' for targeting moving consumers – emphasises movement. In turn, the advertisement of the car situated in the car's urban environment impacts upon people's own understandings of their mobile practices: the glamorous associations of the ads that populate billboards may rub off on the experience of driving in the city, but equally may jar and irritate when juxtaposed with the reality of traffic jams and pollution. The understanding of consumers as increasingly 'on the move' (and therefore aptly targeted by billboards) is fed back to clients in the promotional material that the media owners produce and circulate. In this material, promotional images typically mimic the movement of traffic by the use of slow shutter speed in the camerawork (see Figure 3.1).

This retroductive looping of measurement data, aesthetics and ideas of mobile reception produces a strange form of dialogue between cars and car advertisements inhabiting those same urban environments.

Figure 3.1 Media owner's promotional image (Courtesy of JCDecaux)

This raises questions which, although intriguing, go beyond the scope of this chapter: if perception is fundamentally embodied in the way suggested by Merleau-Ponty (1962), and if the 'driver-car' is neither thing nor person but 'an assembled social being that takes on the properties of both and cannot exist without both' (Dant 2005: 74), then the embodied experience of driving a car interfaces in complex and surprising ways with outdoor advertisements. The retroductive quality of the outdoor advertising industry instigates a set of relationalities that disturbs conventional configurations of dialogue, agency and mobile experience. Alongside the standard (intended) communication between advertisement and 'consumer', the car ads on billboards 'speak to' the cars passing them via the representational activities of market research. In effect, the data gathering, processing and retroduction into material and aesthetic form connects texts and material cars in new ways and creates a form of mediation not based on standard linguistic communication. So, if the driver engages with the car in a hybridised fashion, and the car is engaged in its own modes of communication with ads, what might this mean for the driver? Might this be another, differently mediated, form of 'mobile reception'? These questions aside, my task in the next section is to imagine how outdoor advertising impacts upon the viewer and their experience of urban space, and to sketch out the ways in which these mobile experiences may create new ways for people to apprehend and understand the city.

Knowing the city through 'mobile reception'

Advertising in urban space is often assumed to be a hegemonic or conservative force. The artist Krzysztof Wodiczko, for instance, claims that,

> An intense presence of historic monuments, advertising, communication media and urban events merge with our daily personal performance into one uniform aesthetic practice dangerously securing the continuity of 'our' culture. (Wodiczko 2000: 87)

But I would argue that outdoor advertising's impact on urban space is far more nuanced and ambiguous than a mere homogenisation of the visual landscape, or hegemonic consumerist force (see Chapters 4–7). Instead of creating a semiotic conformity and deterministic visual coagulation of place, brand and sign, the mobility of people engaging with ads – combined with *ideas* of mobility that are worked into the production of advertising structures and textual content of ads – opens up the visual field in unanticipated ways. Sheller and Urry (2006) ask if mobility is transforming our ways of knowing; below I suggest that in their emphasis on mobility, the outdoor advertising industry's knowledge practices create possibilities for those who move through urban space to know that space differently.

For instance, outdoor advertising continually remakes the perceptual relationship between spatial generality and the specificity of location. People moving through urban spaces are likely to come across the same advertising campaigns many times in different locations and in various formats: on billboards, buses, panels in pedestrian zones, taxis (this is framed as valuable to clients wishing to raise or reinforce 'brand awareness'). This acts to bind together places in temporary, loose formations which are nowhere formally mapped. Advertisements on buses trace out shifting, advertising-intensive patterns in and around urban centres as they travel on their daily routes. Advertising companies rarely have control over where their advertising will be seen as specific buses may work different routes each day – such campaigns are not the strategies of the powerful in de Certeau's (1998) terms – so these semiotic sorties re-pattern the city daily with their commercial exhortations. They help to remake people's sense of the city as amorphous and as mobile. As advertising space on roadside billboards and panels is bought in standard two-week blocks of time, so advertising content changes before any real connection between the billboard's contents and its location can be established. This continual changing of textual content and its spatial distribution disturbs perceptions of place specificity at the same as emphasising the transitivity of what counts as 'the city'.

The London Underground train system is an interesting example of advertising's repatterning of urban space. There are elements of specificity to the practices of siting Underground advertising: companies code certain tube stations as male (Tottenham Court Road station with its proximity to an intensity of shops selling various technologies such as computers and cameras) and others as female (such as Kensington High Street or Sloane Square with their proximity to clothes shops). These codings are then offered to potential clients as spatially gendered modes of targeting. But in general, marketing knowledges of the Underground see it as a spatially amorphous zone and therefore open to opportunity. The Underground map of stations and routes has, at best, an ambiguous referential relationship to the patterns of distance and place that exist above ground (as many a tourist has discovered). This is a strange underworld that Benjamin (2003), thinking of the Paris

Métro, imagined as the subterranean unconscious of the city. As it is denuded of above-ground perspective and signifiers of distance and place such as landmarks, advertising panels can inhabit and mark this underground space more fully than those above ground. Although they may not succeed in permanently associating particular spaces with specific brands, the placing of the panels and their changing textual content etch out a particular a subterranean geography and offer travellers ontological and spatial markers of their relationship to urban space in this barely legible zone. Well-known images, brands and text are distributed in tube stations, opposite platforms and in train carriages, and people's familiarity with the advertising form itself makes this unusual space seem less alien.

This geography is defined first and foremost by mobility (and its companion element of 'dwell time'). Advertising acts to inhabit this dwell time and creates a strange effect of domestication, or making an 'interior' space of an urban exterior, in ways that Perec (1999) and Bachelard (1994) may have appreciated (see Figure 3.2). Place can be seen as 'a knot tied from the strands of the movements of its inhabitants, rather than as a hub in a static network of connectors' (Thrift 2006: 141–142). In which case, in the Underground's rhythms of movement and stasis, the commercial aesthetics of mobility in the ad texts

Figure 3.2 London Underground advertising (Courtesy of CBS Outdoor)

combine to create a curious interior/exterior place. It is a place that is marked by the changing patterns of advertising texts which tie together localities in a space where conventional spatial cues are absent.

This focus on mobility means that the practices of the industry make 'place' as a tension between generality and specificity that is played out in commercial terms. In effect, this facilitates a shift in the terms of referentiality, a shift which allows new configurations of space, mobility and attention and also creates the conditions of possibility for spaces of dissonance. By tying ideas of mobility to understandings of people's attention, the industry's commercial practices open up the visual field to slippages. By producing outdoor advertisements according to the principles of a commercial aesthetics of mobility, the textual content favours bold text and simple messages. But viewed, as intended, when mobile in a car, on foot, on a bus or train, reception of these commercial messages may be reduced to snatches of text and glimpses of colour and images that are detached from the semiotic coherence of the original advertisement.

The result may be unanticipated juxtapositions with the urban environment that may speak of the city to the viewer in ways not intended by the advertiser. Figure 3.3 shows a partial view of a billboard on a busy road near a railway station that may well be representative of how people in motion engage with advertisements. The exhortation to 'expect more' juxtaposed with the debris of urban decay – evidence of the city council's under-funding? exemplifying industrial decline? – speaks to viewers in ways that may be subversive and is certainly quite distinct from the intentions of the company that produced the advertisement. Seen in this disjointed fashion, such fragments of text and image are detached from the commercial orientation of the advertising message and may be received as colourful urban wallpaper – an imagistic substrate – or innocuous conversational gambits of apparently inanimate textual forms (Figure 3.4).

The marketing practices of the industry, and their retroductive relationship to ideas of mobility and aesthetics, thus make available to people moving through urban space alternative ways of understanding that space. The formal measurements of space, mobility and consumers that are produced by the industry do not necessarily create homogeneity or reductive visions of the social landscape. Discussing the artist Julie Mehretu's work, Thrift (2006: 141) argues that while much analysis has posited the metrics of measurement, division and calculation as antithetical to creativity – and, we might add, have understood the commercial operations of calculation as antithetical to the

Figure 3.3 Suggestive juxtapositions between text and the city (author's photograph)

ideals of people's spontaneous, organic, lived reality – it may be more useful to think about metrication otherwise: 'metrics have added in as much as they have taken away, producing not only new practices and apprehensions of motion but also fertile sources of conflict' (2006: 141).

Figure 3.4   Conversational gambit (author's photograph)

Such a combination of calculation and a commercial aesthetics may perhaps allow new ways of knowing the city to unfold, or make available alternative ways of apprehending those very capitalist (knowledge) practices that help constitute the city. Writers have noted how the high visibility that advertising affords brands can rebound and make those corporations prime targets of criticism (Goldman and Papson 2006; Klein 2000). But if, as Park, Burgess and McKenzie (1968: 1) argue, the city is as much 'a state of mind' as a composite of institutions and infrastructure, then might not the mobile imagination of the outdoor advertising industry create new ways of knowing the city that are not necessarily determined by advertisers' intentions or the textual 'steer' of the advertisement?

Venturi, Scott Brown and Izenour's (1972) analysis of commercial architecture and roadside billboards in Las Vegas foregrounded outdoor advertising's impact as visual text on a sign-scape of images, texts and building facades that was oriented towards a mobile consumer. While it is clearly the case that such advertising marks the space in striking ways, it would be wrong to restrict an analysis of outdoor advertising's significance to a straightforward 'input' of semiotic content into a preformed urban context. The outdoor advertising industry takes part in *performing* that space by retroductively incorporating market research understandings of mobility into the form and content of advertising. This, in turn, impacts upon how people experience their mobility in urban space and how they come to know the city. We can see that the relationship of mobility, advertising and cities is long-established; what is new is the intensity and recursive character of these market research practices and their explicit focus on mobile attention. Thus, if we can still imagine the city as a body composed of arteries, the circulation must include not only people but flows of knowledge, scopic regimes, affect and fragments of text. Moreover, the city is a body that produces ways of knowing itself, the most striking of which is mediated by a commercial ontology of the city in which the nexus of energy, time and space that Lefebvre conceived is refined to mobility–time–space.

4
The Commodity Rhythms of Urban Space

This chapter extends the previous analysis of mobility and movement to consider a particular spatio-temporal form – urban rhythms. Using ethnographic data,[1] I examine the outdoor advertising industry's practices of researching and exploiting city rhythms. In parallel, I analyse how these practices make available surprising ways of inhabiting and knowing space. Using the concept of rhythms, this chapter asks: how do media owning companies' practices of segmentation and bartering of specific urban sites and routes function to re-map the city?; what is the impact of advertising structures such as billboards and panels upon people's understanding and experience of urban space?; what is the effect of the rhythmic, cyclical appearance of new advertisements in cities?

Outdoor advertising is primarily a visual form that clearly impacts upon urban space in a visual register. But this chapter explores how advertising practices, and advertising texts and structures, also operate in ways that are not strictly textual. I explore how people apprehend advertising's urban rhythms in a bodily way that extends beyond a 'textual reading' of specific advertisements. On the one hand, this form of perception aligns people's embodied orientation with commodity innovation and particular capitalist temporalities in the city. On other hand, the meshing of personal and urban rhythms can effect new relationalities, and can create routes to thinking the city differently.

The first section of the chapter outlines the practices of media owning companies with regards to urban temporalities. Following the analysis developed in Chapters 2 and 3, I examine how the companies' self-promotional imperative in the competitive arena of advertising provision drives them to generate models for understanding – and targeting – people who move into and around city spaces. These 'pitches'

to potential clients offer mapped city routes for the placement of advertisements that aim to exploit people's temporal and spatial experience
of the urban. The second section of the chapter offers a theoretical
framework for analysing advertising's role in organising city space and
in framing individuals' experience of that space through rhythms. I
argue that advertisements in city spaces are rarely 'read' coherently as
texts; their meanings or messages are not registered in any detailed or
consistent manner. Instead, their significance lies in the materiality and
spatiality of the advertising structures, and these are but one of many
forms that populate public spaces. The very familiarity, and indeed ban-
ality, of advertising in city spaces functions to naturalise the conceptual and lived unit that we know as a city.

But drawing on Henri Lefebvre's framework of city rhythms, I
argue that urban advertising has a further and more subtle impact. By
aligning the city's rhythms of travel and work with the commodity's
rhythms of innovation and promotion, advertising enacts or performs a
new connection between people moving around cities and the massed
populations of commodities. Foucault's (1990) bio-politics focused its
regulatory drive on the human population in terms of birth rates, disease and death. But this new urban power–knowledge formation draws
the rhythmic lifecycle of the commodity and people's urban rhythms
into an uneasy and generative relationship.

Mapping and selling the city

Lefebvre (1991) has argued that city space should not be analysed
solely as a conglomerate of signs, images or texts: rather, it should
be approached as a lived, practised space. This section draws on and
extends previous chapters' analyses to examine how outdoor advertising companies *practise* the city, or map and re-map the city according
to commercial principles. Placing a concentration of advertising billboards or panels in what are framed as commercially valuable spaces
creates new urban intensities. Here mobile currents of bodies, finance
and meanings interface and (provisionally) sediment around the physical structures holding the advertisements.

Time and mobility constitute a key nexus through which outdoor
advertising companies articulate these imaginings. In some theoretical accounts such as Virilio's (1991) notion of the new, technologised
city, time plays a significant role. Here, 'people occupy transportation and transmission time instead of inhabiting space' (Virilio 1991:
14). While some of Virilio's generalised claims about transformations

of cities may be subject to justified criticism, his insistence on the importance of temporality has some resonance with advertising companies' strategic, self-promotional discourses.[2] These discourses of identifying, targeting, and delivering the urban consumer to clients function to segment, package and sell this transportation time to companies wishing to advertise. As the advertising companies emphasise and I analysed in Chapter 3, the significance of outdoor advertising may be growing with potential consumers' increasing mobility. Thus in their pitches for business, Clear Channel and Maiden (now called Titan) promote the fact that increasingly busy roads may create problems for travellers and city planners, but they represent enhanced opportunities for advertising on roadside billboards: 'The Roadside audience has grown significantly over the past decade as a consequence of more traffic on the roads and better located and more impactful panels.'[3] In effect, people are spending more time in cars and buses. This emphasis on roads, traffic flows and motor vehicles tallies with recent analyses which flag the increasing importance of cars and car travel for the social and economic organisation of societies, and the significance of 'automobility' as a conceptual framework for understanding people's experiences of this shift (see Featherstone, Thrift and Urry 2005; Sheller and Urry 2000).

But the case of outdoor advertising, with its parallel stress on sites in train stations, underground train stations and free-standing panels in urban pedestrian areas, also demonstrates the value of non-car travel to advertisers. With travellers' frequent periods of immobility whilst waiting or queuing, these modes of transport capture more of what the industry calls 'dwell time' or 'captive message time'. This is the time travellers spend stationary, which is precisely the time advertising aims to inhabit and mark as its own. Areas such as underground train stations are seen to have a 'captive audience' where 'travellers on the platform or in the carriage often have nothing to do but read the ads and have significant time in which to do it'.[4] This idea of dwell time is a standard mode of conceptualising and selling certain advertising spaces, notably in airports and on train and underground train platforms. A practitioner at the company which owns the contract for advertising space at Manchester airport described dwell time in this way:

> Our sell is on the back of dwell times – the market travelling through an airport. It's normally sort of higher end of the social scale...you know, and sort of association of various social markets with various airlines. We can be quite precise in targeting those markets. So we're

more about specifics rather than mass coverage. (practitioner, media owning company, Manchester airport)

The dwell time or time available to receive advertisers' messages is a significant selling point which, combined with perceived purchasing power of airport users, makes advertising in airports one of the most expensive out-of-home sites. The same practitioner describes how the specific character of airport dwell time is used as a selling point to potential advertisers,

> These are sold in terms of economic value of the potential target markets, but also in terms of the mood of going on holiday ... it's the whole environment ... if you take the business aspect out of it ... there's a happy feel to the place which is probably conducive to people taking messages in, wanting to spend more. Whereas if you look at outdoor as a whole or something like a rail station, most people's vision of a rail station is purely travelling on business or roadside you're sat in a queue of traffic. Here you have ... I suppose it's the excitement of actually going somewhere possibly new or somewhere sunny. (practitioner, media owning company, Manchester airport)

In the promotional nexus of selling advertising space, media owners are keen to exploit opportunities to promote the outdoor ad industry as a whole alongside promoting their own company's specific commercial acumen and material resources. For instance, companies selling advertising space in and around airports suffered from the decrease in numbers of air passengers in the immediate aftermath of the 9/11 attack in New York. The companies responded by claiming that 9/11's effects of intensifying airport security in fact offer increased opportunities to producers wishing to advertise. The outdoor company JCDecaux claimed that, 'The tightening up of security in airports will create opportunities for JCDecaux. The longer time spent by passengers in airports will make this audience – captive almost by definition – more available to advertisers.'[5] These targeting strategies, articulating with shifting social contexts such as that engendered by 9/11, create important spatio-temporal zones which congeal around bodies, 'valuable' spaces and the logics of commodity promotion.

In addition to identifying and selling travellers' dwell time, outdoor advertising companies create complex spatial mappings of people's routes into, around, and out of cities. So although companies claim that one of outdoor advertising's great strengths is its ability to reach a mass audience, companies also claim that they can access and analyse travel data in such a way that enables them to target specific groups of potential consumers. As I described in Chapter 3, the industry collectively funds the site classification and audience measurement system called POSTAR.[6] This research system is used to collate a great deal of commercial information, including the number of people passing any one advertising site. For instance, POSTAR has carried out traffic counts for 10,000 panels (or advertising sites), a travel survey of 7,500 people which tracked 80,000 of their journeys, and 9,000 12-minute pedestrian counts over 18 months across the UK.

In addition to quantitative research, POSTAR carries out interviews to explore how and why people move around a particular city. This material is collated in a complex taxonomy. The following are select examples of POSTAR's criteria that classify and price individual advertising sites according to their potential capacity to reach particular consumers: OTS (Opportunity To See), measuring the potential number of times a person may see a particular poster in a week; VAIs (Visibility Adjusted Impacts per panel), that is, the number of pedestrians who actually look at, rather than merely pass, any one panel; 'minimum duration', or the length of time a person would typically have the advertisement in their line of vision as they passed the panel; 'eccentricity', or the degree a person travelling on a typical route has to turn his head in order to see the panel; 'illumination', the panel's status as artificially lit (this is particularly relevant in winter and affects price); 'import/export', or the movement of people between local television areas and regions (this is significant as certain routes to or through the city may access consumers who see different television advertisements that are complementary to the outdoor campaigns). A spokesperson for POSTAR describes the role of the organisation:

> It is simply our job to say there is a poster site, it's on the high street of wherever, so many thousand people will see it in a day and those people are made up of this type of socio-economic group, their gender, their age but also some other characteristics about them, their exposure to other media, like whether they're heavy viewers of television, whether they've got internet access or have a mobile phone, and a few sort of questions about whether they shop at Sainsbury's or Tesco's for example. So it is possible using our data to say this particular poster site is seen by 5,000 45–54 year-old women who are regular Sainsbury's shoppers who have an internet connection and

carry a mobile phone, for example. That's the sort of data you might get from us. (POSTAR spokesperson)

POSTAR is interested in people's mobility and maps this mobility, but the organisation is most interested in *patterns* of travel:

So we have to identify people's patterns. We do a thing called the travel survey where we interview people and ask them about the journeys they've made. We split the sample. One half of it is the journeys in the last 24 hours, the second half is journeys in the last 2 weeks...they have a diary to help their memories. And the way we collect the data is we basically have a laptop which has a sort of magic A to Z on it and we have trained interviewers and they say 'where did you go yesterday?', and they say, 'in the morning I went to Tesco's', 'which Tesco's?', 'the one there'. And then we use sort of a pen thing that joins the dots basically and that's collected digitally. So we have all that digitalised data which gives us people's travel patterns and that allows us to look at what we call 'frequency' in advertising, the numbers of time they may go past a certain poster site. (POSTAR spokesperson)

Thus, advertising sites can be targeted to particular groups' travel patterns and are priced according to their proximity to bus lanes, schools and supermarkets, and according to the number of traffic lanes of the adjacent road. For instance, Figure 4.1 is a media owner's promotional shot which shows the placement of billboards on a major arterial road.

On the premises outlined above, competing advertising companies produce targeting strategies that they pitch to potential clients. For instance, Primesight promotes its 'School Run' targeting strategy which is aimed at reaching children and parents: 'Displays are located within 500m of primary and secondary schools, the majority head-on to traffic. With school journeys now averaging 1 hour a day, the opportunity to reach this weekday audience is massive.'[7] In a PowerPoint pitch to potential clients, another company claims that outdoor advertising is the perfect medium to reach children as their routines involve travel and spending time outdoors: '36% of school children use the bus every day; 58% of school children have seen advertising on the inside of a bus in the past week; 40% of 11–14 year-olds have seen advertising on the Underground in the past week; 65% of 11–15 year-olds are users of National Rail'.

Figure 4.1   Media owner's promotional image (Courtesy of JCDecaux UK)

Another company, Clear Channel, offers a mapping strategy targeting 'housewives' that has advertising sites on routes to (and within 1,000m of) supermarkets or major multiples of which a third of sites are within 300m. Or, to take another example, Clear Channel offers a strategy to target various youth groups in which panels are sited in proximity to relevant locations (for the 14–17 age group: McDonalds, Top Shop etc.; for the 18–24 age group: universities, colleges, nightclubs etc.).[8] As well as targeting specific groups, media owning companies typically make big claims about the impact of outdoor advertising, and these claims often centre on shifting patterns of social behaviour. For instance, one media owner's PowerPoint presentation asserted that the, 'Average person spends 7 hours of the day out of the home and 46 minutes per day commuting. 88% of the population see OHH [out-of-home] during their daily journey.'

The very placement of the advertisements carves out new urban spaces and routes. Moreover, by siting advertisements on forms of transport such as buses and taxis, the vehicles become mobile carto-graphic devices that re-map and commercialise the spaces through which they travel. Outdoor advertising companies use these ideas to pitch for new clients, as instanced in this claim by Viacom (now called CBS Outdoor) about advertisements on coaches: 'Inter-urban coaches connect the UK's motorways with major population centres and airports. Advertising in a virtually "ad free" zone targets motorway drivers, city dwellers and air travellers.'[9] These commercial research and self-promotional strategies create a proliferation of mappings of urban spaces and of people's movements into, around and out of cities. One outdoor advertising company, Titan (previously called Maiden), tries to win new clients by claiming that it has the most recent and efficient methods of consumer classification. It calls one classificatory strategy 'home net' and 'office net'.[10] 'Home net' targets an evening commuter audience, so the advertising panels face traffic on major arterial routes away from cities moving towards residential areas. These panels have higher illumination to ensure visibility on dark, British, winter evenings. 'Office net' targets a morning audience with advertising panels facing traffic moving towards the city. Maiden maintains that this is a useful distinction for advertisers who may wish to target people according to mood, offering, for example, suggestions for that evening's shopping or entertainment.

Similarly, another media owning company promotes 'day part' advertising as a way of tapping into commuter rhythms. As this practitioner describes, such strategies are driven by client demands for more targeted outdoor promotions:

> You know, you've got all of these different skills sets in there, so we can target 100 metres proximity...you know, we can put panels that only are head-on to cars driving into the centre of town. So things like radio breakfast shows, Macdonald's breakfasts, cereals, cereal bars, Red Bull, coffee, all of the kind of things that you associate with morning advertising, you can then advertise to people just coming into the centre of town. And then conversely, if you use the rear side of those panels on the way back out of town in the evening, you can then target more booze, leisure-related products so that you're hitting people in relevant target markets. So there's...lots of different ways that as an industry we've had to do it, really, because I just don't think that the client side was willing to just move along with 5,000 panels any more. (Practitioner, media owning company)

Time of day and rhythms of commuting are part of advertising strategies in other ways too. The media owning company which has the contract for all advertising on the London Underground has worked with the Underground to address the problem of people fainting on the Tube in the morning. The media owning company has tried to work with

breakfast food advertisers to attempt to persuade people to eat breakfast before commuting to work. Similarly, the heat of summer produces
problems for people using the Underground, so the media owning company engaged in sponsorship deals with a bottled water company and
has distributed free bottles of branded water in summer.

Companies also produce new ways of selling audiences that are not
solely reliant on traditional socio-economic classifications. The media
owning company Titan calls another of its classificatory strategies
'modal targeting' or 'modal advertising':

> Rather than thinking of consumers in terms of demographics – age,
> social grade, gender and so on – it is more useful to think in terms of
> 'modes': working at the moment, in a spending mode, in a relaxing-
> with-friends mode, active versus inactive mode and so on. Instead
> of sequential life stages we should also think of life modes – single,
> in a relationship, single again, with children, without children and
> so on.[11]

By maintaining that outdoor advertising is a 'modally targeted'
medium, such a strategy enables companies to make claims about
their capacity to effectively target groups according to temporal and
spatial patterns, such as travel to work, going on holiday, or shopping with the children. Companies also attempt to tap into other
regular, annual events such as the Ideal Home Show, the Motor Show,
the London Boat Show, London Fashion Week and the Notting Hill
Carnival. One soft drinks company advertised on London taxis during
the Wimbledon tennis tournament and when the British tennis player
Tim Henman was playing, free taxi rides were offered. Another media
owning company bought advertising space in swimming pools and
advertised the film *Finding Nemo* by placing signs saying 'No Nemo'
around the pools.

I am not suggesting that these various strategies offer accurate ways of
classifying individuals, or of effectively persuading potential consumers.
The analysis of this material does not reveal an empirically valid picture of people's use of city space or advertising's impact on consumers.
It demonstrates outdoor advertising companies' discursive attempts to
continually re-map potential consumers according to spatial and travel
status and temporal modes of conduct. This re-mapping, and constant
pitching of 'new, improved' research and targeting strategies, is driven
by intense competition amongst outdoor companies and their need
to promote their commercial capacities to clients. So although town

planners or academics may take issue with their methods, conceptual frameworks and data, outdoor advertising companies – and more significantly, their clients – take the figures generated by research methodologies such as POSTAR very seriously. As one advertising practitioner stated in an interview, 'clients do sit and pour over the [POSTAR] figures. We have huge charts of how many people you're going to hit for this amount of money.'

As I examined in Chapters 2 and 3, the industry's research practices and its use of data are complex and uneven. It is clear that quantitative data is central for media owners, as one practitioner at a research company explains, 'by and large, numbers are currency because the media buyers are used to buying on numbers – market research numbers'. But the use of figures is meshed with intuition or marketing 'common sense'. A practitioner describes the process of pitching to clients: 'I think it's making sure that there is statistical evidence to support common sense arguments.... I think it's quite difficult to draw the line between what is fact and what is a gut feel.' There is also a sense in the industry that practitioners are inexperienced or unskilful in their use of data.

> They've got the data but they don't really know how to use it, so it's not been used in as sophisticated a way as it might be ... . There are a lot of people in the marketing communications business who know a dangerously small amount of things about a lot of things, and that's not surprising because it's ... so complex now and so diverse. To really know everything is very difficult and we're getting more and more sort of siloing happening with specialists looking at in great depth a small amount of what there is to know. (POSTAR spokesperson)

Why clients should be so willing to accept research methodologies and figures as accurate – and to believe that advertising is a viable solution to commercial problems – is a complex issue which has been explored more fully elsewhere (see Cronin 2004b, c; Miller 1997; Schudson 1993). For the purposes of this chapter, I would instead like to emphasise the significance of the companies' complex mapping of city space according to potential commercial value and rhythms. Should we see outdoor advertising as 'invasive' and corrosive of the social fabric as Borden would have it (2000: 105)? How should we understand the impact of advertising on people's experience of the city?

Advertising's urban rhythms

The knowledge generated by outdoor advertising companies – driven by strategic, commercial demands – does not offer an adequate account of advertising's significance in urban spaces or of its impact upon people's experiential relationship with cities. Advertising is in dialogue with urban spaces in ways more subtle and less instrumental than those highlighted by the commercial rhetorics of those companies. On one level, this interface with the urban results in some advertising sites becoming integral to the character of certain cities or sites, such as Piccadilly Circus in London and Times Square in New York. But advertising also inhabits and organises urban space in ways more mundane and less spectacular: in a complex and heterogeneous manner, advertising marks the everyday, routine experience of travelling to and around cities. It becomes a staple, taken-for-granted element of most Euro-American cities and, I suggest, plays a key part in producing what Michel de Certeau (1988: 96) describes as 'the disquieting familiarity of the city'. In effect, advertising contributes to the generation and maintenance of an ambiguous sense of familiarity with the structure, look and feel of urban spaces.

By dispersing well-known brands around urban space, advertising can make even unknown cities seem strangely familiar. Although we may never have visited the city in question, advertising can make its urban spaces feel more 'like home', or may apparently render more legible new cultures that initially seem opaque. Advertising's brands and logos make available the unfamiliar city to the visitor by bringing it into an established frame of reference. But advertising's impact is more subtle and ambiguous than this, drawing not only on brands, logos or the textual content of particular advertisements, but also on its ubiquitous presence and its status as an established cultural form. Advertising has an impact regardless of whether or not we register the textual messages of specific campaigns: advertising's very presence in the urban landscape makes familiar and naturalises the particular social arrangement of structures and flows of people that we call 'a city'. Thus, the way in which advertising has insinuated itself into the familiar fabric of the urban everyday gives a certain 'alreadyness' to the city as both a conceptual and lived unit.

But this is not to suggest that advertising companies' strategies of mapping and selling urban space to clients fully determine people's experience of advertising in cities. The panoptic, and what de Certeau (1988: 93) calls the 'geometrical' space of the visual that is constructed by city planners – and, I would add, commercial planners who own and organise advertising sites in cities – does not fully determine individuals' experience and use of city space. 'The ordinary practitioners of the city' develop unspoken and barely legible tactics and ruses that are neither captured nor determined by the systems in which they develop (de Certeau 1988: 93). For de Certeau, these tactics and ruses constitute 'the network of an antidiscipline' defined against the disciplining imperative of city planners and, in this case, advertising companies (1988: xv). Thus, the statistical investigations carried out by planners and advertising companies are unable to fully capture the nature of individuals' movements in city space. As noted in the previous section, it is certainly the case that the complex research practices carried out by outdoor advertising companies have no guarantee of efficiently targeting consumers. Even if advertising is creative, striking and well-situated, there is no guarantee that it will have any affect on its viewers and an accurate assessment of an advertising campaign's commercial effect on sales is equally problematic (Cronin 2004b, c; Miller 1997; Schudson 1993; Tunstall 1964).

This is recognised within the industry. The spokesperson for the Outdoor Advertising Association notes that, 'there are so many other factors in play: competition, price, the weather, you name it'. But this recognition tends to be glossed in media owning companies' promotional activities. Certainly, the power–knowledge formations mobilised by advertising companies are not top-down, super-efficient disciplinary regimes. Rather than operating an omnipotent ideological machine, advertising companies function on a more provisional, reactive basis, attempting strategic interventions for competitive advantage. Thus, just as people in urban spaces develop tactics and ruses as resistance to disciplining regimes, so also 'practices of oppression are themselves created by skilled improvisations' (Thrift 2000: 404). Using de Certeau's insights, and seeing the efforts of advertising companies themselves as tactical ruses, the companies' efforts at statistical representation of routes and potential consumers can be understood as tactical improvisations or skilful self-promotional gambits in a competitive field. But they also constitute a uni-dimensional transcription, and indeed flattening out, of the movements that occur in the city. The research frameworks established by advertising companies artificially arrest and fix these movements for commercial purposes into quantifiable routes and demographic units. They produce urban mappings of trajectories, speeds, social groups and experiences in ways that are instrumentally oriented towards selling or promoting that data as efficient consumer targeting material.

De Certeau's attention to detail in analysing the experience of movement in cities, and his emphasis on resistant practices, has led him to be described as 'a forensic romantic' (Thrift 2000: 399). This forensic detailing of practices and symbols at street-level offers an important analysis of the potential for resistance, albeit 'clandestine', 'unsigned', 'unreadable' resistance (de Certeau 1988: xiv, xvii). But for me, de Certeau's account is limited by a tendency to textualism that risks reducing embodied acts and experience to 'reading' and 'writing'. Whilst de Certeau (1988: 97) argues that unreadable ruses proliferate in city spaces, and that embodiment (in, for example, the form of footsteps) makes available 'tactile apprehension and kinesthetic appropriation', the main body of his analysis frames practice and spatiality as text. He writes, for instance, of 'the ordinary practitioners of the city...whose bodies follow the thicks and thins of an urban "text" they write without being able to read it' (de Certeau 1988: 93). I will turn to Henri Lefebvre's work to supplement de Certeau's insights better to grasp the complex interplay between the structuring impetus of advertising companies and the embodied experience of those passing through or moving around the city.

Lefebvre (1991, 1992, 1996) tries to apprehend these patterns of regularised, but not fully disciplined movements by thinking about a city's *rhythms*. Conceived as a 'pluridisciplinary' project, Lefebvre's (1996: 31) 'rhythmanalysis' draws on a range of approaches and methods such as chronobiology and the rhythms of speech and music to capture the experience and fabric of the urban. For Lefebvre, cities are composed of many such rhythms, some of which are more immediately evident than others as they exist in the foreground of our everyday awareness – the rules of traffic control, the pattern of children going to and from school, or the opening and closing times of shops. Whilst playing an equally significant part in framing our experience of the city, other rhythms are less apparent in our everyday urban imaginary, for example, the rhythmic cycles of a city's trees and other plants.

Lefebvre (1996) maintains that such an analysis must attend to the ways in which rhythms *animate* the urban. Yet this animation should not be confused with movement, speed or a mere repetition of gestures – such a conflation risks casting rhythms as purely mechanical or as socially structured in a deterministic manner, thus overlooking their reciprocal interaction, or at times mutual constitution, with organic, natural rhythms (Lefebvre 1992). Lefebvre thus identifies two dominant forms of rhythms: the linear and the cyclical. Linear rhythms are those centred on human activity and the consecutive quality of social relations, such as the rhythms of work and travel to work or school (Lefebvre 1992, 1996). Linear rhythms operate in conjunction with cyclical rhythms, defined as days, nights, seasons, waves and tides (Lefebvre 1992). The linear and the cyclical cannot logically be separated as they interact in complex ways, for example, in the links between the structuring of the five-day working week and its linear patterns on the one hand, and cyclical diurnal spans on the other. Here also, eurythmics – the rhythms of the body, such as the heartbeat, breathing, hunger and menstrual cycles – articulate with socially structured rhythms such as work (and indeed consumption), and in turn modulate the other's contours (Lefebvre 1992).

Lefebvre (1996: 221) calls rhythms 'a sort of meditation over time, the city, the people'. They offer the urban researcher a multidimensional analytic framework which explores how rhythms furnish the backdrop to the speeds, movements and people's temporal experience of cities. And this experience of the city is fully embodied. Lefebvre (1996) argues that no camera or sequence of images can reveal these rhythms as they subsist and are experienced at a corporeal level that interacts with the social structure.[12] Lefebvre's approach thus moves beyond a semiological or textual account of cities. For him, semiology inadequately addresses both the spatiality of cities and the nature of people's interface with these spaces: 'Changing sites into signs and values, the practico-material into formal significations, this theory also changes into pure consumer of signs he who receives them' (Lefebvre 1996: 115). In effect, a semiological or purely textual analysis reduces the space in question to a collection of messages and the experience of living in that space to a 'reading' (Lefebvre 1991: 7).

In this way, Lefebvre's account offers a useful corrective to de Certeau's (1988) textualism and offers intriguing alternative possibilities for analysing advertising in urban spaces. What form might such an analysis take? Lefebvre argues that a rhythmanalyst will be more aware of 'moods [rather] than of images, of the atmosphere than of particular spectacles' (1996: 229). This is an emphasis on multiple modes of perception and an openness to the reception of data or ways of understanding, and mirrors the type of approach promoted by Maiden's 'modal advertising' discussed earlier. Similarly, Roland Barthes (2002) recounts how his experience of orientating himself around Tokyo is reliant on embodied practice. This orientation, he notes, is not framed by the printed materials on which we rely in the west – maps, guides, telephone books.

Instead, he finds his way by 'une activité de type ethnographique' [a type of ethnographic exercise] and by 'la marche, la vue, l'habitude, l'expérience [walking, sight, habit, experience] (Barthes 2002: 381).[13] These modes of apprehension produce forms of knowledge of the city that are 'intense et fragile' and can only be retrieved by memory traces (Barthes 2002).

These insights can help shift understandings of advertising's impact upon cities from a purely textual 'reading' of specific campaigns to a broader understanding of the significance of advertising sites (billboards, panels in rail stations etc.) and the familiar presence of advertising in urban spaces. For instance, Charles Rice's suggestive account of large-scale advertising images in cities proposes that ads function in a 'cinematic' mode and have 'a particular affectivity that is spatialized' (2001: 25). For Rice, the scale of the adverts fosters a 'spatial fantasy' and a sense of 'closeness' between the viewer and the textual content of the ad that enables forms of identification (2001: 26). Despite an emphasis on affect, Rice's account is still premised on the significance of the textual content of ads and on an assumption that people moving through cities actively 'decode' or respond to advertising messages or affective moods that are presented to them. My data on commercial research suggests that individuals moving through cities do not register the textual content or 'message' of specific advertisements in any focused or consistent manner.

It is certainly the case that advertising companies expend considerable time and money attempting to find ways to persuade potential clients of advertising's effectiveness at reaching consumers. The Outdoor Advertising Association, for instance, launched a billboard campaign in August 2003 with the aim of promoting the outdoor advertising sector. The large billboards featured the words 'Bam!', 'Pow!', 'Zapp!' in pop art-style graphics to emphasise the format's visual impact. Although the Outdoor Advertising Association cited this campaign as proof of outdoor advertising's capacity to deliver strong messages, they were unable to prove that people actually registered the specific content of the advertisements. As Simmel (1991, 1995) noted many years ago, cities as centres for the money-economy fostered the 'blasé attitude' (1991: 24). This non-responsive disposition is generated as a protective mechanism in the face of the metropolitan 'concentration of purchasable things which stimulates the individual to the highest degree of nervous energy' (Simmel 1995: 36). Alongside the proliferation of commodities, Simmel (1995) saw the root of the blasé attitude in individuals' response to the increased tempo of economic, occupational and social life: in the face of such stimulation, people retreat into inattention and reserve.[14]

Arguably, advertisements in urban contexts suffer from a contemporary blasé attitude. It seems that people moving around the city rarely distinguish individual advertisements from those of other campaigns and rarely 'read' the advertisement in a classic sense. Media owning companies attempt to quantify such encounters, as evident in POSTAR's 'Visibility Adjusted Impacts' classification. But the 'recall' research strategy, in which people are asked if they have seen a specific advertisement, to describe an advertisement, or to associate an advertisement with the correct brand, delivers notoriously poor results. It appears that people's mode of apprehension of specific outdoor advertisements is one of inattention. Ironically, the sheer aggregate of advertisements in city spaces may itself exacerbate the blasé attitude towards them, confounding their attempts to channel attention and modify (consuming) behaviour.

But outdoor advertising in urban settings may have a significance beyond that of its textual content and commercial impact of individual campaigns. If we consider Lefebvre's emphasis on the structuring interaction between linear and cyclical rhythms – and the interaction between the bodies of people in cities and the fabric of the urban itself – the impact of outdoor advertising can be seen in a different way. For Lefebvre, the body is central in any analysis of space and cities: 'through the mediation of rhythms (in all three senses of "mediation": means, medium, intermediary), an animated space comes into being which is an extension of the space of bodies' (Lefebvre 1991: 207). It is this animated space, I argue, that advertisers attempt to exploit. In the example of targeting commuters in the 'home net' and 'office net' strategy, outdoor advertising companies attempt to adjust to, and tap into, the linear rhythms of commuting to work that are linked to the cyclical, bodily rhythms of sleep, waking and work. But the rhythms of advertising, and the way in which advertising companies attempt to tap into urban rhythms, also bring into being the animated urban space in more profound ways. In 'A Berlin Chronicle', Walter Benjamin (1979: 295) plays with the idea of 'setting out the sphere of life – bios – graphically on a map'. He maps his life through recounting remembered spaces, feelings and moods in Berlin and their dialogue with the major periods, people or events in his life: the parks of his childhood, the house of a family friend, railway stations he frequented. Here, Benjamin is organising his autobiographical account through his encounter with the spaces and temporalities of Berlin and its inhabitants. This produces, in effect, a biography of his own life hybridised with a biographical account of the spatial and affective orientation of Berlin.

Urban advertising stages a similar articulation in its attempts to align or draw into consonance the biographies of commodities and the biographical trajectories of people travelling to and around cities. Things or objects can be seen to have 'social lives' (Appadurai 1986) and 'biographies' (Kopytoff 1986) through which we can track their candidacy and entry into the status of 'commodity'; or perhaps their suspension from the circuits of commodity exchange by attaining the status of heirloom which renders them 'not for sale'. What I am arguing is that outdoor advertising aims to tap into the rhythms of the city and the people who move around the city to create a biographical dialogue – a rhythmic hybrid – linking the rhythms of commodity innovation and commodity promotion with the city's rhythms and the rhythms of people in city space. Simmel has argued that 'a person does not end with limits [sic] of his physical body'(1995: 41).[15] This leaves open a space of intervention through which the biographical unity of a person may be revised or expanded. In an urban context, the money-economy and its emphasis on exchange-value and quantification makes us indifferent to distinctions between things, thus contributing to the blasé attitude (Simmel 1995).

Commercial culture is trying to exploit this homogenising, blasé effect by attempting to emphasise indistinctions between advertisements and commodities on the one hand, and people moving around the city on the other. Thus, outdoor advertising aims to link the cyclical rhythms of bodies, hours, days, months etc. with the linear rhythms of work, commuting and other structured trajectories through the city. It aims to connect people's urban and personal rhythms to product innovation and cycles of promotion. Figure 4.2, a JCDecaux panel in London, illustrates how advertising attempts to target and inhabit everyday commuting and shopping routes and become part of the fabric of people's urban experience.

As owners of advertising spaces in cities sell these spaces in standardised segments of time, the lifecycle of the commodity and the rhythms of promotion becomes interwoven with the everyday, routine experience of moving around the city. Advertising, thus, marks the 'life stages' of commodity innovation, promotion and withdrawal – we see teaser ads for products not yet launched; new ads for new products; new ads for line-extensions of established products; reminder and brand-awareness ads for established products; and last-ditch advertising attempts for products which are about to be de-listed (withdrawn from the market).

Figure 4.2   Media owner's promotional image (Courtesy of JCDecaux UK)

But advertising is not merely a reflection of the biography of the commodity, nor is it simply a passive medium: advertising is itself an active force that influences the rhythms of a commodity.[16] For instance, Schudson (1993) argues that high-profile advertising for a product or brand can enhance investors' (and potential investors') confidence in it, thus making available more funds for that product's further development and advertising. This extends or re-invigorates both the commodity's lifecycle and the cycles of advertising that promote it.

One of the effects of this dynamic is that people become familiarised with the standardised temporal rhythms of advertising campaigns in which most sites are bought for set lengths of time and many outdoor advertising companies have minimum lengths of hire. Furthermore, the changing rhythms of new advertisements mark people's experience of time. As advertising is sited on modes of transport such as buses, trains and taxis, it marks out time spent travelling and impacts upon people's experience of that time. But it also marks time in other, less obvious ways. We may become slightly disoriented when there is a break in the familiar commercial rhythms – returning to London after a holiday and not recognising the new advertisements on the underground train system can jar the temporal framework of our urban everyday. At these disquieting moments, the normally unrecognised comes to the fore – here, the way in which advertising frames our experience and understanding of the passing of time in specific spaces. As I explore in Chapter 6, the gradual deterioration of the material structure of some billboards also marks the passing of time and creates a dialogue between the temporality of commodity production, promotion and consumption and other rhythms such urban decay and regeneration. This further contributes to a particular city's lived biography, co-authored – or, rather, co-performed – by the rhythms of the commodity and the movements of bodies through its spaces.[17]

Seen in this way, advertising's impact on cities goes beyond the potential commercial effects of individual campaigns whether they are promoting specific commodities, brands or events. It also extends beyond the significance of the textual content of specific advertisements. Advertising's well-established presence in city space and the way in which it functions through constant, rhythmic innovation has a marked effect. This commercial temporality and the spatial organisation of advertising-rich routes into and around cities becomes part of our taken-for-granted experience of urban space. Indeed, the temporality of commodity innovation and promotion contributes to creating the experience of urban excitement or raciness – the buzz of the city.

But advertising does not merely *naturalise* commercial culture or commodity relations. As Lefebvre makes clear (1991), cyclical and linear rhythms cannot be thought apart from one another. We cannot therefore say that advertising brings together the distinct realms of the natural rhythms of the body, seasons etc. with the social rhythms of work and travel. But it is possible to say that advertising in urban spaces establishes a time–space of 'commodity rhythms' that attunes people to the rhythms of commercial innovation and promotion, and links our embodied, biographical movements in the city with the biographies of commodities. The speed of these rhythms of commercial innovation is not in itself the most important factor: the real significance lies in the articulation between the lifecycle of the commodity (and its promotion) and the rhythms of the city and the people moving around that city space. This dialogue is recognised and acted upon by outdoor advertising companies, as illustrated in this pitch by Clear Channel: 'The ASA [Advertising Standards Authority] research found that the synergy between ads and normal life is important to consumers and that billboards provide the best opportunity to demonstrate that synergy.'[18] This synergy, and the time afforded by the specificities of the medium and the temporality of travel, is channelled and exploited: 'Outdoor can't be "zipped" or "zapped", you can't turn the page or tune to another channel. It is also consumed in what can be considered "dead time" – there is no additional cost in money or time to the consumer.'[19]

The alignment of people's everyday patterns of work, shopping, commuting, taking children to school etc. with commodity rhythms places a clear emphasis on the interactive, generative quality of the process. Many authors argue that the city undergoes a constant process of configuration and reconfiguration. Other authors suggest that we think about cities as fields of movement and consider, 'how cities are *orders*, and this ordering is often exacted through the design of flows as a set of serial *encounters* which construct particular spaces and times' (Amin and Thrift 2002: 83). Advertising is one of those ordering forces that organises serial urban encounters and continually makes and remakes the city. Through outdoor advertising companies' mapping strategies, advertising can be seen as one of the generative forces that frames movement and carves out urban spaces and routes. But the concept of 'flow' does not adequately capture the temporal quality of advertising's attempts to align its promotional tempo and cycles with the rhythms of the city and people moving around the city. As both de Certeau (1988) and Lefebvre (1991) note, flows assume a direct reversibility – a trajectory that can be retraced in reverse direction, or can be repeated with the same effect, or retrieved with its original pattern or meaning intact. The concept of rhythm on the other hand, can capture the uniqueness and irreversibility of those moments of travel, thought and embodied experience whether they mesh completely with the commodity time–space that advertising enacts in cities or whether they ignore, refract or resist those structuring elements.

And of course a complete ideological hold by the commodity's rhythms is impossible. The contemporary city is, in Foucault's (2000) terms, a heterotopic space where the conventional syntax of place and the process of naming are disrupted. This is, 'not only the syntax with which we construct sentences, but also that less apparent syntax which causes words and things…to "hold together"' (Foucault 2000: xviii). This loosening of meaning, linked to the targeting of city rhythms, allows advertising to impact upon people and the lived routes into and around the city in new, ambiguous ways. On one level, this articulation naturalises and normalises both the contemporary configuration of the city (as a conglomeration of inhabitants, workers, infrastructure, finance, commodities) and the nature of commodity relations (networks of commodified exchange, the embodiment of value in objects, cycles of innovation and renewed consumption).

I would suggest that there are other important implications that are less clear cut. Outdoor advertising in cities attempts a strategic ordering, a kind of bio-politics, but in a rather expanded sense than that outlined in Foucault's (1990) classic account. It attempts to co-ordinate and align populations of people with populations of commodities by creating a consonant relation between their respective rhythms. This is a form of bio-politics that organises not only around the life course of people – birth rates, disease, death – but around the *biographical connections* between people and commodified things in the rhythmic spaces we know as cities. This is a new mutation in the metabolism of the city. Somewhat like consumption, the concept of metabolism implies a calibrated, regulated 'using up' of resources, materials and perhaps people. But metabolism also signals a generative, productive process. The metabolic interventions of outdoor advertising companies attempt to make and remake mapped routes through the city. But their efforts also have other results that are less amenable to control. They produce the frameworks within which new hybrids are made and remade: the lifecycles and biographies of commodities and people moving through the city are rhythmically overlaid one on the other to create a hybrid woven by rhythms. The imbrication of the biographies of people and of commodities that advertising attempts to institute may redefine us as other 'life-forms' – forms of life that exist and are administered in the advertising-rich spaces of the city, and that orient our sense of self, society and space through commercial principles and the promotional cycles of the commodity.

But the heterotopic spatial quality identified by Foucault also means that advertising's ubiquity in cities does not translate into an unequivocal triumph of capitalist ideologies. The widespread presence of advertising raises the profile of certain brands, but this does not necessarily result into commercial success (Miller 1997; Schudson 1993; Tunstall 1964).[20] Indeed, the heightened profile of brands such as Nike and Nestlé renders them very visible as targets and rallying points for protest groups. Other companies may have equally objectionable production practices or advertising strategies, but the high-profile advertising of some companies tends to draw the fire of such criticism. Moreover, advertising billboards and panels make very convenient sites for graffiti and counter-cultural activity as they are, of course, sited for maximum visual impact (c.f. Klein 2000). But these resistant, 'subvertising' practices may suffer the same blank inattention of the blasé attitude that outdoor advertisements themselves attempt to counter. Rather than the text of the advertisement, it may be the alignment of commodity rhythms with city rhythms and people's bodily and social rhythms that now forms the most important site for advertising's attempts at insinuation and also people's new, and perhaps subversive, embodiment through these hybridised rhythms. Just as the future implications of genetically modified organisms are unclear, so too are the future and the political implications of this rhythmic hybrid.

By distancing the analysis from a purely textual account of advertising, it is possible to see advertising's broader impact as a cultural and economic form, and as a spatialising and temporalising agent. I have argued that outdoor advertising taps into and exploits the linear and cyclical rhythms of the city, creating 'a commodity time–space' and 'commodity rhythms' in which there is an on-going set of dialogues between the commercial rhythms of commodity innovation and promotion on the one hand, and the rhythms of the city and the bodily rhythms of its inhabitants and visitors on the other. It is this set of dialogues or new form of metabolism that deserves closer attention as cities grow and mutate. In the next three chapters, I pursue this interest in embodiment, and the structures and spatiality of advertising, and examine what forms of knowing they enable.

5
Fabulating Commercial Spaces: Mediation, Texts and Perception

This chapter challenges conventional conceptions of advertising's role as medium, intermediary or mediator, and opens up questions about its relation to time, space and bodies. Advertising's mediating function is often conceived in both academic and marketing literatures as a dynamic, and indeed transformative, relationship. It is imagined to mediate between producers and consumers (where advertising creatives act as cultural intermediaries); between needs and desires (where advertising is thought to stimulate consumption beyond basic bodily requirements); between materialities and immaterialities (where the material form of the commodity is thought to become enchanted by the imagery of branding and advertising). In previous chapters I have outlined the many different processes within the industry that are understood as 'mediation', for instance, the commercial relations between media owners, media agencies and client firms. I argued that these interactions do not merely link diverse commercial actors and distinct commercial practices; they operate performatively, creating and re-creating productive relationalities and opening up commercial futures in unexpected ways.

In my analysis, then, mediation is not a process in which an object, person or representation stands in-between other pre-existing objects, persons or representations and helps articulate their interaction. Instead, I contend that this mediation is enacted through complex relational processes and alters through various performances. Recent analyses in urban studies have examined this performative quality of social relations and have paid particular attention to the importance of representation, temporality, spatiality and the body. As noted in the introductory chapter, what has been termed non-representational or post-representational theory or 'styles of thought' offer interesting challenges for thinking about these areas.

> These styles of thought treat everything usually regarded as repre-
> sentational (words, concepts, ideas, perceptions, images) as *events*
> in their own right: 'means without ends' rather than media of
> re-presentation ... [they] collapse the long-standing separation of
> the world (reputedly over there, somewhere in the Real) from its
> re-presentation (supposedly over here, somewhere in the imaginary
> and the symbolic). (Doel and Clarke 2007: 897)

Such approaches offer productive ways of thinking about mediation:
they challenge the strict, conventional distinctions between things,
bodies and images – the material and the immaterial – and take 'the
energy of the sense-catching forms of things seriously' (Thrift 2008: 9).
In studies of the urban, non- or post-representational accounts distance
themselves from approaches that 'decode' city spaces as a field of representations or a semiotic map. Instead, they wish to refocus debates onto
an analysis of mediation as a kind of bodily engagement with spaces
that exceeds the scope of conventional textual representation; they
wish to think about the relationalities of space, time and bodies.

But many who are sympathetic to the aims and approach of non-
representational theories also argue that representations should not
be disregarded. Castree and MacMillan (2004), for instance, argue for
a continued academic engagement with representations and indeed
representational politics, while also pursuing the questions that non-
representational theories pose. It is in this spirit that I draw on these
debates. In this chapter, I argue that a narrow conceptualisation of
what counts as a text or an image is unhelpful when trying to understand their significance in urban space. I elaborate an understanding
of mediation and representation though a conceptualisation of spatiality, of temporality, and of embodiment. It sets up the theoretical
framework for Chapter 6's analysis of advertising structures and texts in
Manchester (UK) and Detroit (Michigan, USA).

The first section of the chapter examines how the relationship of cities to representation has been conceived as a form of mediation. Here
I start to open up the parameters of what should be considered 'representation'. I point to its significance for thinking about cities, discussing in particular James Donald's (1999) account of the archive city. The
second section discusses how Henri Bergson's work on perception and
'images' offers a productive entry point for thinking about how temporality, perception, bodies and spaces are linked. I outline Bergson's

analysis of the production of agency through acts of perception and consider how this approach can be useful for thinking about the perception of advertisements. I revisit Henri Lefebvre's (1991) assertion that space is not merely a neutral medium or field in which events take place. Drawing on Elizabeth Grosz's (2001) extension of Bergson's ideas, I ask how spaces might function as active mediators. The 'action' of mediation is thus reframed as temporally and spatially dynamic, and as fundamentally relational. The final section argues that Bergson's lesser-known work on fabulation, with its emphasis on the embodied nature of perception, offers productive ways of analysing advertising texts and structures. I discuss how fabulation is an imaginative process through which we make stories about the world; but it is also a way of opening up or animating futures, and of seeing the openness of spaces.

Cities and representation

In the literature on cities, considerable attention has been paid to the relationship of representation to urban space and to the role of particular media in articulating an idea of the city. Many accounts propose that the city is at same time a physical environment and an amalgam of representations such as photographs and films. But other analyses suggest that the relationship of representations to city space – of urban materialities to what are seen as representational immaterialities – is more creative and indeed performative. In one of the most suggestive of these accounts, James Donald (1999) argues that representations are not merely peripheral or secondary phenomena, but act to constitute our very understanding and experience of the city. Representations such as films, photographs and novels, but also sociological accounts, create an imaginary city – 'the archive city' – which we carry around with us (Donald 1999: 7). For Donald, the archive city embodies an urban paradox. People's engagement with vibrant city space involves 'an immediacy of experience: the *this, here, now,* so beloved of empiricist philosophers' (Donald 1999: 7, emphasis in the original). But the archive city simultaneously acts to mediate our engagement with space:

> this experience of immediacy is mediated through and through by the pedagogies and aesthetics of the city. It involves not immediacy but contingency. The city teaches us the arts, the techniques, and the tactics of living in the present. (Donald 1999: 7)

Donald's analysis highlights the temporal and spatial qualities of the archive city. He suggests that the city as a way of seeing is produced, and in turn produces, urban representations. This operates in a feedback loop: influenced by people's experience of urban space, the representations that constitute the archive city will shift over time and vary according to the specificities of place. In turn, the archive city will shape people's experience of urban spaces and temporalities. As we inhabit and move through urban space, our imagination (mediated by the archive city) enables us 'to live both here and elsewhere' (Donald 1999: 5). Understood in this way, the city is less a geographically situated place than a 'historically specific mode of seeing' (Donald 1999: 92).

As well as analysing the city as a way of seeing, Donald focuses on how the mass media produce representations of specific cities or a generic image of 'the city'. Clearly, media institutions such as Hollywood dominate the production and dissemination of the archive city. But it is important to recognise that media representations may be at odds with people's everyday experiences of their own cities. And alongside the mass media there exist other modes of representationally engaging with the city, such as through family snapshots or tourist photographs (see Edensor 1998; Urry 2002). These will also contribute to individuals' sense of the archive city. But this multi-modal production of the city as representation and as representational device is not the juxtaposition of a false or idealised image of the city against the real, lived experience of people's engagement with urban spaces. The cinema produces not only images but *modes of seeing*, and specifically, the city as a mode of seeing. This is not to say that people impose a mass-mediated visual template of a particular version of 'the city' onto their environments. Rather, it is to argue that a cinematic mode of seeing will be woven into people's spatialised experience in complex ways. Different media will exert more intense influence on this mode of seeing in different historical periods and much attention has focused on cinema's formative relationship with the modern city (e.g. AlSayyad 2006; Clarke 1997). Cinema has certainly played a key part in creating the archive city – and indeed, perhaps, in forming academic geography's optical unconscious (Doel and Clarke 2007). But as Donald (1999) notes, cinema's influence is now waning while spatial organisation – and imagination – is constituted increasingly by multimedia and global flows of information. How we think about an urban representation, and perhaps even a medium, is shifting.

Donald invites us to think about the co-productive nature of the relationship between the material forms of urban space and representations of cities. This putative distinction between the material and the immaterial has recently received considerable attention as it focuses key questions about the nature of cities, the analytic purchase of particular approaches to the city and the character of capitalism. In one account, Latham and McCormack (2004) challenge the assumptions of approaches which appeal for urban analysis to be more grounded in 'the material'. Often emerging from conventional political economy, such analyses tend to frame the material as a welcome 'gritty reality check' to what is seen as geography's recent romance with theoretical abstractions (Latham and McCormack 2004: 702). As well as pointing out that there are many materialities at play in the city, and that materiality understood in political economy terms is not the same as in other disciplines, they argue that 'paying increased attention to the material actually demands that we begin to take seriously the real force of the immaterial' (Latham and McCormack 2004: 704). Here, the conceptual scope of the immaterial encompasses non-representational forces and processes through which matter continually comes into being. Latham and McCormack argue that to speak of the material is to have already invoked the excessive potential of the immaterial. This recent move towards the immaterial takes many forms including an analysis of affect. Indeed, many now propose that affective economies are as important as political and symbolic economies (Amin and Thrift 2002), and that feelings, ideas and imaginaries are as significant in constituting the 'real city' as economics and architectural structures (Pile 2005).

As well as rethinking the strict conceptual demarcation between the material and the immaterial, these debates open up questions about the nature of representation and the nature of embodied perception. Understandings of the body as the material substrate or medium through which we process (what are seen as) immaterial forms such as representations seem wholly inadequate for thinking about the city and representation. Elizabeth Grosz (1995) offers an intriguing approach to the question of bodies and cities, and challenges the presumptions of many influential accounts of this relationship. One such presumption is that the natural body precedes the city and that it functions to orient the design and construction of cities. In such a perspective, the city is 'a reflection, projection, or product of bodies' (Grosz 1995: 105). Here, the city reflects both human consciousness and the physical materiality and energies of the body. Other accounts, she suggests, imagine the body and city (or body and state) as analogues in which 'the features, organization and characteristics of one are reflected in the other.... The state parallels the body; artifice mirrors nature' (Grosz 1995: 105–106). Rejecting these frameworks as inadequate, Grosz instead suggests a model in which the body–city relationship is neither holistic unity nor ecology, but 'a disunified series of systems, a series of disparate flows, energies, events, or entities, bringing together or drawing apart their more or less temporary alignments' (Grosz 1995: 108). The city is thus

> the site for the body's cultural saturation, its takeover and trans-formation by images, representational systems, the mass media, and the arts – the place where the body is representationally reexplored, transformed, contested, reinscribed. In turn, the body (as cultural product) transforms, reinscribes the urban landscape according to its changing (demographic) needs, extending the limits of the city ever towards the countryside that borders it. (Grosz 1995: 108–109)

Grosz is here drawing on the work of Henri Bergson – and Gilles Deleuze's analyses which were inspired in part by Bergson – in order to argue that the body and the city have a co-constitutive relationship. This is a relationship which includes representations not as immaterial shadows or mirrors of reality, nor as mere semantic resources. Bergson inspires Grosz to suggest that representation is always already bodily and that it *matters*. This is a form of mediation that is fully embodied, that confounds conventional distinctions between the material and immaterial. It suggests interesting avenues for thinking through texts, material structures such as billboards, the spatiality of cities, and their relationship to the body.

Bergson, perception and the body

Henri Bergson's work has recently attracted renewed critical atten-tion and holds considerable appeal for those analysing temporality. Many approach Bergson's ideas through Gilles Deleuze's reading and re-working of them. But it is important to recognise that Deleuze's own framing of Bergson's concepts, such as 'the virtual', is markedly differ-ent (Gunter 2004). Here, I focus on Bergson's own works with a spe-cific interest in his understandings of perception and fabulation. I also address recent re-evaluations and extensions of Bergson's ideas, particu-larly those of Elizabeth Grosz (2001, 2005).

Bergson's work is attractive for many as it promises a flexible and cre-ative approach to understanding embodiment, perception, temporality and 'life'. But his ideas have also attracted considerable criticism which often emerges in contemporary discussion of the similarities and differences between Bergson and other later philosophers who disavowed connections with his work (see Al-Saji 2007; Olkowski 2002). For instance, Mullarkey (1994) points to significant and generally unacknowledged connections between the work of Maurice Merleau-Ponty and Bergson. And Fraser (2008) argues that despite Henri Lefebvre's own distancing of his work from Bergson's, and his personal animosity towards Bergson, Lefebvre used many of his insights while also misinterpreting his account of spatiality. My aim is not to engage in a detailed philosophical discussion of these points but it will be useful to focus on two criticisms of Bergson's work: his prioritisation of temporality over spatiality (a criticism I deal with in more depth in later sections of this chapter), and a kind of biologism and romance with science.

Bergson produced his accounts at the end of the nineteenth and in the first quarter of the twentieth century and his work had considerable impact on thinkers of the time. Influenced by diverse scientific developments, discussions of evolutionary theory, and perspectives from cognitive science, he wrote both with and against those scientific understandings (Lacey 1989). Thus Bergson's work inhabits an ambiguous relationship to scientific 'truth' and to the conventional perception of science advancing towards ever-more accurate understandings of the body and the natural world. In many ways, his analysis of perception and embodiment has been superseded by scientific developments, particularly in cognitive science and neurobiology. But as John Mullarkey (1999b) suggests, conceptual strains of his analyses can be found in contemporary paradigms such as chaos theory and complexity theory, and in the work of influential scientists such as Richard Dawkins. Indeed, assessing the relevance and usefulness of ideas of the body – in this case, Bergson's understanding of embodied perception – is complex, for any discussion of biology immediately invokes 'the body' *and* the study of it.[1]

Bergson's philosophy of the body emphasises openness and change, and also suggests that *accounts of the body* should be open to change. It is on this level that I find his work most suggestive. These characteristics of openness and mutability are most evident in his concept of the *élan vital*, or vital impulse, that I introduced in Chapter 2. This is often interpreted as a theory of *life* as biological force. But as Marrati describes, the *élan vital*, 'the essence of life, that which defines its very origin, is nothing but a tendency to change – it is a tendency to move, and to a movement that *creates* divergent directions by its own growth' (Marrati 2005: 1108, emphasis in the original). So while Bergson has been described as a vitalist, and indeed uses the phrase *élan vital*, the emphasis in his work is on the first part of the phrase: 'the vitality in question is a type of time, a type of organisation, rather than any mysterious notion of an *anima sensitiva*, vital fluid or *archeus*' (Mullarkey 1999a: 63). My interest is to explore how such ideas can be deployed to interpret our experience of advertising and urban space; in particular, how bodily perception can weave ideas about the embodiment and life (as change and movement) back into the ways in which people imagine their environments and their own practices.

My concern, therefore, is not to engage in a general discussion of Bergson's philosophical pedigree. My interest is pragmatically oriented to the possibilities that Bergson's ideas offer my analysis and particularly the ways in which his concepts can be put to work – perhaps in impure or disaggregated form – to offer insights into the issues raised in my ethnographic work and photographic study. Bergson's emphasis on rethinking the 'mediation' between the classically distinct categories of images and things, individual bodies and 'external' matter, open up avenues for analysis that link perceptual action, representation, materiality and agency. This practical, strategic approach would not, I think, be offensive to Bergson. Mullarkey (1999b) notes that Bergson himself admitted that he had no 'system' and acknowledged that his individual works did not therefore constitute a coherent whole: 'indeed, Bergson stated that he never began a new work without also forgetting his previous positions and demanding a new effort of research' (Mullarkey 1999b: 5). In this spirit, I take from Bergson suggestive ideas, and ways of formulating research questions, without any expectation of receiving from his works a systematic or comprehensive framework. In what follows, then, I examine Bergson's ideas about perception and embodiment, together with his less well-known concept of fabulation. This work of conceptual framing is then followed through in Chapters 6 and 7 with a discussion of empirical material.

Bergson's work starts from the premise that perception is fundamentally bodily and that we are oriented to the world through perception. But on the visual level, what the embodied acts of perception apprehend are not images or representations defined in the conventional sense. For Bergson, representation is 'the totality of perceived images' (Bergson 2004: 64). But his concept of an image is unconventional and complex; it is not quite the immaterial form of a representation but neither is it quite the material form of a thing. Bergson's 'image' challenges the distinction between realist and idealist conceptions of the world:

> And by 'image' we mean a certain existence which is more than
> that which the idealist calls a *representation*, but less than that which
> the realist calls a *thing*, – an existence placed half-way between the
> 'thing' and the 'representation'. (Bergson 2004: vii–viii, emphasis in
> the original)

The definition of an image, then, is not restricted to a visual rendering of something which exists materially in the world (or even
a visual rendering of something 'immaterial' or imagined such as a
unicorn). In Bergson's account, representation does not function to
mirror matter; thus, the question of the extent to which representations either accurately reflect or distort matter or the 'real world' is
rendered irrelevant. So this is not an act of representational mediation as standardly conceived. Central to Bergson's understanding of
images, materiality, perception and representation is the body, but
not as a simple, fleshy medium: 'I call *matter* the aggregate of images,
and *perception of matter* these same images referred to the eventual
action of one particular image, my body' (Bergson 2004: 8, emphasis
in the original).

'The image' is thus broadly conceived. The brain is an image, the body
is an image, what are conventionally seen as 'objects' are, for Bergson,
images. The body is the centre of these images just as the perception
of images constitute the body. As we develop as infants, we gradually
carve out from the material world the centre of action that we come to
call our body. In that process we come to distinguish our body from all
others: we create the boundaries of our 'self'. In this way, we fashion
conceptual boundaries of the 'inside' of the individual and its 'outside'
(other people, the material world) where in reality their relationship
is fluid, inter-dependent, and co-productive. Thus, the body, perception and matter are inter-related as images. Bergson understands the
material world as 'a system of closely linked images' in which there are
'centres of real action' which are represented by living matter such as
human bodies (Bergson 2004: 21). These centres of action, or bodies,
suppress certain parts of objects that do not interest them by allowing
to pass through them those external influences to which they are indifferent. But for Bergson, this is not a cognitive process of conscious selec-
tion; it is more fundamental, more bodily. Not founded on individual
choice or agency, it is instead a performative process that produces bodies and agency. Thus, the action of perception is not a process of *adding*

to objects – adding, for instance, meanings or perceptual layers – but rather a process of selecting out or filtering. In that process of isolating certain factors which are not of interest to the centre of action (our body), perceptions are carved out.

This formulation of representation, matter and perception, Bergson argues, is difficult to conceive as conventional wisdom holds that the brain in some ways 'processes' visual or other sensory information received from 'outside reality' and prepares or creates representations from this information. To illustrate this, Bergson asks us to imagine perception not as a kind of biological photographic process in which the eyes receive visual data from which a chemical image is developed later by the brain (Bergson 2004). Instead, we must understand that the brain itself is matter – and image – and cannot be conceived as separate from that which it perceives. Controversially, Bergson claims that neither the brain nor nervous system creates or even prepares representations as the brain merely receives and forwards stimulation. To replace the trope of the photographic apparatus and the process of 'developing' an image, Bergson offers the metaphor of a central telephone exchange. 'It adds nothing to what it receives'; instead, it merely transmits communication – or *movement* – or allows a delay (Bergson 2004: 19, emphasis in the original). But the brain can also direct communication: 'the office of the brain is sometimes to conduct the movement received to a *chosen* organ of reaction, and sometimes to open to this movement the *totality* of the motor tracks' (Bergson 2004: 20, emphasis in the original). So the brain merely receives and directs stimulus; it does not create representations or process information other than by channelling it.

But the process does open up the possibilities of action or human agency. Along with selecting the organs to which to transmit the communication, the brain can insert a delay between the reception of stimulus by the nervous system and the motor response. The existence or size of the gap between this reception and transmission is what differentiates higher and lower order beings, as rudimentary organisms have instant responses to stimuli. This Bergson conceives spatially:

> The degree of independence of which a living being is master, or, as we shall say, the zone of indetermination which surrounds its activity, allows, then, of an *a priori* estimate of the number and the distance of the things with which it is in relation. (2004: 23)

So as well as being relational, perception is fundamentally practical and oriented to action, not to 'pure knowledge' (Bergson 2004: 21). As action and agency are tied to bodily perception in Bergson's broadly conceived sense, 'conscious perception signifies choice, and consciousness mainly consists in this practical discernment' (Bergson 2004: 46). Such practical discernment is the understandings produced by our bodily actions and the scope of perception is indicative of the scope of our agentic possibilities, of the indetermination offered to us by perception: 'the growing richness of perception' symbolises 'the wider range of indetermination left to the choice of the living being in its conduct with regard to things' (Bergson 2004: 21). Thus perception's 'amplitude gives the exact measure of the indetermination of the act which is to follow' (Bergson 2004: 23). Bergson's account of perception offers intriguing avenues for exploring embodiment and agency, and opens up questions about the nature of mediation and representation. In the next section, I examine how his work also foregrounds the significance of spatiality and how this is folded together with his better known account of duration.

Space, movement and perception

While Bergson's understandings of temporality and duration appear frequently in contemporary studies, his conception of space and spatiality has been rather less well received. Critics such as Crang and Travlou (2001) argue that Bergson conceives time as dynamic at the expense of space which he frames as inert and passive. Doreen Massey's (2005) critique of Bergson follows a similar line. She argues that Bergson's emphasis on creativity and novelty focuses on temporality and duration in opposition to space which he associates with fixity (and representation). According to Massey (2005: 23), Bergson characterises space as composed of pluralities; however, this plurality is not radical difference (heterogeneity; differences in kind) but 'the dimension of quantitative divisibility'. Unlike time, Bergson's space is composed merely of a 'discrete multiplicity' and does not have the vital, dynamic quality of duration (Massey 2005: 23). Massey wants to challenge this apparent inertia and instead conceive space as a 'dynamic simultaneity' which is the 'dimension of multiple trajectories... the dimension of a multiplicity of durations' (Massey 2005: 23–24).

But others offer different interpretations of Bergson's account of space and its possibilities. Mullarkey (1999a) argues that Bergson presents different conceptions of space and that these shift across his various works. In *Matter and Memory*, for instance, Bergson states that we *imagine* space as homogeneous and empty for our pragmatic purpose of interacting with it – that is, to provide an apparently stable and predictable ground as traction for our actions. As Mullarkey puts it, 'the homogeneity of space results from our need to reduce its native alterity to a general set of possible positions, every one the exact same save for their different co-ordinates, an "empty container" in other words' (1999a: 13). In *Time and Free Will*, Bergson elaborates on this tendency to reduce and systematise our conception of space: it is our nature as *social* beings, our impetus to live together in communities, that encourages us in this homogenising imaginative practice because it facilitates group formation and living (Mullarkey 1999a).

Elizabeth Grosz (2001) takes a positive view of Bergson's conception of space and suggests how we can creatively work with his account. In Grosz's reading, Bergson argues that in conventional thought, space precedes objects when in reality space is itself produced through matter, extension and movement.[2] Along with Mullarkey, Grosz argues that Bergson's space is neither static nor homogeneous; it is not a medium or container, although we may think of it in these ways in order to create practical orientations to help us go about our everyday lives (Grosz 2001). In fact, Grosz suggests that we can creatively extend Bergson's work by employing the same approach to space and spatiality that he uses to understand time and duration. Temporality and action are central to Bergson's account of perception, for 'the past is essentially *that which acts no longer*' and the present is '*that which is acting*' (Bergson 2004: 74, emphasis in the original). Perception is linked to nascent action or what Grosz calls 'action-in-potential': 'perception impels us toward action and thus toward objects ... and objects reflect my body's possible actions upon them' (Grosz 2001: 120, 121). The present is the site of duration and the domain of the actual, whereas the past – as that which no longer acts – exists in a state of latency or virtuality. We can only access the past by taking a leap into virtuality. This is how memory functions.

Memory, inseparable in practice from perception, imports the past into the present, contracts into a single intuition many moments of duration, and thus by a twofold operation compels us, *de facto*, to perceive matter in ourselves, whereas we, *de jure*, perceive matter within matter. (Bergson 2004: 80)

In this process, memory and perception allow for the creation of forms of self-awareness that are thoroughly bodily and material. Indeed, 'the present consists in the consciousness I have of my body. Memory, the past, has no special link with or proximity to my body' (Grosz 2005: 103). Importantly, past and present are interwoven as they are created simultaneously:

> Every present splits into a dual-sided actual and virtual, one of which has effects, the other of which joins to and adds to the past. The present thus directs itself to two series, two orientations at once: to action, in space; and to memory, in duration. The past could never exist if it did not coexist with the present of which it is the past. (Grosz 2005: 103)

Grosz (2001) argues that this virtual co-existence of the past and present is necessary for what we perceive as succession, that is, the idea of one moment replacing another in an even sequence. This succession can only take place because of 'the virtual coexistence of all of the past at each moment of the present' (Grosz 2001: 124). This conception seems incoherent or paradoxical only if we adhere to a conventional understanding of duration produced through the standard model of spatiality (in which one moment is mapped out after another and cannot overlap).

Grosz suggests that, although Bergson himself does not quite do so, we could extend his fluid understanding of time and duration to space. This would create a conceptualisation of space and spatiality characterised not by fixity and singularity but by change, simultaneity and co-extensivity. Such a model would see space not as a simple medium, nor as homogeneous or inert. Instead, space could be understood as radically relational such that different spaces may interact, overlap or create spatial simultaneities in the manner that Massey proposes. Massey (2005: 9) asks us to consider a model in which space is always in process or under construction, the product of interrelations and interactions, and 'the sphere therefore of coexisting heterogeneity'. Developing Bergson's conception of duration to encompass spatiality, Grosz suggests that the spatial present (*here, now*) 'defines its own region, but this regionality both intersects with the regionality of other heres and, like world duration, links to a larger space, a world space or even a universal space, which in no way qualifies or marginalizes the concrete differences between different spaces' (Grosz 2001: 128). In this understanding, the spatial present opens out to other spaces and times and confounds the logic of strict demarcations in which only one 'here' may occupy that particular regionality at any one time. And space – not merely what occupies certain spaces – may have its own materialities. Grosz speculates that we might

> consider spatiality in terms of the coexistence of multiple relations of *succession*, space as a layering of spaces within themselves, spaces enfolded in others, spaces that can function as the virtualities of the present, the "here".... The same attributes of becoming that Bergson accords to duration can now be seen to accompany spatiality: just as the whole of the past contracts, in various degrees, in each moment of the present, that is, just as the present is laden with virtualities that extend beyond itself...so too the whole of space, spatiality, contracts into the specificity of location, and the occupation of any space contains the virtual whole of spatiality, which is to say, the infinite possibilities of my action on and being acted on by matter in space and time. (Grosz 2001: 128, 119)

Unlike 'the possible' in which the future can be predicted from the present, or in which the future exists in preformed version in the present, Bergson's 'virtual' is the nexus of productivity or the means by which invention and radical change can occur (Grosz 2001). For Bergson, the move from the possible to the real involves nothing unexpected. Whereas the shift to the virtual involves surprise, invention, the unplanned, novelty – the virtual has within it the potential for openness, for something radically different and unpredictable.

If we accept Grosz's extension of Bergson's formulation of duration to ideas about spatiality, this would challenge the idea of space as an inert medium or context, over-shadowed by the dynamism of time. Following Bergson on duration, Grosz argues that it is not possible nor perhaps even desirable to inhabit such virtual spaces (or times). But thinking with and through them offers us more adequate analytic tools. They open us to thinking about spatialities and temporalities as relational and over-lapping; they encourage us to think about the virtual quality of spatialities and temporalities. They enable us to think about spatialities as offering the potential for radical change and invention – a potential that is usually only accorded to duration.

I am tolerant of the paradoxes and complexities of Bergson's work because it offers intriguing ways to ask questions about perception, representation and agency in urban space. In Bergson's terms, the body as a centre of action carves out of sensory data what become isolated as, and understood as, *perceptions* in urban space. What we *see* – or more precisely what we apprehend as singular, distinct impressions of objects and movements in urban space – are actually products of a perceptual process of filtering. We select out from the flux of visual and other stimuli in city space that which does not interest this particular centre of action (our body). Following Grosz, we can see spatiality as virtual, dynamic and interwoven with temporalities in unexpected ways. And Bergson reminds us that perceptual processes are always oriented to the practical and to action, not to what he terms 'pure knowledge' (Bergson 2004: 21). Grosz argues that, for Bergson, objects contain

> real action, the indiscriminate action of its various features upon whatever surrounds it and comes into causal connection with it, as well as virtual action, that potential to exert specific effects on a living being of the kind which the being seeks or may interest it. This cerebral delay allows the object's indiscriminate actions on the world to be placed in suspension, and for the living being to see only particular elements of the object. (Grosz 2005: 100)

Thus the zones of indetermination produced by living forms create a filter which diminishes the object's 'real effects' and allow its 'virtual effects' through. It thus 'enables objects to enter unexpected connections, to make something new' (Grosz 2005: 100). What kinds of novelty or invention does our perception of advertisements in urban space articulate?

Seeing the commercial

The outdoor advertising industry makes every effort to tap into and shape these perceptual processes, aiming to influence this process of filtering for commercial purposes. It creates and places adverts in ways that attempt to inhabit and shape this zone of indetermination, or perceptual gap, where our actions are conceived and effected. In exhorting us to *look at this!*, *buy this!*, the industry attempts to capture and shape future possibilities, hoping to fold future (consumer) actions into the present moment of perception.

Figure 5.1 captures a moment on a late winter's afternoon on London's Oxford Street, a key commercial centre which is vibrant with all manner of sensory stimuli. The impression of the movement of vehicles and people is woven together in a sensory amalgam with lighting from shops windows, shop signs, illuminated advertising panels and a handheld advertising board for a Subway sandwich shop. These elements are captured and isolated by the camera to form a representation. As I argued in Chapter 3, media owners' promotional shots of advertising panels are often taken at night with a slow shutter speed to capture trails of car

Figure 5.1   Oxford Street, London (author's photograph)

lights. This is designed to emphasise the impression of many people and vehicles moving past the advertising panels.

In this photograph, I attempted to capture the same sense of movement and the impression of sensory richness. On one level, the photograph draws on 'the archive city' identified by Donald (1999): the city as a way of seeing that is mediated by layers of representations such as films, photographs, novels, academic accounts. It seems to capture the immediacy of experience that Donald argues is characteristic of urban space. This is an intense, embodied sensation – the 'buzz' of city space as a kind of hyper-present tense – which is very immediate and very animated. But Donald argues that the archive city acts at the same time to mediate our engagement with urban space such that this impression of *immediacy* is in fact *mediated* by a myriad of historical and contemporary representations of cities; it is this play of representations and temporalities that enables us, 'to live both here and elsewhere' (Donald 1999: 5). So neither the experience of living *now* or living *then* is unmediated. The spatial present tense – here, now – is lived in and through past urban spaces. As in Bergson's account of temporality, past and present weave together and act to perform our conception of temporality as a succession of instants that extend evenly and predictably into the future.

The sense of temporal immediacy that the photograph captures is, then, ambiguous in several ways. The photograph appears to freeze one 'moment' of the flow of urban stimuli, but in fact the temporalities of the city and of its representations are much more promiscuously interwoven. And according to Bergson (2004), our perceptual process is not analogous to photography; it does not parallel the technological capture and processing of light sources to 'develop' an image of external reality (either through the chemical development of photographs or the organising of pixels in digital images). Instead, perceptions in any sensory encounter are the results of a process of selectivity. That which does not interest the perceiver is filtered out and what remains is the perception. And that which has been filtered or selected out is not available to conscious awareness. So while the outdoor advertising industry clearly attempts to orient viewers' practices towards purchase, or at least a favourable view of the brand in question, they do not necessarily succeed. As I have shown in previous chapters, neither advertisements' ubiquity nor their textual dexterity guarantees their commercial efficacy.

It is also important to recognise that the textual content of advertisements operates in the register of 'the possible' in Bergson's terms. The possible is the predictable, the foreseeable, that which can easily be read off from present conditions. While advertisements may use aspirational images or messages, they tend to frame these goals in very accessible terms: they want people to feel that they can go and buy the product, not that the product or ideal is beyond their reach. This is markedly different from the register of 'the virtual', the form and content of which is not constrained by the present. The virtual points to the unexpected, the novel, the radically new. Although advertisements are oriented to the new – presenting new products, promising a 'new you' – they do so within the familiar and structured framework of consumer capitalism and market relations.

But outdoor advertisements' impact is not limited to the commercial intentions of their creators. Outdoor advertisements become part of a larger tapestry of urban images, ideas, colours, movements; they cannot help but contribute to the intense mêlée of urban sensory stimuli in ways that exceed or even contradict the ads' commercial remit. Indeed, I have discussed how the industry expends considerable energy attempting, often unsuccessfully, to prevent advertisements becoming part of an urban 'wallpaper' that is unseen and disregarded. This urban space is 'noisy'; it is multiple and its texture is 'lumpy'. Following Grosz, I argue that this simultaneity and overlaying of spaces should not be understood as a practical impossibility; it is instead the very way in which we habitually experience busy cities. Figure 5.1 with its extended exposure tries to express this sense of multiplicity and of movement, the multiple spatial presents or *here-nows* that perceiving bodies in urban space produce. But in order for us to inhabit and move around urban space practically we create certain conventional understandings of space. We imagine space as extending evenly in all directions and functioning as a neutral container for things or as a context in which things happen. To create this pragmatic view of space that enables us to act, we imaginatively and practically draw on the interconnections and relationalities between spaces. Our perceptual practices perform the body-space. They create and maintain a practical conception of the boundaries of our body; they individuate us and provide us with traction in order to co-ordinate ourselves, to move and act.

These boundary-securing practices, of which we are usually unaware, enable us to imagine ourselves to be situated 'in space' thus creating a practical orientation that facilitates our actions. But analysing these perceptual practices points to the relationality of our body-space with other spatialities – things, images – and, moreover, highlights how these spatialities are multiple, over-lapping and simultaneous. The awareness of 'I am here' that the creators of the Subway advertisement draw on and attempt to orient is simultaneously spatial and temporal. But it also relies on a history of spatial and temporal relationalities; it points to virtualities and the multiple potentials in any one spatio-temporal moment-space. And it points to how our understanding of our position in urban spaces is shaped by the archive city and the way of seeing that this effects.

This offers another perspective on why people do not appear to perceive, 'read' or decode outdoor ads in any coherent manner. It is not simply that we are distracted or overwhelmed by the richness of visual stimuli in urban space, but rather that our perceptual processes allow to flow through us that which is not of immediate relevance or use. This filtering process is not *the result of* choice or agency: it produces the zone of indetermination, or temporal gap, in which agency is made possible. The case of outdoor advertisements foregrounds how this is not only temporal (inserting a delay which allows us to resist immediate response to stimulation), but also spatial – it is indeed a *zone* of indetermination. It is produced in and through multiple, over-lapping spatialities of the body moving in space, the spaces of urban structures, and spatiality of the archive city. It opens up opportunities for acting and allows objects, images and persons to interact in novel ways, ways that may confound commercial intentions and resist prediction.

Like Bergson's duration, Grosz (2001) argues, this radical simultaneity means that any location contains the whole of spatiality, contracted but full of infinite possibilities. Understood in this way, it is clear that these urban spaces have their own materialities composed of cluttered pavements, imposing shop fronts, and roads and pavements that channel the traffic of vehicles and pedestrians. But it is equally clear that these spaces are made up of what are often considered immaterialities – images, ideas, sensations, sounds – but which Bergson sees as interwoven with matter and duration, and we can see as interwoven with spatiality. One element of these immaterialities is agency, potential action or the capacity for choice – the zone of indetermination that perception constructs in its filtering process which is spatial as well as temporal.

Bergson's work on perception and temporality, and Grosz's extension of his account to the virtual quality of spatiality, offers useful conceptual resources for thinking about urban spaces and advertising. Their accounts point to how we *practice* perception, how we practice space, and how these practices are interwoven. But questions still remain about how bodily forms of perception and Bergson's broadly defined 'images' articulate with the production of images and texts such as outdoor advertisements that populate urban space. This perceptual activity involves imaginative work or the activity of making connections. In the next section I outline how the addition of Bergson's concept of fabulation to the conceptual framework of perception, time and space discussed thus far can help think through the relationships between advertising sites, advertising structures, advertising texts, city space and people's bodily experience of them. And it can help analyse how these texts and contexts performatively engage with the processes of commercial production within the industry that I have described in earlier chapters. In this way, we can begin to conceptualise the visual or symbolic economy of cities in a broader way than originally conceived by Zukin (1991, 1995, 1996). We can examine how the advertising industry tries to inhabit the visual economy of the city and link it to the virtual economy of advertising effects, profits and commercial relationships.

Fabulation, animation and production of agency

To summarise the analysis thus far – Donald (1999) argues that we understand the city not only through the striking immediacy of its sights, smells and the material presence of its structures; we also understand it through the 'archive city' comprised of multiple renderings of the urban over time through the mediation of films, novels, academic accounts etc. This produces not merely a pool of semantic resources with which to make sense of the city, but also creates the city as a historically specific *mode of seeing*. Bergson's account of perception adds a bodily dimension to this way of seeing and emphasises its temporal quality: past and present weave together to create for us practical understandings of time as an even succession of moments. Bergson argues that this pragmatic understanding is spatial, mapping one instant followed in predictable tempo by the next. But Grosz (2001) pushes this further by suggesting that spatiality should also be conceived in this relational way. She argues that spaces are multiple, layered within each other, over-lapping, simultaneous and *virtual*: 'the whole of space, spatiality, contracts into the specificity of location, and the occupation of any space contains the virtual whole of spatiality' (Grosz 2001: 119). Thus, we create understandings of space – practical conceptions of the relations between our bodies and other material forms including spaces – in order to provide a grounding and point of purchase for our actions. This enables us to move and arrive at our destination, and allows us to pursue plans of action. Just as the movement between past and present creates for us a practical understanding of time, so the (virtual) movement between spaces recognises the fundamental relationality of spatiality and creates practical, action-oriented understandings of space.

I suggest that this movement between spaces, or play of relationality, can be *imaginative*. For Bergson, of course, body and mind are not separate. Perception is bodily, the actions of the brain are bodily. But he did develop a specific concept of what we might call imagination – fabulation. It is Bergson's conceptualisation of fabulation that enables us to make the link between bodily processes of perception and the ways in which we make sense of the world through historically and culturally specific representations. It also helps analyse how we conceive spatiality as a practical, liveable 'context'. In his own works, Bergson did not explicitly outline the links between fabulation and perception, but as Mullarkey argues, it is logical to see perception itself as a form of fabulation:

> they both fragment our experience of 'the real', but to some degree they are also both redeemable, defragmentable (to borrow an ugly word from computing), through art and through philosophy. Only what makes fabulation really interesting is that without it, without the faculty of *seeing as*, we couldn't have the art that redeems the fragmenting activity of perception! (Mullarkey 2007: 59–60)

For Bergson (1962: 112) 'la fonction fabulatrice', or fabulation, is a capacity for creating 'phantasmic representations' (2006: 108). This is centrally important for Bergson's attempt to understand the importance of religion, superstitions and myths in human societies. In *The Two Sources of Morality and Religion* (2006) Bergson devotes considerable attention to analysing various forms of belief including animatism, animism, theism and pantheism. He understands these as forms of representation, or ways of making sense of the world, that involve attributing mindfulness or intention to various worldly forms (natural events, landscapes, animals etc.). The root of the creation of these belief systems, Bergson contends, is in humans' biological characteristics of intelligence, instinct and sociability. Bergson (2006) has famously argued that life has a demand for forward movement – a vital impulse or *élan vital* – and that life is oriented towards the effort to obtain certain results from raw materials using invention (the capacity that intelligence affords us). But intelligence can also offer hindrances in life's goals. For while it affords us imagination and the capability to anticipate possible consequences of actions, that same capacity can generate a paralysing awareness of dangers and thus all manner of anxieties – it acts to 'open the door to the unforeseen and let in the feeling of risk' (Bergson 2006: 138–139). In addition, intelligence creates in us an awareness that we will die and this self-consciousness is antagonistic to life's impetus as it is 'depressing' and it acts to 'slow down in man the movement of life' (Bergson 2006: 131, 130).

Fabulation, then, acts as a kind of 'virtual instinct', the function of which is to counter that paralysing sense of danger and depressing awareness of our own mortality (Bergson 2006: 110). Bergson argues that to achieve this, fabulation acts to arouse 'an illusory perception' or 'a counterfeit of recollection' (2006: 122). Fabulation is used by Bergson to understand religious belief: the very intelligence that gives humans the awareness that they will die also works with the virtual instinct found in fabulation to create stories that promise an after-life to thwart the depressing and unproductive realisation of the inevitability of death. I am interested less in Bergson's explanation of religion than in his more general account of fabulation or story-making in the social world and how these fabulatory acts can 'animate' the lifeworld. Clearly, fabulation can be seen narrowly in terms of the production of fiction such as novels, films and other cultural products that create understandings of the world. But it can also be understood as a more general imaginative practice. 'Imagination' has been conceived in a range of ways, but most often as a form of cognitive practice. In Bergson's account, fabulation (as a form of perception) is a fundamentally bodily practice. It is produced in, and by, the body and it orients the body to practice. As I discuss below, it also creates understandings of the natural and social world that mirror human bodily characteristics and capacities; it animates the world and attributes mindful personality and intent to happenings and objects. This process of fabulation, then, is in no way 'immaterial' for it is fundamentally perceptual and bodily, and it engages with the materiality of the social world.

Fabulation is therefore a productive analytic tool for it can address the multiple strands of my project: advertisements as texts (cultural products that have been 'fabulated' by advertising creatives, that can then be used by people to fabulate and make sense of the world); the role of consumerism and consumption as a material and imaginative mode of engaging with the world; the material structures of advertising panels that inhabit urban space; and the market practices of advertising practitioners in media-owning firms. These make productive fictions of 'the consumer' in urban space and circulate 'animated' understandings of capitalism and commercial process. These are certainly different forms of fabulation and they circulate in different ways. They have traction in the social world to varying degrees, but they share some important characteristics of animation and performativity.

Bergson (2006) argues that the vital impulse manifested in fabulation is essentially optimistic and imagines overcoming obstacles. This sets it in direct contrast with the way in which intelligence imagines potential problems, a function which can helpfully encourage us to be circumspect but can also overwhelm us with anxieties about potential risks. Fabulation thus helps us overcome the representations that intelligence produces about the 'depressing margin of the unexpected between the initiative taken and the effect desired' (Bergson 2006: 140). Bergson conceives this through the objectification and partial anthropomorphisation of external forces. He argues that this fabulatory function can be identified in the practices of people in earlier societies who imagined or fabulated external forces to help them achieve their goal, for instance, in conjuring a spirit to which they could appeal in order to help their arrow meet its mark.

Bergson suggests that the same objectification and animation that we see in the superstitions, myths and religious beliefs of earlier times can be found in how people fabulate about the world today. He gives several striking examples including First World War soldiers' fear of bullets and how people come to conceive of earthquakes as 'events'. Bergson describes how an officer in the war noticed that soldiers dreaded bullets far more than shells or shrapnel even though it was clear that the latter posed far greater risk of death or injury to the soldiers. This can be explained, Bergson argues, by the fact that soldiers imagined that bullets were individually aimed at them by someone who had the intention of killing them. In contrast, the clearly devastating impact of shells and shrapnel seemed far more impersonal and thus less threatening. Bergson describes the soldiers' thought process in these terms:

> 'To produce the effect, which would mean so much to me, of death or a serious wound, there must be a cause of equal importance, there must be intent'. A soldier who, as it happened, had been hit by a splinter from a shell, told us that his first impulse had been to exclaim: 'How silly!' That this fragment of shell, projected from a purely mechanical cause, and which might just as well have struck anybody, or nobody, should nevertheless have come and struck him, him and not somebody else, appeared to his natural intelligence illogical. (Bergson 2006: 146)

Whereas death or injury by a bullet which had been aimed with conscious intent seemed a fitting counterpart to the momentous consequences for the person hit by the bullet, the possibility of being hit randomly by shrapnel seemed somehow implausible. It does not fit with our self-narration that puts ourselves at the centre of our world, and sees happenings around us reflecting that fact. Equally, it jars with our belief that the magnitude of events affecting this centre should reflect the magnitude of their impact on us.

Bergson illustrates this further with the example of a tile falling from a roof in a high wind and killing someone. This will usually be framed as 'chance' or bad luck, and because the consequence of the tile falling or shell exploding into shrapnel has such impact upon the person hit, the cause must be understood as of equal import to the life of that person. The happening is understood in terms of human significance, or more precisely, impact upon human life (either of an individual or human society more generally). And as we understand import in terms analogous to human capacities, so we frame 'chance' as having some kind of intent, malign or otherwise. This forms a contemporary parallel with early societies' understandings of spirits or other anthropomorphisms. 'Chance is then mechanism behaving as though possessing an intention…. Chance is therefore an intention emptied of its content' (Bergson 2006: 148–149). It is agency or energy without a specific aim and is understood as deriving from something like ourselves, a living being or power.

The same form of animation or personalisation can be seen in how we tend to understand 'events'. Bergson (2006) gives the example of an earthquake and argues that where once people saw this as a supernatural warning or a retribution by a deity, the same fabulatory practice can be seen in contemporary understandings of earthquakes as events. The fear that occurrences such as earthquakes elicits risks overwhelming us, but our capacity for fabulation intervenes and avoids our becoming paralysed by fright by creating understandings of what is happening. We achieve this by aggregating the various disturbances surrounding the earthquake, and fabulating that the disturbances were *caused by* the earthquake. We imagine the earthquake as a singular causal entity and attribute it a form of intent or mindful personality. Describing Bergson's account, Mullarkey (2007: 58) argues that 'the naming of an event makes it the event; that is, naming it individuates it, for an "earthquake" itself is simply a disparate set of processes. But with a name, we individuate the earthquake as the *cause* of these processes (rather than the set of them)'. Thus we can better see intention behind the processes.

> The disturbances with which we have to deal, each of them entirely mechanical, combine into an Event, which resembles a human

being, possibly a 'bad lot' but none the less one of us. He is not an outsider.... It lends to the Event a unity and an individuality which make of it a mischievous, maybe malignant, being, but still one of ourselves, with something sociable and human about it. (Bergson 2006: 157–158)

Like the perceptual processes Bergson (2004) describes in *Matter and Memory*, fabulation is practical, oriented to action, and helps us function in a world that we perceive as full of risk. It enables us to act partly because that which is thought to be intended or in some way mindful – a being in some way like us – may be more easily acted upon or resisted. By fabulating a living intention in occurrences in the world, we can call up understandings as aids to our capacity to act. As noted above, one of these is the idea of luck or chance. Bergson describes how the gambler sees luck as that which intervenes in the gap between the initiative taken and the effect desired. He says that at the roulette table we might see the gambler,

make a movement with his hand as though to stop the ball: he is objectifying his will to win, and the resistance to this will, in the form of good or bad luck, in order to feel the presence of a hostile or friendly power, and thus give its full interest to the game. (Bergson 2006: 146)

Alongside our aggregation of occurrences into events, this animation or partial anthropomorphisation of a force in the world (in this case, its naming as luck or chance) helps us act by giving us a sense of agency, a sense that we might have some impact on what unfolds in our lives.

We can understand fabulation as a kind of mediation, although not in the sense generally deployed in studies of the media which see social institutions such as radio or television shaping, reflecting or relaying certain ideals, discourses or ideologies. Following Bergson we can understand mediation as sensuous and bodily, as practically oriented and as productive of agency, and as a process which breaches the conventional distinctions of bodily boundaries (inside/outside, self/other, material/immaterial). This mediation is fundamentally bodily in that perception is tied to our biological capacities and in turn acts to construct our perceived boundaries of selfhood. And in turn, we perceive the world as paralleling our biology – we imagine the world as enlivened, full of intentions, and as exhibiting the same characteristics of agency and movement as human beings.

In his use of Bergson's work to understand contemporary film, John Mullarkey argues that the fabulation of life is 'a type of "seeing as"' and can help explain how we perceive movement '*as* something life-like' (2007: 54, emphasis in the original). Mullarkey's concern is to understand how viewers engage with films and can feel genuine emotions for what they recognise as fictional characters. Using Bergson, he argues that 'fiction makes events (and the people involved in events) come *alive* for us, not just in make-believe, but at a very present and real (although primitive) level of our perception' (Mullarkey 2007: 54, emphasis in the original). The willing suspension of disbelief that fabulation makes possible is the core of our engagement with various forms of fiction. But, Mullarkey argues, what is also being fabricated is *time* and the illusion that the events on screen are unfolding at the very same time of viewing.

Discussing the film *Titanic*, Mullarkey argues that viewers feel the desire to influence the well-known events of that night as they are being presented to us on screen, particularly during the dramatic scene which depicts the ship approaching the iceberg. Although we are familiar with the historical event of the ship hitting the iceberg and sinking rapidly, the experience of viewing this unfold on screen – in the present tense of viewing – encourages viewers to urge the ship to miss the iceberg and so alter the ship's destiny. We thus fabulate alternatives by (partially) anthropomorphising processes as having mindful personality and intent. As Mullarkey (2007: 63) argues, 'it is not that the iceberg is made human, but the *collision* with the iceberg is made into an event with intentionality – and what has intent can have that intent thwarted'. By attributing intent to processes we feel that we can act against them and so alter the course of the cinematic ship *Titanic's* history on screen. Here, fabulation operates not only by aggregating disparate occurrences into a coherent 'event' and animating or anthropomorphising that event, but also by creating a present tense (and thus re-opening the ship's destiny to alternative futures).

Hoping to change the event of the Titanic's collision doesn't come only from making the event live and feel, but also from having it present, reliving its present, and so reopening its future. We believe we are seeing it happen *now*, and it is from *this* temporal state of *actuality* that our paradoxical beliefs, desires, and so on, may follow. One could argue that fiction-making is, by the same token, present-making, for the present, broadly understood, is what is alive for Bergson: movement is actuality and animation (literally), for to move is one condition of being alive that, primitively, allows us to animate things even further. (Mullarkey 2007: 66)

Mullarkey's argument here concerns how film, as the moving image *par excellence*, encapsulates Bergson's ideas about our vitalisation of the social world. Film illustrates Bergson's understanding of fabulation as a (primitive) bodily, perceptual process which apprehends movement as life-like. Bergson argues that movement is fundamental to perception in that our perceptions rely on cerebral movements which are, in turn, bound up with the social world: 'perception as a whole has its true and final explanation in the tendency of the body to movement' (2004: 41). Movement and perception carve out our understanding of the boundaries of our body and create our body as the centre of action: 'As my body moves in space, all the other images vary, while that image, my body, remains invariable. I must therefore make it a centre, to which I refer all the other images' (Bergson 2004: 43). And in his account, practices of perception have an intimate relationship with temporality for past images mingle with present images in order to facilitate action – the present is that which acts and the past is that which no longer acts. As Grosz puts it,

perception is that which propels us toward the present, the real, to space, to objects, matter, to the immediate or impending future; while memory is that which impels us toward consciousness, to the past, and to duration. If perception pushes us toward action and thus objects, then to that extent objects reflect my body's possible actions upon them. (Grosz 2005: 97)

Outdoor advertisements combine fabulation's characteristic of fiction-making with perception's tendency to see that which moves (things, images, natural phenomena) *as life-like*, enlivened or animated by some force that is similar to human life or energy. While it is certainly possible to see outdoor advertisements, and cities themselves, as texts that can be semiotically analysed, such approaches offer limited analytic purchase. But combining Bergson's ideas about perception and about fabulation promises more subtle and productive analytic encounters. As I argued in Chapters 3 and 4, movement is a key characteristic of the city which the outdoor advertising industry is keen to understand and exploit. There I showed how the movements and rhythms of the city are composed of people's trajectories in cars, trains, buses, on foot, and that the movement of people can become aligned with the rhythms of posting advertisements and practices of commercial innovation. As I argue in the next two chapters, this visually rich tableau of movement, and related perceptions of energy, liveliness or the 'buzz' of the city, offer its inhabitants and visitors ways of thinking of the city as *alive* through movement.

But for Bergson the quality of 'aliveness' that we attribute to natural or social phenomena through fabulation has another important characteristic – that of intention. We fabulate and thus vitalise occurrences, whether earthquakes or luck in gambling, by attributing to them mindful personality and intent. As I have argued, advertising is popularly considered to have very specific, identifiable intentions – to sell goods or encourage positive perceptions of a brand. Other media forms such as television programmes or films tend to be considered polysemic and thought to offer a multiplicity of subject positions to viewers. They are seen as complex in their authorial and programming intent, encompassing the aims of entertainment, education, commercial gain and social or political influence. In contrast, advertisements and the advertising industry are popularly perceived as having clear and uncompromising commercial intent, although studies of the industry complicate this picture (Cronin 2004b, c; Miller 1997). This attribution of intent can shape a view of advertising as a social phenomenon which, if not exactly *alive*, may seem vital, full of energy, or having the capacity to exert some form of influence. Indeed, advertisements themselves are often discussed in both academic and popular registers in anthropomorphic terms – they are framed as persuasive, seductive, mendacious, irritating, amusing. More than just ventriloquised forms of the advertising creatives who produced them, advertisements themselves are popularly seen as mindful personalities full of intent.

The forms of fabulation that I have described in this chapter are complex and multi-dimensional. Writing at the turn of the twentieth century, Bergson's examples of fabulation draw on ideas of the social world, the biological (particularly human bodies) and natural forms and forces: earthquakes, soldiers' perception of risk, gamblers' fabulation of 'luck', and falling roof tiles. Unsurprisingly, the way in which Bergson drew these elements together reflected the concerns of the time, particularly scientific understandings of biology. But while there are differences in the particular configurations, today's western societies also mobilise understandings of these elements. Indeed, many studies have argued that contemporary capitalist institutions and practices draw together the natural and social in distinctive ways (see Franklin, Lury and Stacey 2000; Haraway 1997; McNeil 2007).

In my study, the forms of fabulation take a particular shape: 'the market' as animated or in some way 'alive'; the popular understanding of ads and the advertising industry as possessing a form of intention; perception as a spatialising imaginative movement; urban space as characterised by movement (both temporal and spatial). In Chapter 2, I explored the performative character of commercial practices within the outdoor advertising industry. There and elsewhere (Cronin 2008a, b), I argued that one way in which practitioners in my study conceive and enact 'the market' is by partially anthropomorphising it. By animating it in this way, practitioners imagine the market as full of 'energy'. Although, as an animate form, the market is thought of as unpredictable, practitioners also imagine that they could attempt to capture and channel some of this energy for commercial gain. In the light of the argument of this chapter, this imaginative practice can be framed as a form of fabulation. It is a practical understanding that is produced by people to facilitate actions – in this case, to help market practitioners act in creating profit and maintaining market relationships with the aim of securing commercial futures. It aggregates various processes and occurrences, and names them as the 'the market' (of this particular industry); it enlivens this form and attributes to it a kind of personality and intent.

In Chapter 6, I analyse in more detail how these ideas about spatiality are productive for thinking about cities, and how fabulation operates with understandings of urban movements. In Chapter 7, I expand on fabulation and intention, and examine how these concepts can be used to analyse contemporary public space. How people fabulate advertising and its texts can function to animate or enliven understandings of advertising. And by attributing intent or some form of mindful personality to advertising, this fabulation also offers viewers the capacity to act – to buy the goods or services, to actively ignore the advertisement's blandishments, or, in a counter-cultural mode, to deface or subvert the advertising texts. Like Bergson's gambler who fabulates 'luck' as a form of living being that can act for or against her, perceiving and fabulating advertising as a mindful, intention-oriented being constructs ways of acting for the viewers. These ways of thinking are compelling for us because they make sense to us on a primitive, bodily level.

If advertisements can be fabulated as life-like or animated, what other contemporary urban forms might also be anthropomorphised? Examining fabulation's processes of animation reveals that space as well as time can be considered active. Mullarkey (2007) notes that fabulation is a process of fiction-making, but in its animation, is also a process of present-making. The impression of sensory immediacy of the urban that is so familiar to us is produced through the inter-relation of: the urban movements of people, vehicles, images, soundscapes which make the city seem animated (and can be fabulated as enlivened or life-like); our bodily processes of perception which are fundamentally temporal (weaving together past and present) and practical (oriented to future actions); and the potential fabulation produced through the presence of advertising texts and structures such as billboards. These billboards create their own temporalities and thus can be fabulated as enlivening, but also offer textual resources for people's practices of fabulation. Our perceptual, fiction-making practices create an urban present, and for Bergson, the present is that which is acting.

In the following chapter, I explore how fabulation also opens spaces to their potential futures. These are futures which are not just 'possible' in Bergson's terms – that which can be predicted by present conditions – but virtual. Through Bergson and Grosz we can see that the interweaving of past and present creates a virtuality, and we can also consider space in this way. Grosz (2001) argues for an understanding of spatiality as dynamic such that the whole of space contracts into any one location; spatialities are creative and inventive, and can facilitate not only 'the possible' but also the virtual. Past and present co-exist because there is a co-dependent movement between past and present to create a practical, liveable version of time as a succession of moments. So, too, a *movement* between locations or specific spaces creates a practical sense of space as extending evenly and predictably in all directions.

But, I suggest, this movement between spaces can be *imaginative*, and perception and fabulation is one way that we engage in this spatial play. Fabulation allows the play of virtualities and makes visible the ways in which spaces, like temporalities, are dynamic or virtual. It enables us to make surprising (and productive, practical) connections between objects, spaces, images, ideas and bodies; we can make something new. As with Donald's (1999) account of the archive city, fabulation can enable us to live imaginatively *both here and elsewhere*, a positioning that is temporal and spatial, virtual and dynamic, political and full of potential.

6
Perceiving Urban Change in Detroit and Manchester: Space, Time and the Virtual

How people experience cities has long been of interest to urban studies. This chapter asks how people's experience of cities is framed through their perception of urban change. In asking this I place the body, and people's understandings of 'life' and embodiment, at the centre of the analysis. Drawing on the theoretical framework set up in Chapter 5, I explore how the structures of urban spaces and perceptual processes are materially interwoven in ways that are both temporal and spatial. I examine how the specific temporalities of urban regeneration and urban decay are embedded in advertising spaces, texts and structures. Alongside the many other everyday forms such as buildings and streets, these produce an urban vernacular through which people make sense of cities, city life and the multiple capitalist processes that shape cities.

How people perceive their city, and how they think about urban change, is gaining an increased significance at regional and national levels. I have shown that commercial knowledges and commercial practices are performatively folded into the production of urban spaces by advertising texts and structures. A similar conceptual approach can assess people's understandings of urban change that are produced through their perceptual practices. In the UK, city councils, urban planners and developers are increasingly seeking out people's views on their cities, a process of consultation that is becoming framed as 'public participation' and the incorporation into planning decisions of 'stakeholder' interests. Indeed, today 'public participation is central to the practice, legitimacy, and dominant normative principles of spatial planning' (Ellis 2004: 1549). In the US, too, this notion of public participation in planning has been developing for some time in what has been called 'the communicative turn in planning thought' and practices of 'collaborative planning' (Campbell and Marshall 2000: 321–322). In this way, people's perceptions of their city and its future possibilities are being woven into processes of urban planning and urban change. This does not grant to city residents or workers any great influence over changes that may occur in their city. Campbell and Marshall (2000) note that as a practice of democratic participation the process is flawed in many ways. But it does open a space, however contested, in which people's understandings of their city circulate and have some impact. This may shift the terms of urban change in small but significant ways.

Focusing on the perception of the urban environment, this chapter extends Sharon Zukin's (1995) concept of the urban symbolic economy in order to consider representation and meaning in other ways. Zukin argues that western cities now capitalise on culture in unprecedented ways by using it explicitly as an economic base. In this trend, the 'symbolic economy' plays a significant role alongside the 'political economy' (centred on land, labour and capital). The symbolic economy is divided into two parallel productions systems: (1) the production of space, 'with its synergy of capital investment and cultural meanings', and (2) the production of symbols which 'constructs both a currency of commercial exchange and a language of social identity' (Zukin 1995: 24). In previous chapters I have shown how outdoor advertising companies produce understandings of urban space, invest in advertising billboards, and trade in the cultural meanings of cities, potential consumers and the advertisements themselves. Equally, the companies trade in symbolic production and engage in complex self-promotional strategies in competition with other companies.

But this chapter argues that the symbolic economy also needs to be understood in terms of how people experience cities and particularly urban change – an analysis which does not focus solely on representations of cities in place marketing initiatives or cultural products such as films or novels. Zukin argues that both capital investment and cultural meanings and symbols are central to the production of (urban) space, and many other studies have shown this to be the case (e.g. Cronin and Hetherington 2008; Hall and Hubbard 1998). But urban space is also shaped by processes which fold people's understanding of cities into the very production of urban space. Zukin (1995) has signalled the significance of this by suggesting that urban spaces form a kind of public language or vernacular, although she does not elaborate on this insight. This chapter outlines how some of these understandings are produced through the perceptual engagement with ordinary city forms and structures; this forms a particular urban vernacular which shapes people's conceptions of spatial capitalist processes, particularly urban regeneration and urban decay.

Drawing on Bergson's framework of perception and fabulation outlined in Chapter 5, this chapter extends the insights of classic studies such as Zukin's by conceptualising visual engagement with urban space as active, practical and political. Perceptual practices in urban space are not merely 'immaterial' or secondary phenomena; perception is a series of actions that in themselves orient the body to action. This operates on an individual level, practically orienting a person through urban space in a series of motor actions; but it also operates on a more collective scale by shaping people's sense of the temporalities and spatialities of their city, how they might act, and how their city could be otherwise. Bergson's work frames perception as bodily in two ways. It is an embodied process of engaging with the environment. And a particular form of perception – fabulation – is a practice that draws upon *ideas* of the body, life and animation. It attributes them to other phenomena in the world: natural forms, objects, animals, social processes. For Bergson, perception is a broad-based sensory activity that encompasses not merely sight but all the senses. My focus here is on the visual as outdoor advertising operates primarily in that register, but my conceptual scope leaves open the space to include other sensory engagements. In my account, then, the body is productive of vernacular understandings of city in its perceptual engagement with urban forms; and conceptions of the body, 'life' and animation play a key role in shaping understandings of the urban environment.

The chapter draws on case studies of Manchester (UK) and Detroit, Michigan (USA). These cities provide interesting sites for exploring how the visual cityscape offers people material for fabulating capitalist processes. Studies of advertising, consumption and the urban have tended to focus on glamorous, spectacular cities such as Los Angeles or New York. But analysing the less glitzy, de-industrialised cities of Manchester and Detroit offers another perspective on the relationship between advertising and the city, and between material urban forms and capitalist processes. As one-time manufacturing centres, these cities gained their prominence through production rather than consumption. But in the latter half of the twentieth century, these cities took rather different post-industrial paths. So although the analysis of Detroit and Manchester does not offer a direct comparison of industrial trajectories and urban structures such as buildings and billboards, there are significant synergies between the two cities. Both cities have industrial roots and have had to address the aesthetic and financial legacy of old industrial buildings. Their structures reveal something of the temporalities of capitalism in the decline of the industrial era in the west. I focus particularly on the temporalities of urban regeneration and urban decay as they are tied closely to practices of placing advertising structures. But the two cities reveal how these temporalities can operate very differently: in Manchester, the advertising structures embody and make visible a sense of economic buoyancy and positive momentum, whereas in Detroit the advertising structures materialise and make visually tangible a sense of stagnation.

The chapter uses my own photographs from case studies of these two cities. This ethnographic material is qualitatively different from that which I produced through the observation, interviews and document collection that I drew in on Chapters 2–4 in my discussion of the outdoor advertising industry. As discussed in Chapter 1, these photographs acted as documents or fieldnotes during my fieldwork: they mapped and recorded what I saw in different parts of these cities. My understanding of Manchester and Detroit is also drawn from statistical data and other academic analyses of the cities. The photographs that I include in this chapter, therefore, act as illustrations of my visual encounters with spaces of these cities interpreted in tandem with the data and conceptual material gained from other academic studies of Detroit and Manchester. They speak *alongside* other studies' accounts and this dual analysis produces a particular set of understandings of the cities. But while acting as illustration, the photographs are also end-products of a process of *seeing*. The camera provided me a way of seeing, and thus of understanding, the urban spaces of Manchester and Detroit. In turn, the form of visuality that the photographic process offered was also important in shaping my encounter with the other studies of the cities that I draw on. The photos and my readings of other studies performed certain understandings – of temporalities, of perception, of spatiality. In her photographic studies of urban spaces, Helen Liggett (2003: 120) notes that 'when used to make connections to the city, the camera is not an instrument of representation; it is a way of making space and attracting meanings'. In this spirit, my photographs can also be seen as enactments of perception in how they engage with spaces (and, indeed, make other spaces within the photographic frame). Their potential meanings reach out and intermingle with potential meanings to be extracted from other forms of data (population statistics, histories of racial segregation, analyses of industrial decline and material ruination).

But photographs do not mirror practices of perception accurately for they freeze or fix spaces and times. In a study of industrial ruins, Tim Edensor (2005: 16) argues that his photographs 'can reveal the stages and temporalities of decay'. His photographs record his encounters with ruined factories in a striking manner that, for me, evokes a range of interesting sensory and intellectual responses. But I think his photographs have the same analytic limitations as my own: whilst they capture *moments* of decay, they cannot so easily speak of *processes* of ruination and dereliction. It is only in their encounter with other forms of knowing – other studies, data etc. – that they can illuminate the processes of ruination and regeneration that I am interested in here. My photographs, then, do not speak for themselves. They are *part of* the analysis, not the focus of the analysis. They help imagine the relations of urban times and spaces that are not easily extracted from 'empirical data'; equally, the understandings they help create cannot simply be 'tested' for validity against the empirical. In this sense, they are part of this chapter's project of speculation.

The first section of the chapter explores specific commercial temporalities of the industrial urban: ruination and regeneration. Here, I analyse the synergies between advertising texts and structures such as billboards on the one hand, and urban change evident in regeneration and decay on the other. The next two sections focus on the case studies of Manchester and Detroit, and the final section considers how fabulation as a perceptual process can imagine both the city in the present-tense and also the city of the future.

Commercial time and the city: ruination and regeneration

My photographic studies of Manchester (UK) and Detroit (USA) revealed the striking symbiosis of advertising structures with processes and temporalities of urban decay and urban regeneration. In the UK, billboards are very often placed around sites undergoing demolition or rebuilding where media owners can rent space from the developers. Billboard structures may be placed around the perimeter fence of the redevelopment, or 'wraps' or mega-posters printed onto vinyl or mesh may be stretched across the entire face of the building undergoing work. Both these types of site are popular with advertisers as they offer good potential visual contact with passers-by in central urban spaces or, in the industry terms, good VAIs (Visibility Adjusted Impacts or Contacts). It is very difficult for media owning companies to secure city council permission to construct new billboard or panel structures in city centres, so these alternative advertising opportunities are welcome. City councils perceive benefits in the way that ad wraps obscure unattractive building works. The managing director of a media owning firm specialising in large advertising wraps described the benefits of a particular redevelopment site in Manchester:

> The total façade area is 800 plus square metres. We love that because we had access to the scaffold company nice and early so we could design a frame system where it hides everything. You don't see anything other than a beautiful picture frame and the advert. And the reason we like that is because we know that the planning authorities as well as clients, everyone likes that style because it's neat, it's tidy, does exactly what it says on the tin, it covers up a building works, a nasty bit of development.... I say nasty as in it's not very pleasant to walk past the builder's arse, the scaffold and what have you, and if you can put something... if you can dress it, if you like, then not only do we make money but also the clients get exposure to consumers out there, the city gets something in return. It's window dressing. (Managing Director, blowUP Media)

But such wrap sites are temporary, tied to the time-scale of the redevelopment. Also temporary, although with a potentially longer life, are billboard structures set around urban sites of decay or ruination. These are sites which have either been discarded or not yet purchased for development; they might be industrial ruins or old housing areas no longer in use. City councils in the UK will grant permission to companies to erect panels around such sites for they are thought to serve a positive function of concealing these areas of urban dereliction. Indeed, just after the Second World War large numbers of billboards were erected in Britain, masking the bomb damage to urban architecture.

In what follows I explore how advertising makes visible urban temporalities and spatialities in ways which make sense to people in a bodily way. Advertising feeds off, and acts to frame people's understanding of these specific urban temporalities of decay and regeneration. But as Hubbard and Lilley (2004) argue, while many accounts of urban modernisation focus on the increasing speed and pace of cities, it is important to recognise that there is an uneven production of time and space, spacings and pacings. These temporalities of regeneration and decay operate in different ways in the two cities I will be discussing: Manchester (UK) the regenerated urban centre of nineteenth-century industrial capitalism, and Detroit (USA) the classic 'rust-belt' post-industrial city of America.

In my account I will consider both the advertising texts themselves and the panel structures. Many studies have argued that the materiality of architecture embodies not only ideas and ideals but financial resources; as Dovey suggests, 'all built form has inertia, it "fixes" a great deal of economic capital into a certain form in a certain place, stabilizing the spatial "order"' (2008: 208). It is certainly the case that buildings and other structures can impact upon the perceived stability of a spatial and social order, and that they require financial investment to create and maintain. But the city is always shifting according to multiple temporalities in its visible, material form and in its configuration of people, ideas and finance (Amin and Thrift 2002; Graham and Marvin 2001; Latour and Hermant 1998). It would be more accurate to say that some forms are more temporally fluid than others but none are completely 'inert'. Thus their potential effect of stabilising spatial and social orders must be seen as contested or at best as provisional.

Analysing the relationship between billboard structures, commercial practices, perceptual processes and urban temporalities offers one point of access to the times of capitalism. I will argue that people understand society and social processes in part through their engagement with their immediate environments. In an urban context, advertising and advertising structures form part of the environment and help shape people's fabulation of the social and natural world. As advertising has an immediately evident relationship with capitalist temporalities (see Chapter 4), it offers an interesting entry point for analysing the urban vernacular which shapes people's fabulations of social processes, urban change and ideas about capitalism. Linked to recent analyses of how capitalism and commercial practices operate performatively, Bergson's work on what he defines very broadly as 'images' offers some conceptual tools to address this task. Bergson argued that each image is articulated with all other images. And because matter counts as image, the social and biological world must be understood as constituted through interconnections:

> does not the fiction of an isolated material object imply a kind of absurdity, since this object borrows its physical properties from the relations which it maintains with all others, and owes each of its determinations, and consequently its very existence, to the place which it occupies in the universe as a whole? (Bergson 2004: 11–12)

In this framework, we can see the material, built forms of urban space as 'images', images that connect in complex, shifting ways with other material forms including our own bodies. For Bergson, our experience of the world is derived from our centre of action (our body). Perceptual action, broadly conceived, is what forms the particular configuration of our 'self' with the world. Indeed, perception is practically oriented and it is this concept of practice that articulates agency and our connection with what are conventionally thought of as material things: 'perception ... measures our possible action upon things, and thereby, inversely, the possible action of things upon us' (Bergson 2004: 57). In Chapter 4, I explored how the specific rhythms of urban advertising impact on people perceptually as they move through urban space, aligning their rhythms of work and travel with commercial rhythms of commodity and marketing innovation. Here I will examine the specific temporalities of urban ruination and regeneration and how these may frame people's understanding of cities and their futures.

Walter Benjamin noted how urban sites of ruination or demolition can offer tools for thinking about the nature of capitalism: 'Demolition sites: sources for teaching the theory of construction' (Benjamin 1999: 95). He was particularly interested in nineteenth-century shopping arcades when they were falling out of fashion and into disuse. In their visible state of progressive decay or dereliction, Benjamin saw this period in the life of the arcades as offering ways of seeing through the glitz and glamour of consumer spectacle and thus of perceiving the transitory, fragile nature of capitalist culture. When their original aura had decayed, and their dazzling visual appeal had faded, the arcades' nature as empty capitalist cathedrals of consumption becomes evident and possibilities for political imagination are opened up. While Benjamin was writing of decay and demolition of sites of consumption, others have examined how sites of capitalist production can also offer unsettling or counter-cultural perspectives on contemporary society.

Tim Edensor's (2005) work on industrial ruins shows how the visible presence of derelict factories and the disorder that they embody can offer a critique of the contemporary normative modes of ordering cities and societies. The decayed structures of the factories, disused and rusted machinery, old signs, are all charged with the traces of power that are now redundant, a feature which serves to highlight the transitive qualities of hierarchies and particular social formations. The visible presence of these ruined factories acts in tension with dominant systems of representation because these edifices and the sites they inhabit cannot be commodified without being completely transformed. According to Edensor, they thus remain an unsettling presence in the modern city.

Industrial ruins signal other times,

> yet ruins do not merely evoke the past. They contain a still and seemingly quiescent present, and they also suggest forebodings, pointing to future erasure and subsequently, the reproduction of space, thus conveying a sense of the transience of all spaces. (2005: 125)

Edensor argues that the ways in which industrial ruins inhabit and shape multiple temporal dimensions – past productivity, present decay and present-tense interpretation, and future developments – jars with the way in which some social commentators paint the contemporary world as a flux of speeded-up flows. The industrial time of these sites is still evident in their material remains such as 'clocking-in stations, dockets, scheduled programmes of work and delivery, and timetables'. But the dominant temporal form of the ruin is the rate at which it decays (Edensor 2005: 125). So, in marked contrast to what are often seen as intense speeds and flows of the contemporary city, 'the ruin is a shadow realm of slowness' (Edensor 2005: 126). As I suggest in the following sections, these speeds and times can elicit varying responses from different groups of people. What George Steinmetz (2008: 211) calls 'ruinscapes' – areas dominated by decaying or dilapidated man-made structures – can function as evocative, nostalgic triggers for some groups, while signifying mere rubble for others. Ruins may reference past glories, or may signify a rapidly decaying sense of hope for the future economic and social prospects of certain cities.

People's perception of urban temporalities and urban change has long been a focus for academic studies but it merits revisiting in the light of more recent work on capitalist temporalities. Kevin Lynch's (1972) study, *What Time is This Place?*, provides a good entry point. Lynch was interested in how time is embedded in the urban environment, how we *see* and experience this time in a bodily way, and how urban planners can best organise cities to offer people the most wholesome, enriching experience of urban life. In an approach similar to Lefebvre's (1991, 1992) rhythmanalysis, Lynch uses a photographic study to examine the multiple temporalities made visible in Boston, USA. These temporalities are perceptually available to us in: the juxtaposition of old and new buildings; outdoor clocks, parking meters and parking tickets on cars; the rhythms of shops opening and closing; monuments and plaques; old street names; buildings in the process of renovation and signs explaining what is being constructed; trees in leaf; graffiti; cemeteries and museums; peeling layers of old posters; old railway lines disappearing to nowhere.

Lynch argues that perceptions of temporality and especially futurity are crucial for sustaining social life and that planners must incorporate a sensitive understanding of this as they shape cities. Lack of attention to this can lead to a disorientation as we move around the city; but it also can produce a more profound ontological disorientation because the city acts as a social and spatial grounding for many of us. This may lead to a sense of individual disengagement with the social form that is the city.

Lynch identifies various modes through which people experience the relationship of the urban environment to time. These are modes that planners can influence for the social good. 'Temporal collage' is a form in which the juxtaposition of old and new speaks of the passage of time and often takes the form of layering in architecture and leaving traces or fragments of former structures. This is a mode which refers to pro-gression and historical change in which 'time is "borrowed" to enlarge a present' (Lynch 1972: 173). 'Episodic change' is a primitive mode of sens-ing time in which there are discontinuous recurrences which refer to an underlying continuity, evident in the way we perceive seasonal change in trees losing their leaves. In this mode, 'the future is here with us because it will be like something we knew in the past' (Lynch 1972: 174). The 'direct display of change' is an immediate experience of the city's shifting character exemplified by people watching the destruction of a building by fire, or by the creation of urban spectacle by planners using lights to pick out the flow of traffic. Both examples visualise a particular form of change in the city. 'Design for motion' draws on Lynch's argument that the moving view is the primary way in which we engage visually with the city. It leads him to argue that planners should use sequencing design more often to enhance people's sense of movement linked to all scales of change in the urban environment. And 'patterning of long-range change' refers to how we perceive the processes of altering the city on a broader temporal scale, for instance, in the processes of constructing a building. Lynch suggests the use of art and technology to make visible and more legible these processes of change over time, for instance in creating a three-minute film that compresses the construction process.

This emphasis on rendering change visible and legible is the basis of Lynch's analysis. Reconnecting people's embodied, temporal per-ceptions of urban space in an organic way with the processes of struc-tural and infrastructural change, he argues, is the path to social and political engagement. Without an appreciation and implementation of this, 'the boarded-up buildings of a "renewal" area have become a visual symbol of the futility of public action' (Lynch 1972: 196). Lynch's insights show the importance of thinking about the *interplay* between the visible temporalities of decay and ruination on the one hand, and rebuilding work and more general economic regeneration on the other. His analysis highlights the way in which these temporalities are political – their legibility is pivotal to how the citizens imagine their city and what future they imagine for it. In effect, citizens articulate and shape the hope for the city through their visual engagement with urban temporalities. This is crucial, for without a vision of the city shared by planners, business people and residents – a vision which goes beyond the entrepreneurial emphasis on place marketing – then there is little hope for the city. With today's increased emphasis on public participation and stakeholder opinions in planning processes, this visualising of the city and its potential takes on a heightened significance.

As part of the everyday urban environment, billboards and panels articulate certain temporalities and spatialities, and help shape people's sense of engagement with these changes. In my study it is clear that billboards, wraps and panels tap into and shape the temporalities that are produced both by the dereliction and ruination of old buildings, and by sites as they are being demolished or regenerated. In the following sections I use Bergson's account of bodily perception, temporality and fabulation that I outlined in the previous chapter to interrogate these multiple temporalities and consider how people may *live* them. Lynch's analysis points to how visualities and temporalities operate differently in particular urban contexts. The analysis which follows considers this through case studies of Manchester and Detroit, cities which have certain similarities in industrial heritage but which in many other ways are very differently positioned.

Manchester: city of change

Manchester has been seen as the urban centre of the industrial revolution in the nineteenth century. Known as 'Cottonopolis', the city's factories or 'mills' produced a range of textiles. As an industrial heartland that was fed by the finance and products of the British Empire, Manchester has always been part of, and helped shape, a global economy (Dicken 2002). One of the most famous nineteenth-century commentators on Manchester was Friedrich Engels. In his classic text, *The Condition of the Working Class in England* (1987 [1845]), Engels describes many of Britain's industrial cities but pays particular attention to Manchester, claiming that 'the modern art of manufacture has reached its perfection in Manchester' and that 'Manchester is the classic type of a modern manufacturing town' (1987: 82, 83). But the system of industrial production had disastrous consequences for the workers of Manchester:

> The degradation to which the application of steam-power, machinery and the division of labour reduce the working man, and the attempts of the proletariat to rise above this abasement, must likewise be carried to the highest point and with the fullest consciousness. (Engels 1987: 83)

As well as detailing manufacturing processes and factory conditions, Engels famously described the living conditions for the working class of Manchester. One particularly poverty-stricken area of Manchester, on the south bank of the river Irk, is described in vivid terms:

> Everywhere half or wholly ruined buildings, some of them actually uninhabited, which means a great deal here; rarely a wooden or stone floor to be seen in the houses, almost uniformly broken, ill-fitting windows and doors, and a state of filth! Everywhere heaps of debris, refuse, and offal; standing pools for gutters, and a stench which alone would make it impossible for a human being in any degree civilized to live in such a district. (Engels 1987: 90)

This decay and dereliction was restricted to certain parts of the city. Engels notes that the working class and bourgeois areas of the city were strictly separated and that the bourgeoisie might travel through the city without ever being confronted by the visually striking sights of poverty: 'I have never seen so systematic a shutting out of the working class from the thoroughfares, so tender a concealment of everything that might affront the eye and the nerves of the bourgeoisie, as in Manchester' (Engels 1987: 87). The visual aspect of the city was compelling for Engels as it symbolised the degradation of the working class by capitalism, as well as functioning as documentary evidence of the living and working conditions of the poor. For many observers, the rapid transformation of the city's buildings and layout came to stand for wider social and political processes. Describing Engels' response to Manchester, Patrick Joyce argues that,

> For him and others, this city was a place that was rough and raw in its built forms, or rather in its *building* forms, for what observers were seeing in the 1830s and 1840s was the massive outgrowth of the city into unfinished streets and houses, new districts without seeming rhyme

or reason. Manchester was to them irrational, inhuman, brutish, the 'shock city' of the age, as it has been called. (Joyce 2003: 154)

While Manchester's mills and streets meant a life of poverty and hardship for its working class, the city's industries produced vast wealth for some. It also created a legacy of grand municipal and commercial buildings that are still evident in Manchester's centre today. But the once-vibrant industrial economy declined from the 1960s and this had a major impact upon employment in the city. The effect was not only economic but also dealt a blow to Manchester's civic identity which was tied tightly to the manufacturing sectors (Peck and Ward 2002). Service sector jobs increased, and while manufacturing jobs still played a significant part in local wealth generation (Dicken 2002), the number and type of jobs available to the city's workers had changed dramatically.

The political landscape, too, has undergone various significant shifts. Manchester has seen many changes since the 1980s when the City Council shifted from a form of municipal socialism to an entrepreneurialism or pragmatic interventionalist neo-liberalism (Quilley 2002). It has attracted huge sums of government funding for various forms of regeneration, including the development of retail areas, and the building of a sports stadium, cultural venues such as the Bridgewater Concert Hall, and residential developments (Robson 2002). One of the most dramatic changes to the city's structure and aesthetics came following events of 1996. On 15 June, an IRA bomb destroyed much of the city's commercial centre and while no-one was killed, the impact was tremendous. As many as 674 businesses were displaced and the cost of rebuilding the centre was estimated at £500 million (Holden 2002). But the bomb's destruction of the commercial heart of the city also had the effect of opening up possibilities for large-scale redesign and restructuring. Both private and state capital were mobilised in the redevelopment project, bolstering the idea of public–private partnership and the legitimacy of city entrepreneurialism (Holden 2002).

Peck and Ward (2002: 3) summarise the city's characteristics and planning vision from the 1990s as involving: 'the decline of manufacturing industry, the narrow obsession with city-centre regeneration, the (re)emergence of elite decision-making networks and privatised governance; can-do entrepreneurialism of local agencies, and the search for "joined up" responses to social exclusion'. Peck and Ward argue that while many cities in the UK and Europe can be characterised in this way, Manchester exemplifies these trends more thoroughly than most cities. But the regeneration of the city has focused mainly on its centre and there exists another Manchester: 'the city enveloping the revitalised core – poor Manchester, a city of uncertain employment, lifetime poverty, chronic ill-health and educational disadvantage' (Mellor 2002: 230). Contemporary Manchester is a divided city with large areas of deprivation only a few miles from the prosperous city centre and suburbs, and although overall unemployment levels have fallen over recent years, they still remain high in certain areas (Herd and Patterson 2002). So the Manchester that is often lauded as an exemplar of urban regeneration is in reality very good at the 'political theatre of regeneration' while major problems with poverty, social exclusion and social and political alienation remain (Peck and Ward 2002: 6). Indeed, while those supporting the entrepreneurial emphasis argue that economic benefits will 'trickle down' to the poor and least advantaged, critics argue that these shifts drive Manchester towards the model of an 'Americanised' city in which, 'economic and social polarisation will have been perversely underwritten by a set of policies which effectively legitimate the transfer of funds from social safety-net programmes into the subsidisation of speculative accumulation, zero-sum competition and middle-class consumption' (Peck and Ward 2002: 7–8).

The image of Manchester as a city of economic prosperity has been carefully crafted. In the 1990s, Manchester became an *aesthetic* project in the ways in which private and public developers imagined its architecture, and in how politicians and business elites imagined the cityscape (Mellor 2002; Williams 2004). Indeed, Manchester's 'designscape' drew heavily on the presence of creative industries and while there was some emphasis on heritage evident in the shaping of the new city, far more effort and money were invested in the aesthetic look of the city drawing on Manchester's perceived characteristics of 'modernity, avant-gardism and the symbolic capital of creativity' (Julier 2005: 885). The look and 'vibe' of the city are key for attracting businesses and creating wealth and the City Council's regeneration strategy 'calls for a "feel-good" promotion of the city as a centre of investment, in an era of competitive regionalism' (Herd and Patterson 2002: 190). But the visual aspect of the city was not only oriented towards attracting investment and creating a positive economic image; it also aimed to provide city inhabitants and workers with a positive urban experience. Degen (2008) notes the significance of sensory engagement in the regeneration of areas of Manchester such as Castlefield. And in reaction to the 'unfamiliar and anxious Modernist city' that existed before the IRA bomb, Manchester planners sought to reshape the new cityscape as 'reassuringly legible' (Williams 2004: 210). It was staged as a city of consumption and as such its views and vistas were considered crucial. Commentators agree that the changes in Manchester in the past 20 years have been striking. The shifts signal both a marked contrast with the economic prospects of the city in the 1960s and 1970s and also a transformation of the visual landscape: 'to have visited central Manchester at any time from the end of the Second World War until the mid-1980s would have been to visit a ruin' (Williams 2004: 210).

In the following analysis I outline how advertising structures and texts, which are located in specific urban sites, make visible multiple forms of temporality in the way that Lynch (1972) describes: they reference specific events or times; they embody and bring to legibility a sense of longer-term urban change; and they *create* certain time–spaces. Specific large-scale events are striking instances which render visible, and act to shape, forms of urban regeneration. A good example of this is the 17th Commonwealth Games which took place in Manchester in 2002 and the various projects of regeneration associated with the run-up to the Games brought a range of long-term benefits to the city (Smith and Fox 2007). These included providing employment, training and qualifications for its inhabitants, and supporting businesses and voluntary organisations. The main venues for the Games were sited in east Manchester which was in urgent need of regeneration and the East Manchester Urban Regeneration Company (later, New East Manchester Ltd) was set up to co-ordinate a range of local regeneration projects (Smith and Fox 2007). What interests me here is the way in which the new advertising structures which were built in association with the Games articulated and visualised the temporality associated with this specific event and with the broader temporality of regeneration. In Lynch's (1972) terms, the structures embodied the temporalities of the city through a 'direct display of change' in which regeneration through new commercial initiatives and an emphasis on consumption were made visible. They also embodied the principle of 'design for motion' as they were constructed with the mobile viewer in mind as they entered the city by car or bus (see Chapter 3). Media owners took advantage of the entrepreneurial spirit associated with the preparation for the Games and the openness to private funding associated with this. Normally, securing planning permission from City Councils for new advertising structures such as billboards is very difficult. But in the run-up to the Games, media owners were granted permission to construct large, silver structures in the form of an 'M' for Manchester. These incorporated a large advertising panel and were sited on major roads entering the city centre (see Figure 6.1).

Figure 6.1   M for Manchester (author's photograph)

In one respect, these commercial structures were a form of 'place marketing' as they attempted to create a tangible and highly visible brand for the city. Providing excellent sites for advertisements to capture people's attention as they entered the city, they sold the space of the city and its inhabitants (its mobile consumers or target markets) to potential advertisers. But the structures were also intended to promote an idea of Manchester to its inhabitants: the Council granted permission for their construction as they were thought to embody Manchester civic pride and the positive developments brought by processes of economic regeneration. They marked a specific moment in Manchester's economic and architectural reconfiguration linked to the event of the Commonwealth Games. Indeed, some panel casings were even constructed in the shape of weights to echo the weight-lifting competition in the Games.

But while advertising structures embody the temporality of specific events such as the Games, more significant in my study was their materialisation and visualisation of the broader temporalities of ruination and regeneration – what Lynch would term a 'patterning of long-range change'. Manchester's industrial history and the transformations it has since undergone mark it as a city of change and this change is made legible in various ways. There are striking temporal collages where advertising structures such as billboards surround derelict or deserted sites – often old industrial buildings – or mark the perimeter of sites and buildings undergoing reconstruction. Discussing examples of this in Figures 6.2 and 6.3, I will focus on how these advertising texts, structures and spatial contexts can be understood through Bergson's account of perception. I will analyse how they embody and render visible the zone of indetermination of bodily perception, and how perception should be conceived as a form of present-making that opens the future.

Figure 6.2 shows a Manchester city-centre building undergoing reconstruction with a new advertising panel or 'wrap' installed on its street-facing plane. The advertising panel was temporary and was to be removed as soon as the renovation was complete. A city-centre site such as this is attractive to advertisers as it has the potential to reach many 'targets' and permanent panels in such central areas are very difficult to establish. Figure 6.3 shows a derelict building in Ancoats, Manchester, partially covered in an advertisement for Cadbury's chocolate. This building is almost certainly a small nineteenth-century mill; indeed,

Figure 6.2 Manchester renovation and advertising wrap (author's photograph)

Figure 6.3   Derelict building in Manchester (author's photograph)

Engels describes Ancoats as the area in which 'stand the largest mills of Manchester, lining the canals, colossal six and seven-storied buildings towering with their slender chimneys far above the low cottages of the workers' (Engels 1987: 95). It is unclear if this building is undergoing renovation but its status as dilapidated or ruined is clear. Whatever its status, its positioning makes it valuable. Alongside a busy major road in Manchester, this site has been used to erect a multi-sided advertising 'wrap' or mega poster fastened to the scaffolding. As one practitioner describes, such a site is interesting as it answers the key questions an advertiser might pose: 'is it near to people with money, is it near to retail environments, is it near to major arterial roads? All that kind of stuff will give it its own characteristic which the agencies then in turn will translate into a value for a youth brand or for a motor brand or what have you' (practitioner, media owning company).

   These two panels and the advertising text in Figure 6.3 attempt to inhabit the zone of indetermination that I discussed in the previous chapter. According to Bergson (2004) this is the zone created by per-ceptual action that buffers the human being from the immediate responses to stimuli and allows the possibility of agency. This zone

or gap between stimulus and response constitutes agency or the capacity to act, and by trying to manipulate the temporal delay or inhabit
the zone of indetermination advertisements aim to direct the agentic
response – 'look at this!', 'remember this brand!', 'buy this!'. Clearly,
this does not determine the perceiving subject's subsequent actions; the
response, should there be any response at all, is indeed indeterminate.
Advertising's commercial effects are notoriously difficult to assess
accurately but it is possible to explore other more diffuse influences on
social space that escape advertising's clear commercial intentions. By
constantly referencing – and indeed making hyper-visible – the theme
of consumer 'choice', outdoor advertising brings to the fore an idea of
action, change and openness. Although this is framed by its creators in
terms of consumption, the placing of advertisements in shifting social
space to be received by a range of people who are variously socially
positioned, means that producers' intentions are regularly confounded
(see Chapters 2–4). The ads interface with other elements of the urban
visual environment such as buildings, trees, artwork, street signs, graffiti and shop signs. As Figure 6.4 illustrates, they become part of a chaotic semantic mix and thus may speak to perceivers in ways unintended
by their makers.

Both the rhythms of posting new campaigns, and the ads' textual
content which exhorts us to make new purchases, make public a sense
of change and action. This idea of 'making public' will be explored in
more detail in the following chapter. I wish to emphasise at this point
the way in which these ads open up a more general sense of change and
possible action by making visible and attempting to channel perceivers'
zone of indetermination.

Along with their attempts to intervene in the zone of indetermination, these ads draw on and create time–spaces. Figures 6.2 and 6.3
show how the presence of advertising panels, their rhythms of posting new ads, and the texts of the advertisements themselves, have a
distinctive temporal character. One aspect of this is their implication
in people's perceptual practices that *make the present*. The building in
Figure 6.3 has a clear nineteenth-century pedigree that is easily legible
to any passer-by. The advertising panel is using the fabric of the building as a literal support or kind of screen, and in so doing ties itself to
the particular temporal embodiment of capital that some such as Dovey
(2008) see as a kind of inertia of the built form. This inertia, I have
argued, is better conceived as just one form of temporality that interacts
with other temporalities. This nineteenth-century mill emerged from
the capital produced by industrial capitalism tied to the British Empire.

Figure 6.4 Visual semantic mix, Manchester (author's photograph)

Its moment of construction and the period throughout which it functioned were linked both spatially and temporally to empire. It was connected to a sourcing and distribution network of shipping, canal and
railway transport within Britain and extending around its empire, and

to the temporalities of commodity production and consumption that reached a certain pitch in the nineteenth century.

In Figure 6.3, it is evident how the new advertising wrap drags the dilapidated nineteenth-century building into the present-tense of the changing urban landscape. In one sense, the building's 'foot print' is clearly in the same location – it is rooted in the same ground. But in another sense, the nineteenth-century building is evidently in a new space. It is certainly the case that things have changed in the weak sense that its 'context' has altered: it may have new buildings set alongside it, the view out of its windows may be different and the way that the light enters the building may have changed; its uses and connections with other buildings, roads and people may have shifted. But it is not just that the building is 'out of its own time'; it has also been re-spatialised. Elizabeth Grosz's (2001) development of Bergson's account of duration points to how this can be conceptualised spatially. Bergson conceives of duration as 'the virtual coexistence of all of the past at each moment of the present' (Grosz 2001: 124). Past and present interweave and are co-productive. Extending this formulation to spatiality, Grosz suggests that the spatial present (*here, now*) 'defines its own region, but this regionality...intersects with the regionality of other heres' (2001: 128). Spatiality might then be understood 'as a layering of spaces within themselves, spaces enfolded in others, spaces that can function as the virtualities of the present, the "here"' (Grosz 2001: 128). In this understanding, spatiality is fundamentally relational and creative.

Bergson's account, and Grosz's elaboration of it, show how perception, time and spatiality are folded together. The temporal aspect of this is most easily available to the observer. In Figure 6.3, the advertising wrap creates a disjuncture between its referent of contemporary capitalist society and the nineteenth century embodied in the mill. In Lynch's (1972) terms, this is both a temporal collage and a direct display of change. The temporality of the slow ruination of the nineteenth-century industrial mill is juxtaposed with the rapid temporalities of advertising and consumer capitalism – promoting new products, line extensions of products, and new ideas of what it is to consume. But while this temporal aspect is perceptually immediate, Bergson and Grosz remind us that spatiality and materiality are also woven into this picture. Bergson challenges what he calls the 'fiction of an isolated material object' which in fact owes its existence 'to the place which it occupies in the universe as a whole' (2004: 11–12). Materiality, he maintains, is fundamentally relational and this relationality is also spatial. So, when we see the disjunctive juxtapositions of nineteenth-century and today's capitalism embodied in the material form of the building, what is also at play is that building's spatiality. The advertising wrap initiates a temporal movement, jolting the decaying building into the present-tense of perception. But the wrap also focuses a spatial movement; a creative moment which initiates new time–spaces.

The specificities of this process become clearer when we consider Bergson concept of fabulation discussed in the previous chapter. Bergson conceives fabulation as a form of perception that is oriented to sense-making, a crucial activity that enables us to act productively in a world full of uncertainties. As a form of perception, our capacity for fabulation uses a bodily, primitive understanding of 'life' to comprehend the social and natural world. In effect, we tend to see movement as in some way 'life-like'. In fabulation, we animate or anthropomorphise natural occurrences; create ways of understanding the patterning of happenings (for example in ideas of 'luck' or 'chance'); we attribute mindfulness or intent to animals, landscapes, social encounters or events; create ideas of powerful beings (for example, deities); and aggregate various characteristics of our social world to create ideas of an 'event'. These understandings, I suggested, can be extended to analyse how people conceptualise and act on 'capitalism' and 'the city' fabulated as aggregated sets of processes or characteristics, or as entities that are in some way animate.

Fabulation is thus an imaginative capacity that draws on our own experience of our bodies and attributes some form of life-like characteristics to the social world. Within this process, movement is of primary significance. This movement can be literal motion, as in Mullarkey's (2007) example of the scene in *Titanic* in which the ship approaches the iceberg. Discussing viewers' experiences of the film *Titanic*, Mullarkey (2007) uses Bergson to show how we fabulate that events are occurring *at the very time of viewing*; this creates virtualities and opens up the film's well-known narrative thread to alternative possibilities. As film utilises moving images, and movement is for Bergson the fundamental characteristic of humans, we are drawn into the visual experience viscerally. We perceptually engage with this movement on a fundamental, bodily level. We also fabulate disparate happenings into a unit that we call an 'event'. Mullarkey (2007: 63) argues that 'it is not that the iceberg is made human, but the *collision* with the iceberg is made into an event with intentionality – and what has intent can have that intent thwarted'. In this sense we 'enliven' or animate events such as the collision between the ship and the iceberg. And as well as creating understandings of narrative sequence and causality, we also create temporality. Because we fabulate that the actions we see on screen are unfolding at the time of viewing, we open those actions in the narrative to potential alteration. We are thus able to *will* the ship to miss the iceberg despite knowing the inevitable narrative sequence. This is more than a willing suspension of disbelief, Mullarkey argues, for this operates on a visceral, perceptual level – it makes sense to us *through the body*.

But, I suggest, movement as a *process* can also trigger and shape fabulations. Thus the perception of urban change in the social processes of both urban dereliction and urban regeneration can be seen as fabulation. We perceive the temporal movement in the jolting forward initiated by the advertising wrap in ways that make sense to us on a fundamental, bodily level. This then helps shape the way in which we fabulate social processes – capitalism, urban decay and urban regeneration – as animated. This operates in a feedback loop in which people perceive animation or movement as evidence of 'life'; then people *expect* to see movement in that which is 'alive' or in some way animate. So the perception of movement and its life-like quality further fuels the potential for fabulation, and fabulation makes things seem even more alive. Mullarkey argues that fabulation shows how people may not necessarily 'believe in' a film's characters or narrative truth while at the same time experience both as 'real' or animate as they engage perceptually with movement and an idea of 'life'.

The perception of happenings *as a process* involves seeing movement, but also involves temporality. Mullarkey (2007) shows how fabulation is a form of present-making and Bergson reminds us that while duration involves a co-dependent and co-constitutive relation between past and present, it is the present that is the site of action – the present is *'that which is acting'* (Bergson 2004: 74, emphasis in the original). Bergson's idea of duration is one of relationality and of openness. The whole of the past contracts into each 'moment' of the present in a co-productive relationship. The relational movement between past and present is that which constitutes our practical understanding of temporal succession – in which each moment follows the previous and can be predicted to continue in an even pattern. This practical, embodied understanding of time as extending behind and before us in a smooth line enables us to act in the world. It is in this sense a productive fiction. But Grosz argues that for Bergson, the present is full of potential that cannot, in practice, easily be predicted; it is 'laden with virtualities that extend beyond itself' (2001: 119). So, combined with Bergson's idea of fabulation, we can see how perceptual acts open up the future and virtuality (or radical possibility).

What is perhaps less intuitive is the way in which fabulation – as a form of perception, and as a movement-oriented process – acts to open up spatiality. Following Grosz (2001: 119), we can see that 'the whole of space, spatiality, contracts into the specificity of location, and the occupation of any space contains the virtual whole of spatiality, which is to say, the infinite possibilities of my action on and being acted on by matter in space and time'. Spatiality is not neutral or passive, but active and creative. The 'here', with its relational ties to many 'theres', is *acting*. The perceptual fabulation of our encounter with the ad structures opens up temporalities and reveals past, present and future interconnectedness. But it also reveals the virtual quality of spatiality – its creativity. So when the advertising wrap drags the nineteenth-century factory into the present-tense of viewing and the contemporary moment of capitalism, the building is also jolted into a new time–space. Its virtualities are made evident: the perceptual engagement makes legible the spatio-temporalities of the building showing its multiplicities or the fundamental connectedness of spatialities.

Advertising structures, among many other urban forms, act as 'events' in Bergson's terms – we engage with them perceptually and use them to aggregate and anthropomorphise a range of happenings, processes, ideas and representations. The specificity of advertising structures centres on their consumerist, 'choice' orientation and their capitalist temporalitites (see Chapter 4). By emphasising choice, they further animate and open up the perceptual and action-oriented field (in ways not anticipated by their creators). The advertising wrap in Figure 6.3 illuminates that which is often not visible – spatial connections (e.g. global connections of nineteenth-century industrial production and distribution; contemporary iterations of consumerism) and the activities of space. It is in this sense that we can say that the building is in a 'new space'.

This connectivity between what Bergson calls 'images' is not an even, flattened field of networked nodes. It has specific characteristics, for individual bodies are 'centres of real action' which have qualitatively different engagement with the material world than lower-order animals or what we would call objects (Bergson 2004: 21). And it is also clear that different urban spaces and indeed different cities have specific spatio-temporalities and produce different perceptual fields. Although planners' and politicians' rhetoric of regeneration of Manchester does not always translate into reality, Manchester's shifting urban terrain produces a sense of change. As Williams (2004: 201) argues, 'something about the space of Manchester, its scale, its monumentality, yet very modern lack of density, mean that one is always made aware of the fact of transformation'. Building work and the advertising panels that take advantage of these temporarily available spaces, visualises a sense that the city is changing, but more specifically, a sense that the city is moving forward. This perception articulates that the ruined buildings – which reference both the nineteenth-century glories of the industrial city and, in their run-down state, the economic gloom of the 1970s – are the support surface and founding base for new development, economic prosperity for the city, and hope for its inhabitants. In the case of Figure 6.2, the wrap on the building undergoing regeneration piggybacks on the sense of change and renewal (generally understood as a kind of forward motion), and further animates it.

As a form of perception, then, fabulation creates understandings of the world that enable us to act. It creates productive fictions that we do not necessarily 'believe', but which engage us in a primitive, visceral way. It facilitates useful understandings of how things change, in this case through the temporalities of urban transformation. This draws together various visible urban 'events' and, influenced by planners and councils' rhetoric of forward momentum for the city, shapes the perception of urban change. It creates a sense that cities shift and transform – in Manchester's case, in a generally positive way. It animates the city. Lynch (1972) wanted urban planners to incorporate into their practices ways of visualising change. I have argued that urban change is made visible or legible in many more ways than Lynch imagined. Further, I have emphasised how the perception of these changes forms part of the activity, the creativity and the virtuality of spatiality. Here, change is not merely a temporal process but is fundamentally spatial. If we introduce a discussion of a very different city – Detroit in Michigan, USA – we can begin to appreciate the specificities of these spatialities and how the perception of urban change can have a profound influence upon how people imagine the future of their cities.

Detroit, dereliction and hope

Manchester shares with Detroit its status as a one-time industrial centre. Whereas Manchester's history and wealth lay in its textile factories of the nineteenth century, Detroit's industrial past lay in its status as the famous 'Motor City', or 'Motown', of Henry Ford's twentieth-century car factories. Both cities have suffered industrial decline and great deprivation for their inhabitants, and there is also one direct link. In the early twentieth century, Trafford Park in Manchester became the site of the first automobile plant built by Henry Ford outside North

America (although this was later relocated to Dagenham, UK), and many other American firms subsequently developed in and around this area of Manchester (Dicken 2002). But Detroit's history, tied to its specific spatialities, is otherwise distinct. In the 1940s, Detroit was one of America's fastest growing 'boomtowns' whose industries provided relatively highly paid blue-collar jobs (Sugrue 1996). These jobs enfranchised African-American workers such that, in the period 1967–74, 'more than anywhere else in the United States, the movement led by black workers defined its goal in terms of real power – the power to control the economy, which meant trying to control the shop floor at the point of production' (Georgakas and Surkin 1998 [1975]: 5). But Detroit is also famous for its racial inequalities and the riots of 1967 in which 43 died and 7,231 were arrested (Sugrue 1996).

Economic decentralisation has impacted upon Detroit more forcefully than other American cities as many of the jobs it provided were high-wage and low-skill industrial posts, primarily in auto production and often filled by African-Americans (Thomas 1997). Over the years, manufacturers have continued their flight from the city and there has been little success in attracting new industries. New jobs focus on service sector work in hotels and restaurants which is often part-time and insecure (Sugrue 1996). And in tandem with industrial decline, Detroit's central business district has declined, destroying many retail jobs in the centre. The decline in both industrial and retail jobs hit Detroit's African-Americans very hard and they did not have the resources to travel to the new suburbs for the jobs that were springing up there (Thomas 1997). Although significant numbers of white people remained in the centre of Detroit, the phenomenon of 'white flight' or out-migration from the centre to the suburbs was significant in shaping the nature of the city (Thompson 2001). The suburban housing boom, the suburbs' many amenities, growing affordability of cars and the building of highways made suburban living appealing for those who could afford it. This 'pull' factor was combined with a 'push' factor for some white residents who did not want to live in racially mixed city-centre areas (Thomas 1997). US Census Bureau figures estimate that 82.8 per cent of the current population of Detroit City is Black or African-American (compared to 12.4 per cent nationally), and 10.4 per cent white (compared to 74.1 per cent nationally).[1] The Census Bureau data point to the trend of general population decline, estimating Detroit's population in 1990 as 1,027,974, in 2000 as 951,270, and in 2007 as 916,952.[2]

But while Detroit has faced severe economic problems over the last decades, commentators argue that it is important to recognise Detroit's positive characteristics: 'strong public and nonprofit institutions, an accessible location, and a record of successful redevelopment projects' as well as assets such as opportunities for redevelopment on vacant sites (Thomas 1997: 221). There are city residents who defend Detroit and point to residents' creativity and hardiness evident in 'large-scale urban farming enterprises, guerilla gardening, ad hoc public transportation systems, green building experiments, "found object" constructions, food cooperatives, co-housing enclaves, and vigorous art and music installations and performances' (Vogel 2005: 19). But it is impossible to deny Detroit's significant problems. In 1996, Sugrue argued that 'the city is plagued by joblessness, concentrated poverty, physical decay, and racial isolation' (1996: 3). And with the economic crisis of 2008 onward, things have deteriorated further. Sharon Zukin noted in 1991 that Detroit could not rely on the steel and auto industries for rescue. Writing in 2000, Farley, Danziger and Holzer argued that Detroit's configuration of problems with the labour market, housing stock, racism and particularly industrial decline make it especially vulnerable to fluctuations in the global economy: 'when recessions occur, Detroit will likely be hard hit, since at present – as in the past – there are no major industries to cushion slumps in vehicle production when the business cycle turns sour' (2000: 248). Their prediction has come true and the impact on Detroit's residents has been intense. But even in the years just prior to the global economic crisis, Detroit's longer-term decline had made itself felt. Using 2005–2007 figures, the US Census Bureau estimate that only 54.9 per cent of the population over 16 years of age is in the labour force, and that families' per capita income is $14,916 compared to a US national average of $26,178. In Detroit 32.5 per cent of individuals are thought to be living under the poverty line, compared to 13.3 per cent nationally.[3]

The economic depression in Detroit clearly has very tangible effects on the city's residents. The long-term decline of Detroit, as well as the more recent economic crisis which has impacted forcefully on the automotive industry, is made material and visible in the city in many ways. The material forms of buildings and the city's infrastructure manifest certain ways of knowing the city. These run parallel to, and may indeed make more sense to people in everyday ways, than bald reports of economic figures or complex descriptions of global financial processes. Among the many urban structures and texts that materialise urban change, advertising and its billboards embody and present a moment of consumer capitalism particular to Detroit.

It is important to recognise certain specificities of billboard advertising in urban space. Such advertising texts and structures capture the various social and political relations of US cities in striking ways. Mitchell and Greenberg's (1991) study of outdoor advertising in four New Jersey cities found that black and Hispanic neighbourhoods were far more likely to be targeted by companies advertising alcohol or tobacco products than were white areas. Equally, studies of billboard advertising in Chicago by Hackbarth, Silvestri and Cosper (1995) and Hackbarth et al. (2001) found that poor and minority areas of the city were disproportionately targeted by alcohol and tobacco campaigns. In many studies, the placing of billboard structures has been linked to ruined or derelict areas of cities. In their study of outdoor advertising panel density in predominantly African-American neighbourhoods in New York City, Kwate and Lee (2006) emphasise the racial targeting of ads and the significance of sites of dereliction. They found that black neighbourhoods had more advertising space than predominantly white neighbourhoods and that alcohol and tobacco featured disproportion-ately in these ads. They noted how advertising panels and billboards often populated vacant lots in African-American areas of the city, arguing that this may be due to the fact that

(a) deteriorated space may be perceived by advertisers as markers of a community that may not be as well able to fend off unwanted outdoor ads, and/or one in which municipal regulations are minim-ally enforced; (b) landlords may be more inclined toward the finan-cial rewards conferred by installing billboards on their buildings; and (c) deteriorated spaces simply create more available space within which ads may be placed, compared to neighborhoods that are more fully built up. (Kwate and Lee 2006: 22)

But not only do derelict or abandoned urban spaces attract billboard construction; the high concentration of billboards acts to label and stigmatise certain areas: 'the visual disorder caused by a high density of outdoor ads may reproduce inequality by marking neighborhoods as "the ghetto" and reducing assessed value by residents and business owners. Indeed, billboards have been described as symbols that visually define ghettos' (Kwate and Lee 2006: 29).

John L. Jackson Jr's (2003: 344) analysis of advertising panels in Harlem, which has been called the 'capital of Black America', points to the uneven temporality of urban regeneration. He notes the strik-ing presence of large billboards and huge advertising wraps covering the sides of buildings. Combined with initiatives providing grants for community redevelopment and job creation, and an influx of corporate financing to Harlem, the presence of glitzy ads gives the space a sense of economic possibility and forward-motion. The visual aspect of this area of New York is crucial for its image of possibility and potential: 'To glimpse Harlemworld in 2003 is to catch sight of a place in motion, a spatial mobility writ literal by the movement of money, businesses, tenants, homeowners, shoppers, shopkeepers, investors and speculators bobbing in and out of the community on a daily basis' (Jackson 2003: 346). But this redevelopment is not even, a fact made tangible by the massive advertising wraps that cover abandoned, dilapidated Harlem buildings which incongruously abut regenerated buildings. This creates a powerful visual dissonance. Other wraps drape over abandoned residential buildings offering a 'shorthand lesson in racial visuality as told through architectural desertion and reappropriation' (Jackson 2003: 350). Other ads take the form of huge semi-transparent mesh panels which cover the windows of inhabited apartment buildings, representing the financial need of the residents who have agreed to such a deal. This reveals a certain complexity of temporality that Lynch (1972) among others have noted: 'Advertisements atop abandonment also mark the slowness of Harlem's current transformations – a re-invigorated interest than [sic] can't quite completely cover up/over a history of neglect' (Jackson 2003: 348).

These studies of advertising in US cities highlight important issues about racial targeting. They explore the link between specific urban areas, the potential for selling goods, and the social capital that only certain groups can mobilise to resist the proliferation of billboards in their neighbourhoods. Kwate and Lee's study (2006) focuses on the correlation of the presence of billboards, decaying urban spaces and racial targeting of advertisements. They note how the perceived economic value of land is tied to economic possibilities for advertisers who wish to sell space. Jackson (2003) notes the multiple temporalities of not only the dereliction of the buildings but also the stalled urban futures that the advertising texts reference:

> But not only are the apartments themselves abandoned, a palimpsestial remnant of the tenants who once lived inside; I would argue that the advertisements themselves are abandoned as well – left to dangle for a futurity not yet realized, tethered to a material present of brick, glass, and cement that exposes the injustices of pasts rife with restricted covenants qua overcrowded apartments qua absentee landlording. (Jackson 2003: 349)

The presence of billboards in the areas discussed by these studies shows that outdoor advertising companies are able to sell that advertising space to clients, and that these clients perceive that at least some of the people who live in these areas are able to buy the products they advertise. As target markets, the viewers of the ads are considered to wield some (limited) economic power as potential consumers. But in my photographic study of Detroit, it was clear that the poor, African-American areas of the city were not densely populated with billboards. Indeed, the few billboards that were present tended to be empty or abandoned.

Figure 6.5 shows a typical scene near the city centre in which a billboard's peeling advert is promoting its own ad space (unsuccessfully). Figure 6.6 shows an abandoned advertising panel, only its metal frame remaining. Such empty or discarded advertising space would not be present in more economically vibrant cities such as Manchester where space is at a premium and target markets are perceived as lucrative.

What temporalities does advertising in Detroit tap into and shape? What do Detroit's spaces create? Detroit's cityscape or visual economy has attracted considerable attention from academics, social commentators, artists, journalists and film-makers. It is clear that Detroit has been used by people all over America and beyond to symbolise a range of social processes and characteristics, such as industrial decline and racial disharmony. It has been used as the crime-ridden dystopian setting for the futuristic city in the film *Robocop* (1987, dir. Paul Verhoeven) and as the city that symbolises social disintegration in the film *8 Mile* (2002, dir. Curtis Hanson). Jerry Herron (1993) argues that Detroit has become for many Americans a dystopian, worst-case urban scenario. People are deeply invested in the idea that Detroit is atypical and that 'outside war, or some sort of national emergency, it's hard to imagine anything – especially anything domestic and urban – that people could agree on and get behind, except, perhaps, for the wish to keep "Detroit" from happening to where they live' (Herron 1993: 15). Journalist Tony Allen-Mills describes how the sale of a three-bedroomed house for $1 became a news story that symbolised to the rest of America Detroit's unravelling:

> The house on Traverse Street tells part of the story of a decline so dizzying that other cities around America have begun to talk fearfully of 'Detroitification', a seemingly irreversible condition of urban despair that slowly takes grip of once-flourishing communities and strips them of value and life.[4]

Figure 6.5   Advertise here, Detroit (author's photograph)

In the context of the global economic crisis of 2008 onward, it must be much harder for Americans to imagine that 'Detroit' could not happen to their city. But I think that Herron's point that Detroit functions as a horrifying 'other' and cautionary tale holds true. National and

Figure 6.6   Abandoned advertising billboard, Detroit (author's photograph)

international media coverage of Detroit has long focused on violence, decay and despair. While these tales of urban horror may operate for non-residents as a prophylactic, they do not offer Detroit residents a narrative that speaks to them.

> Like gawkers assembling at an accident scene, where the urge is to see the worst, and by looking upon disaster to gain mastery over it, the level of courage becomes an indicator of dread. But the more stories that get told, the less relevant storytelling seems to the task at hand. No matter how true the tales may be – as accounts of people or places or things – they end up like other historic markers; they stand for a kind of memory that nobody who lives here still looks to for explanations. (Herron 1993: 27–28)

In what follows I argue that both the media's coverage, and residents' personal experience of the material and visual cityscape of Detroit, is understood better as fabulation than simple symbolic association. People use the visible material of Detroit, especially its ruined buildings, to fabulate. As a form of perception, fabulation helps deal with the various social fears or memories that Detroit elicits – either in its form as trope or sign of urban disintegration or, for residents, its embodiment of their everyday problems. As a thoroughly bodily process that takes as its point of reference 'life', it is unsurprising that fabulations can unfold variously for people marked by race and class in different ways. I will explore how the perception of urban space is framed by temporalities, particularly of disaster or ruination, in these different ways. The confluence of various factors has led some commentators to argue that Detroit can be seen as a 'slow-motion disaster' caused by 'the long-term collision between corrosive structural processes, counterproductive social policies and vulnerable populations' (Draus 2009: 368, 361). How, then, do we *see* such temporalities and how do we imagine the future of Detroit?

As evident in Figures 6.5 and 6.6, the decaying visual cityscape of Detroit lends itself to ideas of ruin and ruination, and many academics have explored this avenue. George Steinmetz's (2006, 2008) analyses of Detroit signal how the abandoned and dilapidated buildings of Detroit function as ruins of a sort, but ruins that signify differently from the nostalgia-infused dilapidated sites in other cities. Discussing his documentary film, *Detroit, Ruin of a City* (2005) created with Michael Chanan, he argues that Detroit can be understood as a city of ruins but that, 'these ruins are widely perceived as embarrassing and ugly, as a reminder of a painful history that would be best forgotten, and as targets for the wrecking ball' (Steinmetz 2006: 491). But it is clear that people see the dilapidated landscape of Detroit in differing ways.[5] Most of the city's residents, he suggests, see these remnants of buildings as 'mere rubble and breeding grounds for crime' (Steinmetz 2008: 216). Unlike in some other cities, these industrial ruins are not preserved as forms of heritage although they can attract what he calls 'ruingazers', predominantly outsiders and suburbanites who seek to revel in a kind of exoticised, dystopian vision of urban decay (Steinmetz 2008: 216). Others include residents who seek to revalue the architecture of Detroit, some of which is now ruined or well on its way to dereliction.[6]

Others view Detroit, or an idea of Detroit, with a vivid nostalgia. As Sperb argues, Detroit and its representations are subject to intense nostalgia in ways which are clearly marked by the city's racial history: 'for many white residents past and present, steeped in nostalgia, Detroit is an absence – a city, an industry, a modernity, that *was*' (Sperb 2008: 185). In a similar vein, Steinmetz argues that the ruins of Detroit signify for some a nostalgia for Fordism, 'a desire to relive the past, to re-experience the bustling metropolis as it is remembered or has been described' (Steinmetz 2008: 218). This is also a nostalgia for a working class solidarity that has been lost to contemporary neo-liberal, individualistic competitiveness. This nostalgia is, 'the sense of having lost an entire sociohistorical context and the identifications bound up with it' (Steinmetz 2008: 220). Ruins therefore are more compelling and semantically rich than restored buildings because they make visible temporalities in a striking way: 'ruins function like Rubin's vase/profile illusion, allowing the viewer to see the intact object and its disappearance at the same time' (Steinmetz 2008: 232). In effect, ruins facilitate understandings of *process* and change.

The unsuccessful plea for advertisers to buy space on the billboard in Figure 6.5 and the abandoned billboard frame in Figure 6.6 also make visible these temporalities. They may reference a time of more economic buoyancy in which more people could afford to buy the products advertised, and more companies could afford to invest in advertising. But advertising texts and structures do not afford nostalgic visions in the same way that ruined buildings may. Unlike the findings of studies of other US cities, outdoor advertising in Detroit does not disproportionately target African-Americans – indeed, those groups are seen as too poor to be worth targeting. Billboards do not spring up more intensely in black areas of the city. What is most evident alongside decay and ruination in Detroit is absence and emptiness.

Figure 6.7 shows a typical scene not far from the city centre. The old, rather grand houses are boarded up and appear deserted, although many people still attempt to live in them. They are material testament to Detroit's history of white, middle class out-migration to the suburbs and nearby small towns. This exodus has left a patchwork of derelict housing areas and empty lots. It is estimated that 22.2 per cent of Detroit's housing units are currently unoccupied.[7] Bill McGraw (2007: 294), journalist and long-term resident of the city, writes that emptiness seems to define Detroit: 'it seems as if much of the city has gone missing'.

> In addition to the large tracts of the city that are broken down, significant portions of the landscape are simply vacant; they have been razed of all man-made structures, and those areas have devolved into lush fields of lamb's quarters, spreading knotweed, milky purslane, spready spurge and Russian thistle. It is not unusual to see ringed-necked pheasants in the tall grass ... . Along with empty land, Detroit also has thousands of empty buildings. It has derelict downtown skyscrapers with large trees growing from roofs. It has vacant homes, churches, schools, fire stations, police precincts, libraries and armories. (McGraw 2007: 290, 293)

Figure 6.7   Dilapidated housing stock, Detroit (author's photograph)

For those visiting Detroit, this emptiness is striking and creates a sense of viewing the aftermath of some disaster. As Sugrue argues, 'whole sections of the city are eerily apocalyptic' (1996: 3). Part of this disaster is economic decline and its effects on the city's residents, and part of it is the history of discordant social relations. Indeed, the past lives visibly in the city's structures – the property damage inflicted during the riots of 1967 is still apparent on the abandoned buildings of Detroit and in its vacant lots (Sugrue 1996).

Detroit's empty spaces are just as socially and visually significant as the city's buildings. The architects Perez and Daskalakis (2001: 81) argue that the voids or *'terrain vague'* of Detroit do not produce a *tabula rasa*: rather, there is a complex interplay between presence and absence, erasure and construction. Steinmetz (2008: 231), in parallel, sees Detroit's many empty spaces as a counterpart to ruins and suggests that we understand them as 'negative ruins'. Steinmetz emphasises the processual character of decay and ruination and argues that attempts to deal with the visible remains of buildings by demolishing them will only proliferate ruins in a new form – negative ruins or ghostly forms of social and natural processes of dereliction. Perez and Daskalakis suggest something similar:

> The act of erasure or voiding is not and can never be complete; there is always the residue of something that is no longer there and the expectation of something that could be there. There is always the trace of something that has occurred and the anticipation of something that is about to happen. (Perez and Daskalakis 2001: 82)

These architects suggest that such voided spaces are unsettling, inspiring, and their 'sheer magnitude, pervasiveness, and *otherness* force us to recontextualize what we thought we knew' (Perez and Daskalakis 2001: 84). They are writing from their position as architects and planners whose professional experience and knowledge is challenged by the evidence of vast areas of 'unbuilding'. And Steinmetz is writing from the perspective of the social analyst wishing to stress how social processes – industrial, political, racial – become tied up in the material remains of buildings and also in the voids of those buildings when they are pulled down.

But what of Detroit's residents' experience of the cityscape? People live in, and pass through, these 'voided spaces' and it is unlikely that they experience these spaces as forms of 'otherness' as these architects do. This is not an ethnographic study of people's attitudes to the material forms of Detroit's landscape. But I wish to explore conceptual frameworks that can start asking questions about people's complex engagement with urban spatiality and temporality. Bergson's account of perception and fabulation can help make sense of the ways in which Detroit's ruins speak to people. As Steinmetz suggests, ruins are compelling as they act as the Rubin's vase/profile illusion which reveals simultaneously both the object and its disappearance. I am arguing that ruins make visible *processes* (natural, social, political). These processes, understood as forms of movement and animation, make sense to us in ways that draws on bodily processes of perception and attributes ideas of bodies and life to those processes. This is not, then, a merely cognitive process of story-making. Seeing movement as 'life-like', fabulation offers ways of understanding how people make sense of their environment through embodied perception.

Fabulation also offers ways of dealing with (social and personal) anxieties. Herron (1993) shows how non-residents confect ideas about 'Detroit' as a frightening, atypical example of urban collapse and social disintegration. This is not mere symbolism. It can be seen as a fabulation in which people conceptually draw together disparate social processes (industrial decline, growing unemployment, racial tension, infrastructural disintegration), and attribute them to a unitary, causal, animate force. Bergson and Mullarkey emphasise this as an 'event', but it can also been seen as a more temporally distributed form – an event-as-process. Thus Detroit as a 'slow-motion disaster' (Draus 2009: 368) can be fabulated as a process which is nonetheless unitary, causal and animate. Abstract, global economic forces do not make sense to people in the direct and compelling way that embodied perceptual engagement with their changing urban environment does. In Bergson's terms, we fabulate the city as in some way animate through our perceptions of urban temporalities. Writing in 1961, Jane Jacobs recognised the significance of process in urban analysis but also insisted that understandings of urban processes are available to all:

> For cities, processes are of the essence…. The processes that occur in cities are not arcane, capable of being understood only by experts. They can be understood by almost anybody. Many ordinary people already understand them; they simply have not given these processes names, or considered that by understanding these ordinary arrangements of cause and effect, we can also direct them if we want to. (Jacobs 1972 [1961]: 454)

Fabulation is one such mode of understanding. It does not rely on access to specialist knowledge, skills or data, but produces understandings through an embodied, perceptual engagement with the urban environment. These understandings loop back on themselves and feed their performance – thus perceptions of temporal and spatial movements further facilitate our understanding of the city as life-like, as shifting, as animated. Thus Detroit becomes 'Detroit' and a process of 'Detroitification' becomes precisely what other cities seek to avoid.

This focus on process foregrounds the significance of temporality and particularly futurity. This is crucial for making sense of how people imagine the possible future of their cities. Barbara Adam and Chris Groves (2007) provide an interesting account of how paradigms for imagining the future shift over time and facilitate particular social formations. They argue that capitalist models of time articulate the future as emptied of content, abstracted from context, and amenable to calculation. It is a future that appears available to be filled by anything and that can be commodified. But in fact, 'the empty future of contemporary economic and political exchange is fundamentally uncertain and unknowable' (Adam and Groves 2007: 12–13). These models of imagining time encourage us to disconnect the future from the present and thus have had a detrimental effect on societies and on the globe, storing up a range of problems such as environmental degradation. Adam and Groves argue that we need to change our relationship with the future, beginning with a shift in our concepts of time and futurity:

> We must draw into our thinking, imagining and feeling the 'shadow side' of futures as latent processes on their way to emergence. Instead of conceiving futures simply as the products of our actions and activities in the present, we have to understand the futures societies create as swelling up within them, always on the way to unfolding. The future in this sense is not abstract, not empty, and not simply open to transformation, but is instead *living* within the present. It inhabits the relations that establish the interdependence of things, and which contain the potential for producing unintended and unforeseen consequences. (Adam and Groves 2007: 122, emphasis in the original)

Such a model, Adam and Groves argue, would facilitate a more responsible, more ethical stance to future generations and to the globe. What interests me particularly is how their concept of the 'living future' resonates with Bergson's ideas about temporality and fabulation. Imagining the future as that which unfolds, which lives within the present, which has some form of animation, and which is oriented to action can be seen as a form of fabulation. It also sits alongside Bergson's idea of the 'virtual', perhaps an unsurprising connection as Adam and Groves are influenced by Deleuze and Guattari's thinking which in turn draws on Bergson: the living future 'refers to halos of evolutionary potential that surround and permeate individuals and make it possible for them to transform others and be transformed by them in surprising and unintended ways. It is neither pre-formed and pre-determined nor fully indeterminate, empty and open to endless transformation' (Adam and Groves 2007: 198). The openness of imagining cities' futures is thus tied to how we understand the present and its potential (or virtualities). Within these imaginings, the perception of certain temporalities that are understood as 'processes' play a key role. As I have argued above, the understanding of urban processes is not limited to those with special knowledge. In Adam and Groves' terms, this is the 'lived future' which is 'the way humans and other living entities experience their world as something in the process of being made, anticipate its changing form and participate in its production' (Adam and Groves 2007: 198).

But these modes of understanding – Bergson's fabulation and Adam and Groves' 'living future' – can have interesting consequences as they are played out. One effect of the anthropomorphisation of 'Detroit' that I have described is that the attribution of causality and indeed blame becomes easier in commonsense terms. As Steinmetz argues, 'the city's ruination bleeds metonymically into a discourse about "human ruins" who are blamed for the damaged condition of their environment' (Steinmetz 2006: 503). This certainly appears to be the case, but there is another level operating here. The material form of the city itself, folded into the embodiment of its people, comes to be seen as an entity that is life-like. Through processes of fabulation, the city itself comes to be seen as the cause of its own problems. These fabulations of Detroit as a distinctive, agentic entity may offer some form of relief for Americans who fear that the social and economic processes that they see there may happen to their own cities.

But as Bergson argues, fabulation also offers other practical orientations to action. Creating out of disparate social and natural forces an idea of a being rather like us – unitary, agentic, mindful – we are given traction to act by creating something to *act against*. Fabulation as a form of perception should not be considered an abstract, secondary phenomenon subordinate to other modes of knowing and doing because 'perception is a measure of our virtual action upon things' (Grosz 2005: 102–103). In this vein, the city's visible material forms, whether buildings or advertising structures, can be conceived as 'events', as tangible co-minglings of spaces and times. Detroit's past – of industrial manufacture, of social unrest – is everywhere materially visible in the city, and Steinmetz (2006, 2008) shows how some people engage with the visible remains of buildings in a nostalgic fashion. But also visibly available are the present and future – the living future. Perez and Daskalakis (2001) hint at this in their discussion of voids by arguing that while they always leave a mark of something in the present, these voids also *anticipate* that something might happen. People's visual engagement with urban material forms as 'events', I suggest, are virtual actions which draw together past, present and future in ways which are spatialised. Understanding the building or advertising structure as event involves the perceptual, fabulatory action of aggregating social, political, economic and natural processes. It accesses duration as understood by Bergson – involving the co-mingling and co-productive nature of past, present and indeed future. And it engages the radical connectedness of spatiality in the way elaborated by Grosz. These 'spaces' of what people come to see as 'events' (buildings, ad structures, voids) are opened up and we apprehend their virtual nature. They describe their own distinctive location in the geometrical sense of describing a circle. But they also reveal how they are interwoven with other spatialities, and may overlap, co-exist, intertwine, or jar in ways which are uneven and unpredictable.

This shows how *spatialities* as well as temporalities are active and creative. Following Bergson, Grosz outlines how the (virtual) movement between past and present acts to create temporality as we understand it (which is a practical understanding that facilitates our actions in the world). Like others such as Lefebvre (1991), Grosz emphasises that spatiality, too, must be seen as active and creative. I have argued in this and the previous chapter that fabulation should be seen as a kind of (imaginative) movement. It helps us act in the world and it engages with, and helps performatively reproduce, spatiality as creative. In the case of fabulating urban space and the temporalities of capitalism, we can see how understandings of the past may be formed and how people may attribute the causality of social processes. But we can also see that the virtual (spatial and temporal) movements involved in perceiving material urban forms as 'events' opens up the *future*; as in viewing a film, we are offered the chance to actively write the script as events are unfolding. This is a (virtual) space and can be a space of action and hope – a 'living future' which reconnects present actions with responsibility and ethical concerns.

I have shown how this is enacted very differently in two cities. In Manchester, the temporalities of urban regeneration written into the city's visible, material forms offer a positive sense of forward-motion and economic growth. In Detroit, the decay of the cityscape offers complex engagements with ideas of, and hopes for, the future. Sugrue argues that 'what hope remains in the city comes from the continued efforts of city residents to resist the debilitating effects of poverty, racial tension, and industrial decline' (1996: 271). This is certainly the case, but one important way that people resist these effects is through fabulating alternative futures. This should not be understood in the loose sense of merely imagining something different. For Bergson, 'the possible' is that which can be read off from or predicted from the present – nothing radical or unexpected is involved. In contrast, 'the virtual' is the site of novelty, difference, invention, and can involve the unpredicted (Grosz 2001). Fabulation enables understandings that are embodied and *felt* as potentially real (in some future). This is a form of virtual spatial and temporal movement. It can create a sense of hope that is embodied (and not reliant on nostalgic forms of engagement with the past). So despite the very real, tangible effects of unemployment and economic decline in Detroit, fabulation can help people engage with their world in ways that enable them to act, for instance, against unproductive city council initiatives or against media representations which pathologise their city. These fabulations may be far less influential in changing cities than global forces of finance, but may have small but significant longer-term impacts through, for instance, the practices of public participation and stakeholder consultation.

This chapter has examined representation and visuality in ways which differ from classic accounts such as Zukin's (1995) urban symbolic economy. As in previous chapters, I have explored the idea of representations as performative and not merely as simple expressions of, or resistances to, the 'real' economic baseline of cities. In earlier chapters, I have shown how commercial understandings (of people and spaces) are performatively woven into the industry's practices which in turn contribute to the production of the urban. Here, I have extended this analysis to consider how people's engagement with the material forms of urban space is thoroughly embodied. Our perceptual practices act to create 'events' as spatio-temporalities and open up ideas of the future beyond the idea of the possible. In the next chapter, I draw the insights of the previous chapters together in order to examine the nature of contemporary urban 'public space' and its synergies or tensions with 'commercial space'.

7
The Commercial Vernacular of Advertising: Public Space, Commercialisation and Public Address

Advertising is often thought to symbolise the expansion of the commercial world and the increasing commercialisation of public space. In many accounts, the proliferation of advertising forms and media represents the reach and power of the advertising industry, and advertising texts represent the ideological hold of consumer capitalism. In parallel, the visual impact of outdoor advertisements on urban space is often read in popular, policy and academic discussions as a sign of the encroachment of commercial life into public life. But my analysis throughout this book has pointed to the complexity of the relationships between industry practices, representations, spatialities and advertising effects. In the light of this analysis, and considering advertising's long pedigree and the many claims made over the years about its powers, how should the impact of contemporary advertising on space be assessed? A more nuanced analysis of the 'commercialisation' of space requires attention to the specificities of advertising. It also requires an exploration of its temporalities, material forms and commercial practices. I have examined these issues in various ways throughout the book but this chapter offers an additional point of entry by exploring them through the lens of 'publicness'. In parallel, it offers an analysis of publicness, public space and public address through the practices and forms of urban advertising. In this way the chapter explores the character of 'the commercial' in relation to the urban in the contemporary west.

This chapter introduces new empirical material and also draws together the analyses of previous chapters, reframing them in terms of ideas about publics, public spaces and public address. I highlight and develop four key points that explore the issue of 'commercialisation' in relation to publicness: (1) The practices of the outdoor advertising industry produce 'the public' (as consumers, viewers of ads, people-in-space) but this 'public' has a complex relation to real people. (2) In my analysis of these industry practices it has emerged that the production of 'the public' is interwoven with the production of urban spaces and is shaped by commercial imperatives. Issues relating to 'the public' and 'the commercial' have long been controversial and I frame my account in relation to studies of nineteenth- and early twentieth-century outdoor advertising and in relation to a brief survey of studies of contemporary publics and public spaces. (3) My data reveals how the production of 'the public' and urban spaces as 'public' is processual. More specifically, this process has a recursive character: industry practices, the commercial presentation of data, imperatives embedded in commercial relationships, research practices, and the production and placing of ads operate in feedback loops which are generative. Industry practices attribute openness to their own research data and to urban spaces and, by incorporating these understandings into their practices, *produce spaces as open and malleable.* I explore how this finding facilitates analyses of the commercial character of urban, 'public' space. Instead of simply suggesting 'increased commercialisation', it reframes questions in terms of newly intensified forms of performative knowledge and spatial practices in today's capitalism. These feedback loops produce new formations that are undetermined, open, and loosely coupled, and whose processes and outcomes are not easily predicted. (4) One of the outcomes of this generative feedback process of advertising practices, texts and spaces is a particular form of public address. Although advertising has always functioned as a (varying) form of public address, I identify how outdoor advertising today facilitates a specific form of address. Industry practices make possible forms of animation through fabulation. Publics and spaces are being made (in part) as commercial, but this commerciality is not tightly determined – it is a loosely woven set of relations whose implications are not fixed. One consequence is that advertising texts, spaces and temporalities are produced as sufficiently 'open' to form a vernacular through which people can understand their everyday urban experience. Clearly, it would please the advertising industry to create a consumerist vernacular which people accept as their own and which acts to channel experience. But as I explored in Chapters 2 and 3, such a vernacular cannot be controlled by the industry; advertising speaks to, and of, 'the popular' in ways which resist prediction or commercial forecasting. Advertising can help fabricate both a vernacular and a 'publicness' that generates a range of (unexpected, embodied, discordant) understandings of consumption and commodities, and of capitalism itself.

Within my analysis, representation emerges as a key pivot for debates and practices associated with advertising and public space. This includes representation in the conventional formulation of (advertising) texts and images, and in the representational strategies of the industry's research and data presentation practices. But it also includes the sense of democratic political representation as discussed by authors such as Iris Marion Young (2000). Advertising's texts, spatialisation and industry practices draw on, reshape, and co-articulate these two senses of representation. Throughout the book I have examined representation in terms of ad texts and industry research practices. And I have expanded its conceptual scope using insights from non-representational theory associated with authors such as Thrift (2008). It is an analysis of the shifting articulations of these senses of representation with that of democratic politic representation that offers a useful entry point to understanding the commercial character of today's urban spaces.

The chapter outlines and develops the four points noted above. The first section of the chapter presents recent debates about public space, the creation of 'publics' and the nature of 'publicity'. The second section introduces and analyses data on the ways in which the advertising industry produces spaces and produces publics. The final section draws together the arguments of the book and explores the significance of advertising's public address.

Publics, urban spaces and publicity

Given the intense contestation over conceptualisations of public space and publics, beginning with a rigid definition of 'publicness' would be counter-productive. This is due not only to the sheer range of definitions, although it is true that there are as many conceptualisations of public space and the public as there are studies of them. A fixed classification of what constitutes publicness would obscure the *processual* character of the changing formulations and practices associated with it. These cohere at particular moments in particular cultures to create 'public space' as idea, practice, pivot for political action, and location – and even these provisional coalescences are hotly contested. A more productive starting point might be a review of some recent studies' specific interventions in 'publicness'. Instead of a broad-brush account of the nature of public space today, I hope that this approach will offer a more textured and suggestive opening for analysis. Neither comprehensive nor detailed, the next section is a loosely thematised snap-shot of some recent explorations of public urban space and publicness.

Ideas about public urban spaces draw on and pull together a wide range of concerns and practices. Loukaitou-Sideris and Ehrenfeucht (2009), for instance, argue that US sidewalks function as spaces in which people demand and enact their rights as participants in society:

> Access to public spaces...is a mechanism by which urban dwellers assert their right to participate in society, and these struggles over the very the right to use public spaces take different forms. One distinction can be made between a demand to access a space for its defined use (as was the case with desegregation movements over public transportation and public facilities) and the right to define a space's use (such as a fight against a public sleeping ban). (Loukaitou-Sideris and Ehrenfeucht 2009: 7)

In their account, public space functions as a zone in which conflicting interests are played out. But they also show that what counts as such space – space which is truly open to public access – is a matter of contention and this involves the core rights of participation in society. They draw out distinctions between people's claims to access space for the use intended by its creators (planners, architects) and its regulators (police, city councils etc.), and claims to access space for unintended use, particularly homeless people's use of sidewalks as places to sleep. In addition, their account highlights definitional practices – who counts as 'the public' that might demand access to public urban spaces?

Loukaitou-Sideris and Ehrenfeucht produce a useful analysis that shows how classifications of 'the public', the parameters of public urban space, and rights of social participation are knotted together in complex ways. Their distinction between intended and unintended uses is helpful as it highlights tensions, contestation, regulation and resistance, issues that have a long pedigree in urban studies. Recent studies pursue this distinction. Rivlin (2007), for instance, frames as 'found spaces' those locations that are not formally designated as 'public'. In her account, too, people's actions are central in producing such spaces, for example, in people's use of buildings' steps as a place to eat lunch. Similarly, Fernando (2007) explores the 'open-ended' qualities of urban street spaces, identifying as their key characteristics not only people's practices, but those spaces' material forms. Some are restrictive and 'tighten' public space – bollards with chains, fences, locked gates around public plazas – but others, such as streets unconstrained by fixed features like benches, allow open-endedness, adaptability and a greater richness of civic street life (Rivlin 2007: 54). Franck and Stevens (2007: 2) argue that people's use of urban space in this range of unintended ways, such as skateboarding, produces spaces as 'loose' and this looseness can feed back in positive ways: 'the indeterminacy of loose space, along with free access, opens the space to other possibilities: to activities not anticipated, to activities that have no other place' (Franck and Stevens (2007: 17).

Such practices associated with the looseness of space may not be framed in overtly political terms but other actions in space are oriented to specific political ends. Enguix's (2009) discussion of Lesbian, Gay, Transsexual, Bisexual Pride marches in Spain, for instance, shows how such actions do not merely occupy public space but actively produce that space and certain identities in politically inflected ways. In parallel, Lee's (2009) analysis of how people's actions have produced Tiananmen Square in China as a public space notes how those actions also confer on people rights to that space.

Such analyses focus on political representation and actions associated with such representation. Other accounts explore textual representational interventions in the production of public space that might be considered political in other ways. Senie (1999) argues that the space of billboards can articulate the relationship and the tensions between commercial advertising and what is framed as 'art'. Art on billboards does more than challenge the distinctions between 'high' and 'low', and 'gallery' and 'commercial' work; it asks 'implicitly if artists are capable of communicating directly with a general public, if art today is able to create even temporary disturbances in the fields of mammon' (Senie 1999: 15). Such interventions imply a public that is being addressed, and in construing such a public, opens up a space for action. This is most evident in 'culture jamming', 'adbusting' and 'subvertising' where representational actions aim to challenge mainstream ideas, corporate culture, consumer practices or even capitalism itself (see Harold 2009; Klein 2000;). Often sited in public spaces such as streets, then photographed and circulated on the internet, such interventions may take the form of defacing or 're-purposing' advertisements. By mimicking and subverting the texts of adverts, Lasn argues that culture jamming 'cuts through the hype and glitz of our mediated reality and momentarily, tantalizingly, reveals the hollow spectacle within' (Lasn 2000: 131–132). Inspired by Guy Debord's work and Situationist activities, Lasn demonstrates faith in the power of counter-speech in public and confidence in a public that can engage in such speech.

While some culture jamming interventions may aim at a very broad target, other representational actions in public space have a more specific political focus. Heon, Diggs and Dorin (1999: 56) outline the 'Your Message Here' project organised by the artists' collective Group Material and the Randolf Street Gallery in Chicago, USA. The collective worked with activist groups in Chicago to produce billboard posters that would be situated in their neighbourhoods. The Chicago/Gary Union of the Homeless made a poster that read 'We May Not Have Homes/But We Do Have Names/ And We live Here too' and was covered by the signatures of homeless people living in the area. This was a striking representational act that used a public space to challenge people's perceptions of who counts as 'local residents' and 'the public'. It used a familiar form of public address – the billboard poster – to articulate social rather than commercial concerns – in this case to render visible the fact that the homeless count as local residents who should have access to rights associated with 'the public'. Such examples demonstrate that urban art and the representations produced by culture jammers do not merely take place in public space. They hijack, or reformulate, forms of public address and actively constitute publics and the very urban spaces that they utilise (see Deutsche 1996; Miles 2004).

Other accounts articulate the relationship between capital, definitions of public space, and visions for ideal urban life. Kayden's (2000: 1) study focuses on 'privately owned public space', a phenomenon which he argues was inaugurated in New York in 1961. City planners offered various concessions such as floor area bonuses to office and residential developers if they included in their designs spaces such as plazas, atriums and arcades that, although privately owned, would be available for the public use. Kayden's (2000) and Németh's (2009) later study reveal that this practice has spread throughout the US but its success in providing meaningful or useful social spaces for city residents is limited. Kayden notes the incidence of locked gates and missing amenities in such purportedly public spaces. Németh argues that the definition of the public mobilised by such practices is very restricted and the management approaches to the spaces 'severely limit the ability to have an inclusive and diverse public realm, as the institutional arrangements governing these spaces enable owners and managers to filter and order users based on fiscally driven priorities and mandates' (Németh 2009: 2482). Such accounts point to the ways in which definitions of public and private are constantly shifting and have an important relationship to capital. They also signal the importance of attending to the specificities of their enactment and to any tensions in the rhetoric deployed by actors in the field, in actors' practices, and in the resulting impact on city residents.

Many other studies reveal how social difference is a key axis for the production and contestation of public space. Stoker's (2003) analysis of the eruvim of Hasidic Jews in Montreal, Canada, illustrates the complexities involved in practices of public space and the rights of 'the public' linked to ethnicity and religion. An eruv is a wire stretched high up between buildings which constitutes 'a symbolic extension of the walls of the Jewish home into the public domain' (Stoker 2003: 18). Stoker details the controversies surrounding this practice in Montreal where, for some of the non-Hasidic residents, the eruvim symbolised 'an offensive territorial marker that threatens to create a Hasidic ghetto' (2003: 19). Stoker's analysis highlights the contestation of public urban space in relation to differing perspectives on the most appropriate management of religious and cultural diversity. Space acts as the site of conflict and also as one of the sources of conflict. In studies such as these it is clear that notions of public rights and who constitutes 'the public' are active and contested rather than firmly established. It is also clear, as Watson argues, that 'differences, in all their embodied and psychic complexities, will always enter and be performed in the public spaces of the city' (2006: 171).

Similarly, Houssay-Holzschuch and Teppo's (2009) study of a shopping mall in post-apartheid Cape Town, South Africa, shows complex performances of race and ethnicity. But here spatiality is understood to be active, and spaces are seen as constantly produced and reproduced. The authors argue that public spaces such as the mall which are now open to diverse groups 'sustain and support novel ways of asserting social identities in a new political situation' (Houssay-Holzschuch and Teppo 2009: 351). The space itself is shaped by Cape Town's patterns of newly desegregated ethnic relations but also facilitates new social relations. Other studies focus on how social relations and forms of appropriate sociality are enacted in, and produce, forms of public space. But people's actions that produce space may be oriented towards emotion rather than the kind of rationality that underpins Habermas's (1991) model of publicness, public debate and deliberation. For instance, Durham and Klaits' (2002) discussion of funerals in Botswana outlines how social relations are recognised through the extension of emotional states between people at such events and they give rise to a public space and a civil discourse that is based on sentiment.

Studies of public space and social difference often take as their focus issues of inclusion and exclusion. Analyses of gender, and the ways in which gender is always already cross-cut with class, ethnicity, sexuality, reveal the processual and contested character of constructing public space (see Bondi and Rose 2003). De Koning's (2009) discussion of class and gender in Cairo's public spaces reveals how inclusion for one group may involve exclusion for another. The study argues that women's public presence has become one of the most significant markers of young upper-middle-class culture that had developed in Cairo's new leisure spaces in the 1990s. The spaces of the street and public transport are 'marked by constant efforts at shielding the pure, properly sexualized upper-middle-class female body' (de Koning 2009: 534). The discourse of the vulnerable, classed, female body then justifies certain exclusions (of lower class men) from other 'public' spaces such as upmarket coffee shops. De Koning concludes that these women's bodies become the visible site for new class configurations in Cairo's public spaces, but that 'their public visibility can come to stand in for new inequities' (2009: 553).

The representation of women and women's rights can also take a textual form in urban spaces. Rosewarne's (2007) discussion of whether 'sexist advertisements' on urban billboards can be considered sexual harassment raises complex issues that link women's rights (to freedom from harassment) to issues of textual representation. Rosewarne's analysis problematically assumes clear definitions of what constitutes sexual harassment and a sexist advertisement. And the issues she outlines open up questions about public address, public space and representation that prove too complex to be subsumed in such assumptions. Winship's (2000) analysis of controversial UK billboard ad campaigns in the 1990s points to some of these complexities. She focuses on infamous campaigns such as the Wonderbra underwear ads which presented the tag-line 'hello boys' alongside sexually provocative images of women. These, she suggests, become a site for the representation and contestation of ideas about feminism and post-feminism, and of the shifting relations between men and women. The siting of such ads on billboards in urban space gives the ads, and the debates and the controversies that they engendered, a particular character as they challenged the gendered separation of public and private:

> When these ads shift outside of women's magazines that disruption is accentuated: private and intimate feminine fantasies enter public 'media event' space, and the alleged boundaries between commercial and civic speech (and between consumer and citizen) fall away. (Winship 2000: 47)

Accounts such as Winship's reveal how public space can provide the representational arena in which gender relations, gender politics and feminism are contested. Advertisements' public address draws on commercial formats and is shaped by commercial aims but necessarily interfaces with public debate about gender politics. This interface or conversation may have its terms framed in particular ways but its consequences are open and not easy to predict.

This brief sketch of some recent accounts shows the richness and diversity of the work on urban public space and offers useful cues for my analysis. It reaffirms the point that attempts to produce fixed definitions of public space or the public are inadequate. Such moves towards definitional closure are constantly troubled by the shifting character of practices and processes that create public space and publics. Viewed across a broad timescale, it is clear that concepts and practices of public and private shift over the centuries (Boyer 1996; Iveson 2007; Mitchell 2003). And the studies I have outlined point to more micro-level changes and contingencies: particular spaces and ideas about spaces are made and re-made, and their transformation is meshed with social change, for instance in race and gender politics. As Kilian (1998) argues, 'public' and 'private' should not even be seen as opposite points on a continuum. Reifying conceptions of 'public space' and 'the public', even on a continuum with 'private space', fixes an idea of what must be protected and whose interests should be upheld. This risks missing the implications of shifting politics – for instance in new, racially desegregated spaces in Cape Town. Assuming a unified public space also acts to exclude shifting interests and identities as it presupposes what constitutes, and what *should* constitute, public space. As Deutsche (1992: 38–39) argues, discourses of public space that either assume or aim for unity depend on repressing differences and conflict. Put another way, ideas and practices of public space are knotted up with ideas and practices of democracy with all their contingencies and conflicts. As Mitchell argues:

> The central contradiction at the heart of public space is that it demands a certain disorder and unpredictability to function *as* a democratic public space, and yet democratic theory posits that a certain order and rationality are vital to the success of democratic discourse. In practice, the limits and boundaries of 'democracy' seem to be determined as much through transgression … as through legal or bureaucratic ordering. (Mitchell 2003: 130, emphasis in the original)

Despite the problems inherent in stabilising definitions of publicness, many accounts of cities mobilise such reified concepts. This sets up a putative ground from which to claim that public life has declined or that public space has been eroded (see Sennett 2002). Sennett (1992) argues that urban residents' fear of exposure or harm drives city planners and architects to foster a 'being in public' that is neutralised and that limits social contact. Therefore they produce, 'bland, neutralizing spaces, spaces which remove the threat of social contact: street walls faced in sheets of plate glass, highways that cut off poor neighborhoods from the rest of the city, dormitory housing developments' (Sennett 1992: xii). But as Mitchell (2003) argues, if public space (and the forms of public life associated with it) has never been guaranteed nor has ever simply existed as a given, it is hard to claim that public space is being eroded.

It is certainly the case that there are significant shifts in the planning and provision of purportedly public space through private initiatives as Kayden (2000) and Németh (2009) demonstrate. This represents an important development tied to neo-liberal capitalist discourses, but there exist many other practices that complicate the picture. In the brief account above, the tensions and conflicts over public space are made evident in how people engage with material spaces and ideas of 'the public'. As Enguix (2009) shows, the 'publicness' of urban spaces is used strategically by LGTB marches to make visible certain identities, to own the rights to inhabit urban spaces safely, and to claim a place in the classification of 'the public'. In parallel, Lee's (2009) analysis shows not only how demonstrations produce spaces in the city but also articulate a claim to rights. Space is practised and ideas of public space are socially generated and shifting.

Rivlin (2007), Fernando (2007) and Franck and Stevens' (2007) accounts exemplify analytic trends that emphasise the openness or looseness of space. This openness is in part produced by people's spatial practices – of skateboarding subcultures, the mingling of social groups – but is not determined by them: the material forms that help create public spaces themselves facilitate looseness and offer possibilities for surprise and unintended consequences. As Amin and Thrift (2002) note, there is no necessary correlation between the openness that facilitates interaction in public space and the fostering of civic virtue. Such looseness of public space can enable not only the democratic contestation and debate that many hold as an ideal, but also harassment, hatred and violence. Such a point stresses the political character of definitions of public spaces and the practices around it, whether direct political engagement for the rights of the homeless, or the mere presence of classed female bodies in Cairo's public spaces. For although the categories of public and private are constructed and contingent, they are also real and necessary because they are *lived* and they shape lives (Kilian 1998).

Iris Marion Young (2000) attempts to draw together these various strands of publicness in the concept of 'publicity'.

> First, publicity refers to the constitution of a site for communicative engagement and contest. Secondly, it refers to a relationship among citizens within this site. Finally, publicity refers to the form that speech and other forms of expression take. (Young 2000: 168)

The first sense of publicity Young outlines is often formulated in debates on the public sphere in which various forms of media take central place (see Anderson 1991; Hartley 1996; Warner 2002). Habermas's (1991) famous model of a national public sphere as a space of rational deliberation mediated by printed matter has dominated these debates, although later accounts attempt to shift the analysis to the multimedia spaces of a 'post-national' world (Fraser 2007). Young's second two formulations of publicity are also well-represented in public sphere debates. Influential accounts such as Warner's (2002) focus on the production of public spheres through forms of address. These take the existence of common interests and shared worlds as both their premise and their problem. It is the engagement with, and calling into being of a collective imagined as 'the public' that links debates on public space and on the public sphere(s). The public sphere is often imagined as the site or medium through which people are interpellated as a collective, 'the public'. They are asked to recognise themselves as such and engage in debate about their interests. This idea or ideal of the public ratifies claims for public space – 'the public has a right to public spaces'. And many accounts explore how the differing discursive production of key media, such as printed news or television, shapes the specific forms this debate takes.

Young attempts to make these issues cohere in the concept of publicity. Although appealingly comprehensive, the concept is doing rather a lot of work in suturing together these diverse themes and may act to obscure some important nuances. As Iveson (2007) emphasises, we need to tease apart the specificities of publicness and consider carefully how different elements interact. The following sections draw on the idea of public address discussed by Iveson (2007) and others. I consider how the practices of the advertising industry, its textual products, and advertising spaces in the city, act to make publics, make public spaces and create distinctive forms of public address. Emphasising how publics, spaces and forms of address are *produced* acts to denaturalise them; it highlights their status as *made up* and contingent. As Warner (2002: 8) argues, a public is 'a practical fiction'. But its fictionality does not imply a lack of affective engagement on the part of those people who are interpellated; nor does fictionality imply insubstantiality or a lack of material impact.

The commercial production of public space and 'the public'

Does advertising in cities simply commodify or commercialise previously 'public' spaces? Do industry practices merely package and sell people in cities as target markets for potential advertisers? What forms of 'publicness' are produced? In this section I address these questions in terms of the performative approach that has inspired this book, and revisit and add to the analysis of data in Chapters 2–4. I examine how the industry's practices produce 'the public' or 'publics' as objects of knowledge and how this production does not require a strict referential relationship to 'real people' or a baseline 'reality'. Loose couplings of data and practical insights are all that are required to maintain efficient commercial relationships between media owners, media agencies and clients. Aligned with this, I analyse how the industry's production of 'the public' is woven together with its practices of making urban 'public' space. I frame this analysis by outlining how outdoor advertising has long attracted criticism for its practices and products, and these criticisms also articulate wider social concerns. But I argue that a specific form of contemporary advertising practice (and critique of advertising) can be identified.

Outdoor advertising is a truly *mass* medium in an age of media fragmentation. It does not have the reach of other forms such as internet advertising, but its occupation of urban spaces means that it potentially speaks to an audience that is broad in terms of demographic characteristics. Unlike targeted newspapers, television programmes or websites, it is unable to target specific groups without also including in its 'conversation' many other people. Outdoor advertising's particular form of 'public address' linked to its location in public urban spaces, thus gives the industry and its products a particular form and character. But this also opens it to various forms of critique and controversy, and these can be traced back over many years.

Nevett (1982) outlines how nineteenth-century criticisms of outdoor advertising in England articulated a wide range of concerns. These included condemnation of 'obscene' advertisements, 'unsightly' large hoardings, billboards that blighted the beauty of rural landscapes, and flashing electric advertising signs which were thought to cause traffic accidents. The structures themselves attracted censure and not only for their impact on urban aesthetics or for their size; advertising hoardings were thought to act as screens for 'immoral acts' (Turner 1965: 108). There were parallel concerns in America. Bogart (1995: 97, 94) notes how early twentieth-century criticisms of outdoor advertising in New York ranged from its 'intrusiveness and depravity' and its production of 'an overabundance of sensory bombardment', to its detrimental impact on the aesthetics of the city. But such criticisms came from only a few sources. Nevett (1982) notes that in nineteenth- and early twentieth-century England the National Society for Controlling the Abuses of Public Advertising (SCAPA) was a minority, middle-class concern, although it did exert some influence in passing the 1907 Advertising Regulation Act. And SCAPA did shape similar developing organisations in America such as the City Beautiful reformers (Wilson 1987).

Most interesting is the way in which the social positioning of critics shaped both the forms of criticisms of advertising and the urban ideals that such criticisms held up. Gudis (2004) notes that in early twentieth-century America the very presence of billboard advertising became controversial, with various groups of urban reformers seeing correlations between civic virtue, morality and the environment. For the reformers, the presence and number of billboard ads on highways symbolised, 'the increasing disorder of the modern city, whose throngs of different classes, colors, and kinds of people impinged upon both middle class mores and the reform ideal of a socially and technologically engineered environment' (Gudis 2004: 168). The middle-class reformers' articulation of visually harmonious, advertising-free urban landscape was, Gudis argues, an attempt to reassert their status in the face of both the masses and mass marketing.

Gudis outlines how the debates and controversies around outdoor advertising emerged from social ideals and societal patterns. Many of these urban reformers were middle and upper class women who drew on and reformulated gendered discourses of nature, beauty and morality. They framed their objection to billboards in terms of 'moral aesthetics' as part of a wider project of the beautification of urban space (Gudis 2004: 170). And they argued that the integrity of the roadside should be protected from billboards for it was a character- and nation-building resource through which one learnt beauty, civility and morality. In this way, they assigned 'good republican motherhood to nature itself' and extended the 'the idea of the sanctity of the home to the landscape at large' (Gudis 2004: 184).

> The separation of the spheres that had characterized the relationship between women and men, home and workplace, reformers now applied to the landscape at large, where nature became the domestic realm, necessarily separated from commerce and the signs of the city, while women became the upholders of its purity. As such, their ideal for the landscape was consistent with other domestic, middle-class, suburban, and arcadian, ideals. (Gudis 2004: 184)

Gudis concludes that although diverse reformers articulated their critiques of billboards and outdoor advertising in terms of public ownership of urban and rural space, the idea of 'the public' that they called up was narrowly defined in terms of their own middle and upper class values and interests.

In a similar vein, Baker (2007: 1188) argues that outdoor advertising in late nineteenth- and early twentieth-century America had become, 'a lightning rod for debates over the impact of what one critic called a "juggernaut of commercialism"'. The perceived commercialisation of public space by advertising 'precipitated a battle between civic and commercial interests over control of urban space as an expressive medium' (Baker 2007: 1207). But it was the 'symbolic integrity' of urban space that concerned reformers rather than its democratic integrity. They believed that a disciplined urban environment could cultivate 'genteel civility' and what one commentator of the time called 'a proper submission to authority' (Baker 2007: 1208). This insistence on the control of the commercial in public space 'often quite explicitly expressed a longing that it instead be an instrument of class stewardship' (Baker 2007: 1208).

But not all commentary on outdoor advertising was critical. Turner (1965) notes how advertising had become both a familiar form in English nineteenth-century urban spaces and the subject of seemingly affectionate satire:

> The Victorians took an innocent delight in the production of satirical prints showing enormous hoardings on which posters had been pasted, one partly over another, in such a way as to produce 'messages' like: 'Funerals Conducted with Decorum and Dignity by FUNNY FOLKS

EVERY WEDNESDAY with a Band and Chorus of 700 Performers in
A. LYNES AND SONS 13s TROUSERS'. (Turner 1965: 97)

These nineteenth- and early twentieth-century examples show how
criticism of outdoor advertising has a long history. They make clear how
the specific formulation of those critiques reflects social change and
social concerns as well as the class and gender status of those that made
the criticisms. But they also show that critical engagement with ads
and urban space actively creates ideas of the public and public space –
indeed, that the tensions and practices associated with resistance to
outdoor advertising are generative.

In my study, this engagement with ads and urban space centred on
the industry's practitioners but also included an account of criticisms
of outdoor advertising that are filtered through the UK regulatory body,
the Advertising Standards Authority (ASA). Complaints about specific
advertisements from the public, but also from rival advertising agencies
or client companies, are directed to the ASA which has regulatory codes
setting out standards and acceptable advertising practice (see Cronin
2004a). In my study, industry practitioners' own understandings of controversies around the content and placing of ads are significant because
they feed them back into their own practices.

The most striking contemporary manifestations of public controversy
over outdoor advertising is the outrage over the specific textual content
(particularly regarding 'taste and decency'), advertising for products
like alcohol that are seen as unhealthy, and the specific siting of certain texts (especially near schools or places of worship). Media owners
consider that advertising for products such as alcohol may be deemed
acceptable by the public and by the ASA in certain sites. But industry
practitioners think that such advertising in proximity to schools is
likely to cause controversy: 'it annoys people, it upsets people, it upsets
communities' (practitioner, media owning firm). While certain product
types like alcohol may be particularly controversial, the textual content
of an advert for any product may become significant when combined
with specific locations. Adverts showing images of scantily clad women
may provoke no comment if placed in a magazine targeted at young
men, but can cause considerable controversy when sited on a billboard
near a mosque. Practitioners note that this can elicit complaints but
also more direct action: 'sometimes [people] ring up, sometimes they
just get black paint and pour it over the unit, because it's instant then
and they just paint the glass out so the poster is completely covered
up' (practitioner, media owning firm). Describing the controversial

perfume advertisement featuring a naked model, Sophie Dahl, an ASA spokesperson outlines how billboards' status as *mass* media affords them particular impact:

> aside from TV, [billboard ads] are the ones that are likely to generate a large number of complaints, and it is…because it is untargeted, no matter that you as an advertiser are going to have a target, you are going to hit so many more people outside of your target audience…. If someone is running an ad specifically for *Loaded*, say, you would expect them to go in a magazine because they understand that per-haps they can be a little bit more risqué there than you can be on a broadsheet when you're going to just get so many more people seeing it. And that was the thing with the Sophie Dahl poster…. They had started it off as a women's press ad, a women's magazine ad, and we had 3 complaints…when they decided to go up with the posters…we ended up with 900 odd complaints…. Something that's highly stylized can fit in with the magazine's content but when someone is just walking out of their house and they happen to have a 96 sheet poster there and it's got a naked woman on it…. (ASA spokesperson)

Offence is not the only trigger for complaints about the combination of a particular advert's content and its location. There are also con-cerns expressed about the impact upon the safety of spaces. An ASA spokesperson recalls how a female underwear advertisement on a bus shelter near a lap-dancing club provoked complaints: people 'said that they'd seen an ad at a bus shelter and they'd been there late at night and it'd made them feel a little bit uncomfortable'. The female under-wear advert, in its location near the lap-dancing club, was considered by the complainant to sexualise that space and it made her feel vulner-able when using the bus stop at night. Also implied in the complaint was an idea that the textual content of the ad may elicit a sexualised response in (male) viewers impacting upon women's experience of using the bus stop.

These examples of controversies about specific outdoor advertise-ments and their placement mirror general tensions evident in ideas of 'the public' and publicness. As in the overview of studies of publicness and public space outlined above, there is contestation about inclusion, interests, spatiality, rights and values. The tensions in these shifting formations combine to create what is understood as, and practised as, public space. But what counts as 'the public' and 'public interests' are mutable and their characterisation provokes intense debate. Advertising practitioners must work within these parameters, particularly those of 'taste and decency', but there is a constant risk of failure where an advertisement and/or its placement engender outrage. As one practitioner noted, 'it's more and more likely to happen as the culture changes, and that is very difficult for us to track' (practitioner, media owning firm).

In these examples, industry practitioners co-produce an idea of 'the public' against which they gauge the appropriate siting and textual content of ads. This conjuring of 'the public' is based on (fairly rare) actions such as defacing or painting over ads found to be offensive, direct complaints to the media owners or advertisers, and complaints to the ASA. But practitioners' conceptualisation of 'the public' and public space is far more strongly influenced by the research practices and exigencies of commercial relationships that I analysed in Chapters 2–4. There, and as I detail below, practitioners' production of 'the public' is partial, strategic and is understood by all in the industry to have a loose relationship to 'real people'. But my study also shows how practitioners research space and research target markets (or audiences or publics) in ways which weave them together. Publics and spaces are conceived and enacted as enmeshed because this aligns with industry needs of producing data which can be mobilised to maintain profitable relationships.

Outdoor urban space is treated by the industry as a medium but not in the simple sense of a context or backdrop. Unlike most media, the audience is not self-selecting or narrowly targeted, and the advertising message is not shaped or framed by surrounding editorial material (e.g. articles in newspapers, content of television programmes, page content of websites). On the one hand, the industry sees this as a potential problem as some clients may only feel comfortable commissioning targeted advertisements (such as television ads). From this perspective, an advert in a mass medium will potentially 'hit' many people outside its target market, a phenomenon known as 'wastage'.

> It's a very broadcast media. At the same time clients are very narrow cast in their targeting needs. So a client might have a target market as clearly defined as 16 to 24 year old men ABC1. Now that's difficult with posters to answer that brief. A poster on the high street will target those people but it will also target loads of other people so you get this kind of sort of wastage that people talk about in advertising agencies. (practitioner, media owning firm)

But although there is a recognised issue of 'wastage', the industry also frames the mass or broadcast character of its medium as a potential selling point, as one practitioner explained:

> Outdoor is a medium. If you look at magazines, newspapers, every other media has some kind of editorial proposition. When it's cinema it's all about films, getting people in there and the advertising is always an excuse to hit people in the right environment. When you look at outdoor, outdoor has no editorial. It is purely an advertising medium, so what we have to do is to somehow editorialise the panels that we've got and we do that by targeting and mapping. So a panel outside, for example, a petrol station forecourt or outside a newsagent or outside a supermarket, by definition then that becomes their editorial. So ... we editorialise by geography. You know, so where other people may have clearly defined target markets according to what people buy their magazines, read their newspaper, watch the TV programmes, and the thing with outdoor is we target everyone and we don't need people to come and seek out posters, the posters will seek you out. (practitioner, media owning firm)

This practitioner notes that some clients are attracted to specific geographical targeting for their advertising panels. It emerged that clients selling FMCG (Fast-Moving Consumer Goods) such as confectionery are particularly interested in what the industry terms 'proximity'. This is a coding for panels and billboards near 'point of sale' sites such as shops and supermarkets where people may translate the advertising invitation immediately into a purchase.

But while some clients consider specific locations and 'proximity' important, most consider outdoor advertising as a broad, untargeted medium and use that medium accordingly. Outdoor advertising is pitched by practitioners to potential clients as a form of (mass) public address that potentially speaks to all, and offers great opportunities for increasing 'brand awareness'. Practitioners sell this massified urban space and public address by 'editorialising by geography' in part by telling stories about specific types of panel location (e.g. petrol station forecourts as an excellent site for speaking to 'the mobile consumer'). The target market of advertising in a magazine or television programme would be imagined with reference to the magazine or programme content. But here the specific characteristics of these spatialities – for example, panels facing commuter traffic leaving cities – shape how the industry constructs ideas of 'the audience/target/public' that they pitch to potential clients. But more often, practitioners editorialise by imagining a hybridised object of research that they wish to sell – this hybrid is composed of urban space and people-in-space (specifically, people moving-in-space). And it is performed by research practices and an attitude towards research that is shaped by commercial requirements.

As described in Chapters 2 and 3, these industry imperatives involve creating and maintaining commercial relationships (between media owners, media agencies and clients) and fighting for 'point of difference' and competitive advantage. This shapes a view of research – and of audiences/publics and urban spaces – as 'impure', strategically flexible and open. This view steered the practices that I observed in the industry. As one practitioner described,

> [Research] is quite embedded in the way that we approach things rather than it being a separate, pure discipline…. The market is changing all the time and it's a people business. Then research can't be in an ivory tower, it has to be subsumed into the practicalities of what we do on a day-to-day basis. And so it's a moveable feast, it changes all the time and there are no set parameters of what research should be or shouldn't be…. But of course it's taken from a pure base of what we would all like to see, what we'd all like to achieve but we all know that the ideal is never the reality. So although there is the principle of pure research, what effectively takes place from day to day is the practical implementation of the knowledge that we have, and then try and build it and grow it as we go along rather than start out with an ideal or the Rolls Royce of research and then sort of right just try and stick to that principle. It's a moveable thing. (practitioner, specialist media agency)

Industry practitioners thus see research practices as 'messy' and the resulting data as strategically viable rather than empirically valid (in the sense of being replicable or having a direct representational relationship to 'reality out there'). They attribute great importance to ways of researching people and spaces that are 'creative' and 'organic'.

> [Research is] very messy. It's not as purist as people probably think from the outside…. The reality is it's much more organic and bespoke and we draw on it in all different ways and basically it creates a bespoke argument to fit a particular requirement for that client. And to me that's a better thing than having something which

is immovable, inflexible, purist... sort of like black box of thoughts and research which homogenises people's thinking but then you end up with a factory... it's like an egg factory, everything is coming out the same at the other end. And also from an agency point of view, if that was the case, how would we differentiate from our competitors?... How would we convince them to pay more money to us than our competitors unless we have a point of difference? (practitioner, specialist media agency)

This is a view of research as creative because it is not bound to strict models of empirical validity. But it is also an approach to research that is 'organic' in the sense of being mutable and *generative*. As I argued in Chapter 2, this open attitude to research and data is able to generate commercial relationships and competitive advantage in ways that can respond flexibly to market developments and social change.

Here I want to expand that analysis to include how industry practices fold in and construct ideas of 'the public' (as target markets) with ideas of space and an open approach to research practices. Presenting persuasive accounts of publics/targets, and thus convincing clients of media owners' expert knowledge skills, is crucial for their success, as one practitioner describes: 'Unless you go in to a client and you bowl them over and prove to them that you know (a) their audience, (b) their problem and (c) you've got the solution and there is only one solution, you'll lose the client straight away' (practitioner, media owning firm). Selling outdoor advertising space almost always means persuading clients to transfer some of their marketing spend away from other formats such as television. This means that researching the public/target markets and pitching that knowledge to clients is always bound up with promoting the outdoor sector of the advertising industry. Media owners therefore construct convincing profiles of people-in-space, particularly profiles which reflect poorly on competitor sectors (e.g. television or press advertising), or poach from that catchment:

I mean predominantly outdoor's audience tend to be light TV viewers... by definition people out and about a lot, they tend to be young, more affluent, upwardly mobile, and those people watch less television especially now the way that the TV market has fragmented. So you sell it in a positive and say outdoor actually acts as a way of reaching a TV audience in a much more cost effective way to hit not all the broadcast audience, but one element of it, which are the light

TV viewers. I think you bring data from any source you can possibly bring to show that. (practitioner, specialist media agency)

In earlier chapters I discussed how research carried out by the industry tends to show that people's perceptual engagement with outdoor ads is light or fragmented. This is certainly an inconvenient finding which cannot be easily glossed by the industry. Therefore, practitioners have to incorporate into their research angles and their pitches to clients a conceptualisation of the public as a less-than-attentive collective. Conceptualisations of 'the public' as a number of target markets are folded into industry formulations of moments of attention as Visbility Adjusted Impacts or 'eyes on panel' (see Chapters 2 and 4). At the same time, the industry has to incorporate a recognition of the limited nature of this attention and the difficulty in proving a direct correlation between outdoor ads and increased sales of the product in question. One way the industry finesses this is by framing outdoor advertising as a 'low involvement' medium which is nevertheless very well-suited for 'branding building' or increasing 'brand awareness':

> most of outdoor is about branding, is about perceptions...yes, it has a sales knock on effect as well. Yes, it's about shifting cars, jars of tomato ketchup, whatever it happens to be. There is a bottom line to all of that, but outdoor...doesn't tend to be used too much as a direct response medium where there's a direct correlation between investment versus sales. It tends to be used much more in a branding sense, about raising awareness public perceptions of the brand. (practitioner, specialist media agency)

The placing and formulation of ad campaigns also involves conceiving 'the public' as potentially recalcitrant receivers of marketing messages. Not only may this public fail to respond to the invitation to buy or to look more favourably on a brand; this public may speak back to advertisements in ways unintended by their producers.

> We were going to do a campaign a while back for Triumph Underwear but one of the ladies was sitting in the chair with her legs slightly apart and that was kind of deemed to be slightly indecent, and they're also worried about...because we do lots of stuff on walls, actually people are quite close to it and so there's the risk of people graffitying it and it's felt that if it's a bit controversial then people will interact with those posters.... Remember the Dove campaign where it's using

real women? They did the one with the large women and then they did one for what do you consider beautiful and they had kind of a very fair skinned lady, a lady with lots of wrinkles, all sort of different character faces, and then they had boxes that you can tick as to whether it's beautiful or not beautiful. Now the creative just took it as it's just creative but then actually people were going around ticking it or going 'no, she's really ugly', so it encouraged people to draw on it. (practitioner, media owning firm)

Although not the kind of counter-cultural or culture jamming intervention discussed by authors such as Klein (2000), this certainly represents a response by people to a perceived invitation to contribute to a public conversation. Some people directly replied to the public address of the advert and this kind of action requires practitioners to imagine a 'public' which is active and potentially playful or hostile.

The above examples show how practitioners 'editorialise by geography', both by addressing specificities of locations such as petrol station forecourts and by using a more generalised concept of urban space as a mass medium. Directed by the exigencies of the industry, they research and conceptualise publics and spaces as folded together and as co-productive. These 'publics' are not only products but productive fictions. Throughout this book I have addressed the ways in which these fictions are practiced although I have not until now framed these explicitly through ideas of publics. In Chapters 2 and 3, I examined how commercial practices, especially knowledge practices in research projects, aim to create particular versions of publics. These publics are textual products that circulate between media owners, media agencies and potential clients in the form of databases and statistics, PowerPoint presentations and mocked-up ad campaigns. They are practical fictions in that they are produced for, and shaped by, the strategic aims of creating and maintaining (profitable) commercial relationships by forming a currency of exchange.

But they also generate something new. As I have described in Chapter 2 and elsewhere (Cronin 2008a), this operates on a commercial level as a mode of manufacturing innovation and thus producing 'point of difference' for companies competing for clients. In these practices, publics and urban spaces are framed as raw, malleable material for practitioners' creative uses and presentation of data. This plasticity enables the practitioners to explore new routes for enhancing their competitive advantage over other media owning companies – they facilitate the creative play that flexible understandings of 'empirical data' on publics and spaces may allow. But these practices also generate something new by opening spaces for the unintended and the unexpected. Shaped by these commercial requirements, the 'publics' that are produced are certainly framed as (potential) consumers – as you might expect in market-oriented practices – but they also have other more peculiar characteristics. The 'units' that compose these publics are not easily identifiable social groups or individuals. Instead, they are framed as hybrids of people-space-movement, or as mere sources of 'mobile attention'. These are abstracted Visibility Adjusted Impacts (VAIs) or 'eyes on panel' that can be sold to potential clients as quantifiable 'hits' who will see any adverts that are placed on that particular site.

These research formulations and the resulting data have material effects: they are processed by media owners, media agencies and clients and fed back into the placement of ad panels and the content of ad texts. In Chapter 3, I showed how the industry's research practices loop back and feed into one another: they frame target markets as mobile; ideas of mobility are fed into the formulation and practices of research projects; such understandings inform the textual content of advertisements; research projects attempt to capture how people engage with such texts and spaces; those ideas are fed into promotional material aimed at potential clients, thus forming a currency which helps create and maintain market relationships. This performs recursively: the ideas, practices and interests make 'publics', make market relations, and make urban spaces in a generative feedback loop. This points to the interweaving of multiple ideas in the city spaces' 'publicness' that Iveson (2007) is at pains to emphasise. The performative character of this enactment has been noted by Warner (2002): publics are performed in the production of texts, and people come to recognise themselves as part of 'public/s', and are fabricated by texts. But in my analysis I show the imbrication of conventional texts (advertisements, statistics, other texts produced by the industry) with practices and with urban spaces, and how this disrupts standard conceptions of representation and textuality.

In Chapter 3, I argued that industry data, ideas, intentions, material forms and urban spaces start to speak to one another in unexpected and certainly unintended ways – not quite the ideal form of public debate that many urban theorists had in mind. This opening up towards the unexpected also extends beyond the intentions of its commercial creators and acts on urban spaces, people and ideas. By editorialising by geography, and researching in open, loose modes, 'space' is put into play *as active*. It is performed as having a creative, generative role in the production of publics as target markets.

To sum up, ideas of space and ideas of the public are *practised*. Industry practitioners fold ideas about space and publics into their commercial practices, which then operate in positive feedback loops. And they are practised as hybridised forms, not as distinct entities of 'spaces' and 'publics'. These practices are generative, and act to make spaces and publics. These formations are contested and contingent, and they reach out and intertwine with wider social issues (such as gender politics). 'Representation' is revealed as complex and shifting; here, it encompasses ideas about the representation of publics, and ideas about textual processes and products. In this context, the 'commercialisation of public space' is less a linear process that transforms one type of space into another, than a multi-dimensional relationship of ideas, practices and interests.

Public address: advertising as vernacular in soft capitalism

I have outlined how industry practices create 'publics' and urban spaces. I will now develop these insights in order to reconsider advertising as a form of public address. Reviewing my analysis of bodies, perception and fabulation in Chapters 4–6, I will extend that analysis to reformulate advertising's status as a social, spatial and representational form. In those chapters I explored how the industry's production of city space is informed by ideas of the body and people's everyday life; in parallel I examined how these practices of producing texts and placing advertising structures impact upon people's embodied engagement with urban space. Such engagements are not 'readings' of 'urban texts' but are more diffuse, bodily, perceptual interactions. The significance of this analysis sits uneasily with the many accounts that, following Habermas, construe acts of reading and models of textuality as primary modes of creating publics. Although his own analysis is based primarily on textuality, Warner questions 'to what degree the text model, though formative for the modern public, might be increasingly archaic' (2002: 16). The issue of periodisation raises interesting questions, including the extent to which the 'other-than' or 'more-than' textual was always a significant influence in creating publics. It is this significance that I explored in Chapter 4 where I showed how advertising practices aim to tap into city rhythms and people's routine rhythms of living in, working in and moving around cities. In doing so, industry practices facilitate ways of knowing that are *felt in the body* and make sense on a visceral level. Their address, which at the same time assumes a (receptive) public and fabricates that public, is not based on a simple decoding of textual messages (to be either accepted or resisted).

In Chapters 5 and 6, I extended the analysis of the embodied nature of perception and people's engagement with cities by exploring how perception is also temporally and spatially animating. I offered a speculative account of how perceptual knowing makes spaces and imagines futures in ways that are shaped by processes and tensions in capitalism (particularly those of urban regeneration and urban dereliction). 'Publics' as generated through perception, and as fabulated as enlivened, extend into futurity in the perceived temporalities of urban spaces. Allowing the play of virtualities, fabulation renders visible the ways in which spatialities, like temporalities, are virtual and dynamic. Thus publics and urban spatialities are co-produced (as virtual, open, generative and politically charged). The fabulation and enlivening of space enables us to make unexpected connections among objects, spaces, images, ideas and bodies.

The relationship between cities and bodies has been explored extensively (e.g. Sennett 1994), as has the relationship between bodies and ideas of *public* space. As Deutsche argues, 'how we define public space is intimately connected with ideas about what it means to be human, the nature of society, and the kind of political community we want' (1996: 269). The analysis I have presented offers a development of these ideas to consider how animation, fabulation and 'life-likeness' also shape public space and ideas about society. At this point it will be useful to revisit accounts of advertising in order to reframe how advertising today might be understood.

Many studies have pointed to advertising role's as mediator between products, people and ideas (Leiss, Kline, Jhally and Botterill 2005), and role as powerful ideological form (Goldman 1992; Williamson 2000). Raymond Williams's (1980) highly influential account of advertising as a magic system elegantly draws together many of the concerns of such accounts. Williams argued that advertising is crucial for the functioning of contemporary capitalism as it 'preserves the consumption ideal from the criticism inexorably made of it by experience' (1980: 188). For Williams, the serial consumption of goods results only in the serial failure of those goods and consuming experiences to fulfil basic human needs and desires. Advertising's role is to gloss over this failure and to project important social values and ideas of happiness ever-forward onto new goods. This can occur, Williams argues, because of a general social failure whereby western societies can find no adequate means of public debate and decision-making about our needs and our social organisation. In this void, advertising can operate as magic – 'a highly organized and professional system of magical inducements and satisfactions, functionally very similar to magical systems in simpler societies, but rather strangely co-existent with a highly developed scientific technology' (Williams 1980: 185).

Williams notes that advertising is thought by many to reflect an overly materialistic tendency in today's western societies. But he argues that advertising's ubiquity instead suggests that we are *not materialist enough*. If we were genuinely materialist in our approach to living with and using things we would find advertising with its promises and blandishments to be of 'insane irrelevance' (1980: 185). In a differently organised society, we would not look to advertising for important meanings and values for they would be available to us in our social relations. Thus for Williams, the continual production of advertisements constitutes an always-unsuccessful attempt to provide meaning and values, and acts to obscure real needs.

> If the meanings and values generally operative in the society give no answers to, no means of negotiating, problems of death, loneliness, frustration, the need for identity and respect, then the magical system must come, mixing its charms and expedients with reality in easily available forms, and binding the weakness to the condition which has created it. Advertising is then no longer merely a way of selling goods, it is a true part of the culture of a confused society. (Williams 1980: 190–191)

Williams's account is striking and persuasive. But put into dialogue with Henri Bergson's (2006) concept of fabulation that I outlined in Chapters 5 and 6, it is possible to offer a more nuanced account of advertising as text, as industry and as socio-spatial form. Williams sees as dissonant the co-existence of magical thinking (which he associates with earlier societies and with advertising) and contemporary scientific understandings and technology. In contrast, Bergson's account of fabulation sees the myth-making practices of earlier societies as *consonant with* the sense-making activities of contemporary societies. They could both be considered forms of magical thinking and are not troubled by developments in scientific thought. Bergson conceives fabulation as a practically oriented 'virtual instinct' which tempers the problems created by human intelligence and helps us to act in the world. The magic, anthropomorphic powers or spirits that people once fabulated have the same roots as have contemporary ways of thinking about chance, events and causation.

Williams sees advertisements as illusions or fictions that distort or mask true human needs; they can gain traction when the social organisation fails to provide adequate means of sociality and meaning-production. But Bergson sees our capacity to fabulate, to create 'phantasmic representations' (2006: 108) or an 'effect of mirage' (2004: 30), as a core part of our humanity, not as a result of social failure. Our capacity for fabulation creates counterfeits of real experience but these are productive, helpful fictions that enable us to engage with the world and facilitate our actions. In his account, our use of stimuli to fabulate is part of our material, practical involvement with the social and natural world. Williams is right to consider advertising as a part of wider social processes and the social fabric, and writes convincingly of its appeal which often operates on an emotional or affective register. But a narrow focus on advertising as falsehood, or gloss over the true material quality or significance of goods, restricts the analysis of advertising's social significance. I found fabulation a useful concept with which to understand the significance of advertising texts, advertising structures and advertising spatiality. This locates advertising as *part of* our material, bodily sense-making activities and as part of our social world. It is not simply a formation that attempts to reflect (and refract) societies, nor does it merely act as a parasite upon societies.

The primary register in which outdoor advertising operates is the visual, and the visual has been identified by many authors as a key, if problematic, aspect of urban design and city life. Discussing the homogeneity of the design of modern towns, Henri Lefebvre argues that,

> They are made with the visible in mind: the visibility of people and things, of spaces and of whatever is contained by them. The predominance of visualization (more important that 'spectacularization', which is in any case subsumed by it) serves to conceal repetitiveness. People look, and take sight, taking seeing, for life itself. We build on the basis of papers and plans. We buy on the basis of images. Sight and seeing, which in the Western tradition once epitomized intelligibility, have turned into a trap: the means whereby, in social space, diversity may be simulated and a travesty of enlightenment and intelligibility ensconced under the sign of transparency. (Lefebvre 1991: 75–76)

Locating the visual in the realm of a consumer culture in which 'we buy on the basis of images', Lefebvre is wary of what he understands as visually oriented urban design and of the way that the visual troubles or prevents true understanding. Sharon Zukin's analysis, although having many resonances with Lefebvre's, is rather more positive about the potential of the visual in cities. Zukin argues that 'as both site and sight, meeting place and social staging ground, public spaces enable us

Figure 7.1a–d   Watch This Space – creating an urban vernacular in Manchester (author's photographs)

to conceptualize and represent the city' (1995: 260). She argues that cities are 'a visual repertoire of culture in the sense of a public language. Their landscape and vernacular are a call and response among different social groups' (1995: 264).

More recent accounts further explore such entanglements of people, materiality and the visual culture of public urban spaces. In a post-human analysis, Ash Amin (2008) sees a modest but significant collective promise emerging from such entanglements. Amin's conception of connection and collectivity can be seen as a kind of vernacular that is visual, material and embodied. It is not a language precisely, nor a set of cognitive responses or physical encounters with other people in urban space. For Amin, such collective potential is 'not reducible to dynamics of inter-personal interaction that prompt a sense of "us" or ease with the stranger' (2008: 8). Instead,

> the collective impulses of public space are the result of pre-cognitive and tacit human response to a condition of 'situated multiplicity', the thrown togetherness of bodies, mass and matter, and of many uses and needs in a shared physical space…. Inculcations of the collective, the shared, the civic, arise out of the human experience of surplus; mass and energy that exceeds the self, that cannot be appropriated, that constantly returns, that has emergent properties and that defines the situation. (Amin 2008: 8)

Zukin's framing of cities' visual culture as a vernacular, and Amin's account of collective connection are loose but suggestive formulations. Using the material of my own study I can offer a more specific and more fully characterised account of one particular vernacular. As I argued in Chapter 6, the visual and temporal scapes of cities can be usefully analysed through fabulation. This follows a different line from Amin's analysis which insists that people's pre-cognitive and tacit responses shape the collectivity of public space. As I outlined in previous chapters, Bergson's fabulation is not a form of *pre*-cognition, but rather reshapes what counts as cognition. Equally, fabulation might be seen as tacit in that its syntax is not that of a conventional language, but it is not a form of unspoken knowing – it creates *alternative* ways of speaking and knowing.

Fabulation offers an alternative perspective on Lefebvre's comment that people 'take sight, taking seeing, for life itself'. I have argued that perception, and seeing 'life' or animation, are central parts of human ways of negotiating the world. Rather than inhibiting understanding, fabulations aid our practical and knowing interactions with our social worlds. Thus advertising can be considered one element that constitutes an urban, visual vernacular. At the same time, it functions as a form of public address that calls into being 'a public' (that is contested, shifting and referentially flexible). Its status as vernacular derives from the familiarity of its presence and form; its population of the everyday urban environment and its temporalities; its links to the popular pleasures (and frustrations) of practices of shopping; and its ties to commodities (as things we live with and use to shape our lives).

This set of analyses complicates the picture of publicity, public address and public space offered by Iveson (2007) and Young (2000). Both discuss cities as key sites for public debate and contest. This is borne out in the examples of political protest outlined above which emphasise how such protest *uses* space but also *creates* space, publics, and rights. Both discuss the importance of public debate. In defining publicity, Young notes the significance of the relationship between citizens within such as space and the form that communications between them takes. But I have suggested there are many other forms of more diffuse 'dialogue' occurring: whether in recursive loops of industry data, practices and spaces, or embodied conversations with cities' rhythms and 'vibe'. Throughout this book I have suggested that as a process that animates, fabulation allows for forms of 'non-standard' communication – between people and spaces, between processes and materialities, between futures and spatialities. Fabulation's engagement with the virtuality of spaces renders legible all manner of connections among histories, people and things. It thus creates forms of awareness and embodied engagement that produces publics as both specifically located (for instance in Manchester or in Detroit) but spatially distributed.

Thus advertising forms one visual, urban vernacular. But as discussed in Chapter 6, the relationalities that compose this vernacular extend far beyond what can be seen. Through fabulation, this vernacular makes senses to us in bodily ways – in ways that are *felt* as real – for its syntax is visceral. As a product of the advertising industry, its address aims to speak to and for 'the people' (imagined as a public of consumers-in-space). But the openness of industry practices and the loose connectivities of its various elements mean that the industry's messages, forms of address and intended outcomes are opened up in unexpected ways. This does more than facilitate a simple resistance, or a tactical subversion of ideologies. It makes an intense, generative field that speaks of, and to, people as publics with interests, rights and conflicting ideas.

A focus on advertising and its formation of a vernacular highlights the commercial and the popular, both areas that conventional political theories of democracy and the public sphere view with suspicion. Certainly, Habermas (1991) was highly critical of what he saw as a turn away from a democratically healthy 'culture-debating' society to a dumbed down 'culture-consuming' society. So the form of public-making and vernacular that advertising and its public address creates is not the kind of publicness that some political theorists might hope for – it is commercial and it is vulgar. But this vernacular is potentially powerful precisely because of its recursive, co-productive relation to commercial practices, and those practices take on a new, intense relationship in the today's capitalism. Many recent analyses have understood contemporary capitalism as performative and adaptive; ideas and practices are processed, reworked and 'act back' upon capitalism in ever-changing ways. Here, capitalism is not a structure but a web of practices in which 'capitalism is "instantiated"' (Thrift 2005: 1). Thrift (2005: 11, 6) describes how in today's 'soft capitalism' knowledge practices such as those of management consultants, the media, and business schools take on a new significance. They become part of the 'cultural circuit' of capitalism:

> This form of capitalism has chiefly been conjured into existence by the discursive apparatus of the cultural circuit of capital which, through the continuous production of propositional and prescriptive knowledge, has the power to make its theories and descriptions of the world come alive in new built form, new machines and new bodies. (Thrift 2005: 11)

This is a capitalism in which knowledge practices fold back on one another, perform connections, and call up formulations that act on the world. It is a capitalism in which there is a constant processes of experiment: it is 'a theoretical enterprise in which various virtual notions...are able to take on flesh as, increasingly, the world is made in these notions' likeness' (Thrift 2005: 6). I have written about these knowledge practices in Chapter 2 as 'commercial experiments' which enact commercial relationships in productive but shifting formations. By framing their research practices and data as 'organic' or full of (commercial) energy, practitioners also perform a kind of enlivening which opens up the commercial futures of their industry in ways they hope to inhabit profitably.

But those practices or capitalism itself should not be considered overwhelmingly powerful or wholly determinant. These commercial experiments also have the unintended effect of opening up possibilities for fabulation – itself an enlivening enactment – and effect the creation of advertising texts, structures and spaces as a vernacular. As potential consumers or target markets, we are not merely experimented upon by the industry's research practices; the possibilities for fabulation that those practices facilitate produce us as experiential and experimental subjects. The commercial knowledge practices of the cultural circuit of capitalism unintentionally offer vernacular knowledge practices to publics. These ways of knowing become woven back into the cultural circuit of capitalism, as I have argued above in relation to industry practices of imagining 'publics'. Of course, commercial practices attempt to tap and profit from these experiential subjects (such as in branding events and 'buzz' marketing). But the ways in which the vernacular has been produced as experimental and adaptive means that it can exceed the grasp of the commercial world. This vernacular can function as a popular knowledge practice that is sensuous, bodily and enlivening. It is not reliant on models of 'reading' the 'textuality' of ads and urban space, nor does it produce standard forms of debate or public dialogue. It encompasses representation (as fabulatory sense-making activity) and political representation of 'publics' (in terms of 'having a voice' and being represented). It is constantly shifting and is not easy to capture.

This vernacular also offers critiques of capitalism and spatial practices that cannot be subsumed by capitalism. It can articulate many concerns and I have outlined how criticism of outdoor advertising over the years has articulated a range of issues such as classed notions of urban aesthetics and gendered notions of value and social order. But the forms of critique that fabulation and advertising's vernacular enable are more diffuse, more visceral, and less easy to counter. They speak of, and back to, capitalism by offering people ways of understanding abstract capitalist processes such as urban dereliction and urban regeneration that I described in Chapter 6. And the recursive ways in which ideas of 'the public' and 'public space' are woven back into commercial and spatial practices means that these active formulations of publics become animated.

This is not to say that capitalism, publics or public space are 'alive'. Capitalism or commercial practices are not *vital* in the sense of having some form of living ontology, nor some underlying structure that replicates itself across time and space. The pair of authors Gibson-Graham (1996, 2006) offer useful cautions against creating understandings of capitalism or markets as naturalised or as having some form of inherent reproductive dynamics (see Cronin 2008a). Rather, I am suggesting that publics, public spaces and commercial practices become animated as they are performed as 'loose', open and generative. They therefore have a range of potentials and futures. This openness should be understood in Bergson's (2004) sense of the 'virtual' rather than the mere 'possible'. That is, the feedback loops of commercial and popular knowledges open publics and public spaces to futures that cannot be easily predicted, nor easily controlled.

This approach does not absolve advertising of criticism, nor does it de-politicise issues around advertising texts, industry practices, or its spatial, urban forms. Rather, this approach broadens the scope of what can be considered political and also opens up the political in vernacular registers. It points to the complexities in the 'commercialisation of public space' and at the same time shows how the commercial 'speaks back' to capitalism. Many academic studies have noted both the power of capitalism and its contingency. David Harvey's (1985) influential account, for instance, explores the influence of capitalism whilst noting that capital's own processes can give rise to forces that can threaten the survival of capitalism itself. My study has discussed this power by analysing the manifold ways in which the commercial practices of the outdoor advertising industry attempt to exploit, redirect and open up the social world to profit. This analysis has not been framed as an examination of capitalist 'structures' or 'institutions', but rather as an exploration of how capitalism is continually performed in practices. These same practices also have the unintended effect of opening up intangible but nevertheless significant forms of urban vernaculars. These may evolve into new shapes and may interface with more organised and openly articulated resistance in ways yet to be conceived.

Notes

1 Introducing commercial spaces

1. See Schivelbusch (1988) for a discussion of lighting in the nineteenth century, and Asendorf (1993), Crary (1993), O'Connor (2000), Rabinbach (1992) and Seltzer (1992) for a contextualisation of the impact of technologies on society in general and visuality in particular.
2. Media owners tend not to call themselves 'advertising agencies'. This term is generally reserved for creative agencies. These generate ideas for campaigns and then execute those ideas, producing the finished advertisement.

2 The industry and the city: knowledge practices as commercial experiments

1. There have, of course, been many studies of place marketing and the marketing of cities to attract tourists and inward investment (e.g. Hall and Hubbard 1998; Kearns and Philo 1993).
2. Advertising Association's Figures. http://www.adassoc.org.uk/aa/index.cfm/adstats/accessed 19/12/09.
3. Director of an advertising agency based in Manchester, UK. Interviewed as part of a pilot study.
4. Director of an advertising agency based in Manchester, UK. Interviewed as part of a pilot study.
5. Why client companies should continue to advertise despite understanding advertising effects as at best indeterminate has been explored elsewhere (Cronin 2004 b, c; Miller 1997).
6. A parallel understanding of this commercial dynamic could be produced by the concept of virtualism developed by Carrier and Miller (1998) and extended by Leyshon, French, Thrift, Crewe and Webb (2005). Rather than merely representing the world, economic abstractions (or theories) contribute to constituting the world. But, they argue, actors' practices must also be considered as they act to constitute such abstractions.
7. Although beyond the scope of this chapter, it is interesting to note how agencies pitch themselves to clients using the notion of the 'energy' of brands (in ways which aim to brand the agency as innovative and skilled in commercial calculation). For instance, a marketing communications agency called Young and Rubicam promotes itself as an expert in identifying and channelling this energy, a form of energy they conceive as having an orientation to the future: 'Some brands are so filled with energy, that they don't just move. They move the market. Brands with energy are surprising and innovative. Constantly reinventing themselves. Setting the standard for their category. They're where consumers are – and they're headed where consumers want to be. At Y&R we invested heavily in understanding this energy phenomenon,

194

using our proprietary BrandAsset® Valuator. And we discovered that Energy™ is a quantifiable value in a brand. Only Y&R can measure it. We know what brands have Energy™. We know how much they have. And why they have it. At Y&R Energy™ is not only what we know. It's what we do. Y&R. We Energise Business'. http://www.yr.com/accessed 3/6/07.

8. On market stabilisation and destabilisation see Slater (2002a).

3 Mobility, market research and commercial aesthetics

1. A slide taken from an industry PowerPoint presentation directed at clients.
2. A slide taken from an industry PowerPoint presentation directed at clients.
3. On experiential marketing, see Moor (2003).
4. A practitioner describes what constitutes a 'media first': 'you tell the press or the media, and they go and take loads of photographs and they write up a thing on it, an exposé, and it's good publicity, not just for us but for the client as well'.
5. A slide taken from an industry PowerPoint presentation directed at clients.
6. See http://www.postar.co.uk
7. A slide taken from an industry PowerPoint presentation directed at clients.

4 The commodity rhythms of urban space

1. In this chapter, material which is openly available on websites is identified by company name. But material collected during my ethnographic work at companies has been anonymised.
2. The issue of temporality has been explored in the literature on advertising in a range of ways, including Raymond Williams's (2003) classic account of advertising's place in televisual 'flow'. Elsewhere, I have analysed temporality in relation to print advertisements (Cronin 2000).
3. http://www.maiden.co.uk (accessed January 2006).
4. http://www.viacom-outdoor.co.uk/UK_Media/interurban.cfm (accessed January 2006).
5. http://www.jcdecaux.co.uk/ (accessed January 2006).
6. The following information is taken from the POSTAR website: http://postar. co.uk/ (accessed January 2006) and from interviews in 2007.
7. http://www.primesight.co.uk/schoolrun.html (accessed January 2006).
8. http://www.clearchannel.co.uk (accessed January 2006).
9. http://www.viacom-outdoor.co.uk/UK_Media/interurban.cfm (accessed January 2006).
10. http://www.maiden.co.uk (accessed January 2006).
11. http://www.maiden.co.uk (accessed January 2006).
12. Other accounts have also placed an emphasis on multiple senses. Even in his paradigmatically visual analysis, *The Image of the City*, Lynch (1960) stressed the need to understand the city through multiple senses. The importance of the sensuous city has been taken up more recently by others such as Degen (2001, 2008), Rodaway (1994), Urry (2000a).
13. Author's own translation.

14. The relationship between distraction (or inattention) and contemplation (or absorption) has a long theoretical pedigree. See Benjamin (1982) and Crary (1993) for discussions in relation to visuality, and Featherstone (1991) for a discussion of the swings between detachment and absorption that are enabled by images in contemporary consumer culture.

15. This challenging of the boundaries of the human body has been taken up more recently by many authors, most notably Haraway (1997) and Latour (1993).

16. Many accounts have argued that advertising should not be seen as a transparent medium, but rather as an active force which impacts upon society in a range of ways. For instance, Raymond Williams (1980: 190) famously called advertising the 'magical system' which works upon social life and people's understandings of themselves in complex ways. Echoing this emphasis on its active role, Leiss, Kline, Jhally and Botterill (2005: 5) maintain that advertising is 'the discourse through and about objects, which bonds together images of persons, products and well-being'. I have elsewhere extended this argument, proposing that advertising's 'mediation' operates on multiple, profound levels, such as its role in performing and maintaining distinctions between objects and humans (Cronin 2004a).

17. I am grateful to Monica Degen for a discussion on this issue.

18. http://www.clearchannel.co.uk/billboards/WhyBillboards/ (accessed January 2006)

19. http://www.maiden.co.uk (accessed January 2006)

20. In fact, the ubiquity of advertising may represent its provisional and tenuous hold on consumers' imaginaries rather than its power. The very fact that advertising requires a constantly re-stated presence and continual innovation may reveal its inefficiencies and its weaknesses as a driving force for consumption.

5 Fabulating commercial spaces: mediation, texts and perception

1. I am grateful to Maureen McNeil for our discussion of this point.

2. Antliff (1999) argues that Bergson's conception of spatiality is not that of empty Euclidean space, but of movement and duration. Real movement, for Bergson, is the transference of a state rather than a thing and thus no entity can change place without changing form.

6 Perceiving urban change in Detroit and Manchester: space, time and the virtual

1. US Census Bureau 2005–2007 figures: http://factfinder.census.gov/ servlet/ACSSAFFFacts?_event=&geo_id=16000US2622000&_geoContex t=01000US|04000US26|16000US2622000&_street=&_county=Detroit&_ cityTown=Detroit&_state=&_zip=&_lang=en&_sse=on&ActiveGeoDiv=&_ useEV=&pctxt=fph&pgsl=160&_submenuId=factsheet_1&ds_name=null&_

ci_nbr=null&qr_name=null&reg=null%3Anull&_keyword=&_industry=
(accessed 15/07/09).
2. US   Census   Bureau   website: http://factfinder.census.gov/servlet/
SAFFPopulation?_event=ChangeGeoContext&geo_id=16000US2622000&_
geoContext=&_street=&_county=Detroit&_cityTown=Detroit&_state=&_
zip=&_lang=en&_sse=on&ActiveGeoDiv=&_useEV=&pctxt=fph&pgsl=010&_
submenuId=population_0&ds_name=null&_ci_nbr=null&qr_
name=null&reg=null%3Anull&_keyword=&_industry= (accessed 15/07/09).
3. US   Census   Bureau   website: http://factfinder.census.gov/servlet/
ACSSAFFFacts?_event=&geo_id=16000US2622000&_geoContext=01
000US|04000US26|16000US2622000&_street=&_county=Detroit&_
cityTown=Detroit&_state=&_zip=&_lang=en&_sse=on&ActiveGeoDiv=&_
useEV=&pctxt=fph&pgsl=160&_submenuId=factsheet_1&ds_name=null&_
ci_nbr=null&qr_name=null&reg=null%3Anull&_keyword=&_industry=
(accessed 15/07/09).
4. Allen-Mills, Tony (2008) 'America's darkest fear: to end up like Detroit', originally published in *The Sunday Times*, 5 October 2008. Reprinted in *The
Times Online*: http://business.timesonline.co.uk/tol/business/economics/art-
icle4881309.ece (accessed 21/7/09).
5. The artist Tyree Guyton's 'Heidelberg Project' is an interesting case in point.
His changing installations in the Detroit streets use a startling array of 'found
objects'. Arens (2001) outlines how Detroit's residents are divided on the significance of this project, some seeing it as art and others as a mass of rubbish
that devalues the neighbourhood. See http://www.heidelberg.org/ (accessed
3/9/09).
6. See the 'DetroitYES Project' created by Lowell Boileau. The website has virtual tours of Detroit's buildings, some of which are still in use, some abandoned, some photographed at the moment of demolition. http://detroityes.
com/home.htm (accessed 20/7/09).
7. US   Census   Bureau   website: http://factfinder.census.gov/servlet/
ADPTable?_bm=y&-geo_id=16000US2622000&-qr_name=ACS_2007_3YR_
G00_DP3YR4&-ds_name=ACS_2007_3YR_G00_&-_lang=en&-
redoLog=false&-_sse=on (accessed 15/07/09).

Bibliography

Adam, B. and C. Groves (2007) *Future Matters: Action, Knowledge, Ethics* (Leiden and Boston: Brill).

Adey, P. (2004) 'Secured and Sorted Mobilities: Examples from the Airport', *Surveillance & Society*, 1(4), 500–519.

Agnew, H. E. (1938) *Outdoor Advertising* (New York and London: McGraw-Hill).

Al-Saji, A. (2007) 'The Temporality of Life: Merleau-Ponty, Bergson, and the Immemorial Past', *The Southern Journal of Philosophy*, XLV, 177–206.

AlSayyad, N. (2006) *Cinematic Urbanism: A History of the Modern from Reel to Real* (New York and London: Routledge).

Alvesson, M. (1994) 'Talking in Organizations: Managing Identity and Impressions in an Advertising Agency', *Organization Studies*, 15(4), 535–563.

Amin, A. (2008) 'Collective Culture and Urban Public Life', *City*, 12(1), 5–24.

Amin, A. (2000) 'Economic Assets' in S. Pile and N. Thrift (eds) *City A–Z* (London and New York: Routledge).

Amin, A. and N. Thrift (eds) (2004) *The Blackwell Cultural Economy Reader* (Malden, MA, Oxford and Carleton: Blackwell).

Amin, A. and N. Thrift (2002) *Cities: Reimagining the Urban* (Cambridge: Polity).

Anderson, B. (1991) *Imagined Communities: Reflections on the Origins and Spread of Nationalism* (London and New York: Verso).

Antliff, M. (1999) 'The Rhythms of Duration: Bergson and the Art of Matisse' in J. Mullarkey (ed.) *The New Bergson* (Manchester and New York: Manchester University Press).

Appadurai, A. (1986) 'Introduction: Commodities and the Politics of Value' in A. Appadurai (ed.) *The Social Life of Things: Commodities in Cultural Perspective* (Cambridge: Cambridge University Press).

Appleyard, D., K. Lynch and J. R. Myer (1966) *The View From the Road* (Cambridge, MA: MIT Press).

Arens, R. (2001) 'The Heidelberg Project' in G. Daskalakis, C. Waldheim and J. Young (eds) *Stalking Detroit* (Barcelona: Actar).

Asendorf, C. (1993) *Batteries of Life: On the History of Things and their Perception in Modernity*, trans. D. Reneau (Berkeley: University of California Press).

Bachelard, G. (1994) *The Poetics of Space*, trans. M. Jolas (Boston, MA: Beacon Press).

Baker, L. E. (2007) 'Public Sites Versus Public Sights: The Progressive Response to Outdoor Advertising and the Commercialization of Public Space', *American Quarterly*, 59(4), 1187–1213.

Barthes, R. (2002) *Œuvres Complètes, Tome III, 1968–1971* (Paris: Éditions du Seuil).

Bauman, Z. (2000) *Liquid Modernity* (Cambridge: Polity Press).

Beck, U., W. Bonss and C. Lau (2003) 'The Theory of Reflexive Modernization: Problematic, Hypotheses and Research Programme', *Theory, Culture and Society*, 20(2), 1–33.

Benjamin, W. (2003) *The Arcades Project*, trans. H. Eiland and K. McLaughlin (Cambridge, MA and London: The Belknap Press of Harvard University).

Benjamin, W. (1982) *Illuminations*, trans. Harry Zohn (London: Fontana/ Collins).

Benjamin, W. (1979) *One Way Street and Other Writings*, trans. E. Jephcott and K. Shorter (London: NLB).

Berg, M. and H. Clifford (1998) 'Commerce and the Commodity: Graphic Display and Selling New Consumer Goods in Eighteenth-century England' in M. North and D. Ormrod (eds) *Art Markets in Europe, 1400–1800* (Aldershot: Ashgate).

Bergson, H. (2006) *The Two Sources of Morality and Religion*, trans. R. A. Audra and C. Brereton (Notre Dame: University of Notre Dame Press).

Bergson, H. (2004) *Matter and Memory*, trans. N. M. Paul and W. S. Palmer (New York: Dover Publications).

Bergson, H. (1962) *Les Deux Sources de la Morale et de la Religion* (Paris: Presses Universitaires de France).

Bernstein, D. (1997) *Advertising Outdoors: Watch This Space!* (London: Phaidon).

Bogart, M. H. (1995) *Artists, Advertising and the Borders of Art* (London and Chicago: University of Chicago Press).

Bondi, L. and D. Rose (2003) 'Constructing Gender, Constructing the Urban: A Review of Anglo-American Feminist Urban Geography', *Gender, Place and Culture*, 10(3), 229–245.

Boorstin, D. (1963) *The Image* (Harmondsworth: Pelican Books).

Borden, I. (2000) 'Hoardings' in N. Thrift and S. Pile (eds) *City A–Z* (London: Routledge).

Bowker, G. C. and S. L. Star (1999) *Sorting Things Out: Classification and its Consequences* (London and Cambridge, MA: MIT Press).

Boyer, M. C. (2001) *The City of Collective Memory: Its Historical Imagery and Architectural Entertainments* (London and Cambridge, MA: MIT Press).

Boyer, M. C. (1996) *Cybercities: Visual Perception in the Age of Electronic Communication* (New York: Princeton Architectural Press).

Brierley, S. (1995) *The Advertising Handbook* (London: Routledge).

Bryson, J. R., P. W. Daniels, N. Henry, J. Pollard (eds) (2000) *Knowledge_Space_ Economy* (London and New York: Routledge).

Bull, M. (2005) 'Automobility and the Power of Sound' in M. Featherstone, N. Thrift and J. Urry (eds) *Automobilities* (London: Sage).

Bullmore, J. (1991) *Behind the Scenes in Advertising* (Henley-on-Thames: NTC Publications Ltd).

Burrows, R. and N. Gane (2006) 'Geodemographics, Software and Class', *Sociology*, 40(5), 793–812.

Callon, M. (ed.) (1998) *The Laws of the Markets* (Oxford: Blackwell).

Callon, M., C. Méadel and V. Rabeharisoa (2002) 'The Economy of Qualities', *Economy and Society*, 31(2), 194–217.

Callon, M. and F. Muniesa (2005) 'Economic Markets as Calculative Devices', *Organization Studies*, 26(8), 1229–1250.

Campbell, H. and R. Marshall (2000) 'Public Involvement and Planning: Looking Beyond the One to the Many', *International Planning Studies*, 5(3), 321–344.

Carrier, J. and D. Miller (eds) (1998) *Virtualism: A New Political Economy* (Oxford: Berg).

Castells, M. (2000) *The Information Age: Economy, Society and Culture, Volume 1: The Rise of the Network Society* (Oxford and Malden, MA: Blackwell).

Castree, N. and T. MacMillan (2004) 'Old News: Representation and Academic Novelty', *Environment and Planning A*, 36(3), 469–480.

Clarke, D. B. (2003) *The Consumer Society and the Postmodern City* (London: Routledge).

Clarke, D. B. (ed.) (1997) *The Cinematic City* (Routledge: London).

Clarke, D. B. and M. G. Bradford (1992) 'Competition between Television Companies for Advertising Revenue in the United Kingdom: the Independent Television Regions Prior to Deregulation', *Environment and Planning A*, 24, 1627–1644.

Clarke, D. B. and M. G. Bradford (1989) 'The Uses of Space by Advertising Agencies within the United Kingdom', *Geografiska Annaler B Human Geography*, 71(3), 139–151.

Cochoy, F. (1998) 'Another Discipline for the Market Economy: Marketing as a Performative Knowledge and Know-how for Capitalism' in M. Callon (ed.) *The Laws of the Markets* (Oxford: Blackwell).

Coquery, N. (2004) 'The Language of Success: Marketing and Distributing Semi-luxury Goods in Eighteenth-century Paris', *Journal of Design History*, 17(1), 71–89.

Crang, M. and P. S. Travlou (2001) 'The City and Topologies of Memory', *Environment and Planning D: Society and Space*, 19(2), 161–177.

Crary, J. (1993) *Techniques of the Observer: On Vision and Modernity in the Nineteenth Century* (Cambridge, MA and London: MIT Press).

Cresswell, T. (2006) *On The Move: Mobility in the Modern Western World* (London and New York: Routledge).

Crilley, D. (1993) 'Architecture as Advertising: Constructing the Image of Development' in G. Kearns and C. Philo (eds) *Selling Places: The City as Cultural Capital, Past and Present* (Oxford: Pergamon Press).

Cronin, A. M. (2008a) 'Gender in the Making of Commercial Worlds: Creativity, Vitalism and the Practices of Marketing', *Feminist Theory*, 9(3), 293–312.

Cronin, A. M. (2008b) 'Calculative Spaces: Cities, Market Relations and the Commercial Vitalism of the Aadvertising Industry', *Environment and Planning A*, 40(11), 2734–2750.

Cronin, A. M. (2004a) *Advertising Myths: The Strange Half-Lives of Images and Commodities* (London and New York: Routledge).

Cronin, A. M. (2004b), 'Currencies of Commercial Exchange: Advertising Agencies and the Promotional Imperative', *Journal of Consumer Culture*, 4(3), 339–360.

Cronin, A. M. (2004c) 'Regimes of Mediation: Advertising Practitioners as Cultural Intermediaries?', *Consumption, Markets and Culture*, 7(4), 349–369.

Cronin, A. M. (2000) *Advertising and Consumer Citizenship: Gender, Images and Rights* (London and New York: Routledge).

Cronin, A. M. and K. Hetherington (eds) (2008) *Consuming the Entrepreneurial City: Image, Memory, Spectacle* (New York: Routledge).

Curry, M. R. (2004) 'The Profiler's Question and the Treacherous Traveler: Narratives of Belonging in Commercial Aviation', *Surveillance & Society*, 1(4), 475–499.

Dant, T. (2005) 'The Driver-car' in M. Featherstone, N. Thrift and J. Urry (eds) *Automobilities* (London: Sage).

De Certeau, M. (1988) *The Practice of Everyday Life*, trans. S. Rendall (Berkeley: University of California Press).

De Koning, A. (2009) 'Gender, Public Space and Social Segregation in Cairo: Of Taxi Drivers, Prostitutes and Professional Women', *Antipode*, 41(3), 533–556.

Degen, M. (2008) *Sensing Cities: Regenerating Public Life in Barcelona and Manchester* (London and New York: Routledge).

Degen, M. (2001) 'Sensed Appearances: Sensing the Performance of Place', *Space and Culture*, 11/12, 52–69.

Degen, M., C. DeSilvey and G. Rose (2008) 'Experiencing Visualities in Designed Urban Environments: Learning From Milton Keynes', *Environment and Planning A*, 40(8), 1901–1920.

Deleuze, G. and F. Guattari (2004) *A Thousand Plateaus: Capitalism and Schizophrenia*, trans. B. Massumi (London: Continuum).

Dery, M. (2006) ' "Always Crashing in the Same Car": a Head-on Collision with the Machinic Phylum' in S. Böhm, C. Jones, C. Land and M. Paterson (eds) *Against Automobility* (Oxford: Blackwell).

Deutsche, R. (1996) *Evictions: Art and Spatial Politics* (Cambridge, MA and London: MIT Press).

Deutsche, R. (1992) 'Art and Public Space: Questions of Democracy', *Social Text*, 33, 34–53.

Dewsbury, J-D. (2003) 'Witnessing Space: "Knowledge Without Contemplation" ', *Environment and Planning A*, 35(11), 1907–1932.

Dicken, P. (2002) 'Global Manchester: from Globaliser to Globalised' in J. Peck and K. Ward (eds) *City of Revolution: Restructuring Manchester* (Manchester and New York: Manchester University Press).

Doel, M. A. and D. B. Clarke (2007) 'Afterimages', *Environment and Planning D: Society and Space*, 25(5), 890–910.

Donald, J. (1999) *Imagining the Modern City* (Minneapolis: University of Minnesota Press).

Dovey, K. (2008) *Framing Places: Mediating Power in Built Form* (London: Routledge).

Draus, P. J. (2009) 'Substance Abuse and Slow-Motion Disasters: The Case of Detroit', *The Sociological Quarterly*, 50(2), 360–382.

Durham, D. and F. Klaits (2002) 'Funerals and the Public Space of Sentiment in Botswana', *Journal of Southern African Studies*, 28(4), 777–795.

Edensor, T. (2005) *Industrial Ruins: Space, Aesthetics and Materiality* (Oxford and New York: Berg).

Edensor, T. (1998) *Tourists at the Taj: Performance and Meaning at a Symbolic Site* (London and New York: Routledge).

Elliott, B. B. (1962) *A History of English Advertising* (London: B. T. Batsford).

Ellis, G. (2004) 'Discourses of Objection: Towards an Understanding of Third-Party Rights in Planning', *Environment and Planning A*, 36(9), 1549–1570.

Elmer, G (2004) *Profiling Machines: Mapping the Personal Information Economy* (London and Cambridge, MA: MIT Press).

Engels, F. (1987 [1845]) *The Conditions of the Working Class in England* (London: Penguin).

Enguix, B. (2009) 'Identities, Sexualities and Commemorations: Pride Parades, Public Space and Sexual Dissidence', *Anthropological Notebooks*, 15(2), 15–33.

Farley, R., S. Danziger, and H. J. Holzer (2000) *Detroit Divided* (New York: Russell Sage Foundation).

Featherstone, M. (1991) *Consumer Culture and Postmodernism* (London: Sage).

Featherstone, M., N. Thrift, J. Urry (eds) (2005) *Automobilities* (London: Sage).

Fernando, N. A. (2007) 'Open-ended Space: Urban Streets in Different Cultural Contexts' in K. A. Franck and Q. Stevens (eds) *Loose Space: Possibility and Diversity in Urban Life* (London and New York: Routledge).

Fletcher, W. (1999) *Advertising Advertising* (London: Profile Books).

Foucault, M. (2000) *The Order of Things: An Archaeology of the Human Sciences* (London and New York: Routledge).

Foucault, M. (1990) *The History of Sexuality: Vol. 1, An Introduction*, trans. R Hurley (London: Penguin).

Franck, K. A. and Q. Stevens (2007) 'Tying Down Loose Space' in K. A. Franck and Q. Stevens (eds) *Loose Space: Possibility and Diversity in Urban Life* (London and New York: Routledge).

Franklin, S., C. Lury and J. Stacey (2000) *Global Nature, Global Culture* (London: Sage).

Fraser, B. (2008) 'Toward a Philosophy of the Urban: Henri Lefebvre's Uncomfortable Application of Bergsonism', *Environment and Planning D: Society and Space*, 26(2), 338–358.

Fraser, M., S. Kember and C. Lury (2005) 'Inventive Life: Approaches to the New Vitalism', *Theory, Culture and Society*, 22(1), 1–14.

Fraser, N. (2007) 'Transnationalizing the Public Sphere: On the Legitimacy and Efficacy of Public Opinion in a Post-Westphalian World', *Theory, Culture and Society*, 24(4), 7–30.

Fraser, W. H. (1981) *The Coming of the Mass Market, 1850–1914* (London: Macmillan).

Gandy, O. H. (1993) *The Panoptic Sort: A Political Economy of Personal Information* (Boulder and Oxford: Westview Press).

Garvey, E. G. (1996) *The Adman in the Parlor: Magazines and the Gendering of Consumer Culture, 1880s to 1910s* (Oxford: Oxford University Press).

Georgakas, D. and M. Surkin (1998) *Detroit: I Do Mind Dying* (London: Redwords).

Gibson-Graham, J. K. (2006) *A Postcapitalist Politics* (London and Minneapolis: University of Minnesota Press).

Gibson-Graham, J. K. (1996) *The End of Capitalism (As We Knew It): A Feminist Critique of Political Economy* (Cambridge, MA and Oxford: Blackwell).

Goffman, E. (1972) *Relations in Public. Micro Studies of the Public Order* (New York: Harper & Row).

Goldman, R. (1992) *Reading Ads Socially* (London and New York: Routledge).

Goldman, R. and S. Papson (2006) 'Capital's Brandscapes', *Journal of Consumer Culture*, 6(3), 327–353.

Goldman, R. and S. Papson (1996) *Sign Wars: The Cluttered Landscape of Advertising* (New York: Guilford Press).

Goss, J. (1995) 'We Know Who You Are and Where You Live': The Instrumental Rationality of Geodemographic Systems', *Economic Geography* 71(2), 171–198.

Gottdiener, M. and A. Ph. Lagopoulos (eds) (1986) *The City and the Sign: An Introduction to Urban Semiotics* (New York: Columbia University Press).

Grabher, G. (2002) 'The Project Ecology of Advertising: Tasks, Talents and Teams, *Regional Studies*, 36(3), 245–262.

Graham, S. and S. Marvin (2001) *Splintering Urbanism: Networked Infrastructures, Technological Mobilities and the Urban Condition* (London and New York: Routledge).

Grosz, E. (2005) *Time Travels: Feminism, Nature, Power* (Durham and London: Duke University Press).

Grosz, E. (2001) *Architecture From the Outside: Essays on Virtual and Real Space* (London and Cambridge, MA: MIT Press).

Grosz, E. (1995) *Space, Time and Perversion: Essays on the Politics of Bodies* (London and New York: Routledge).

Gudis, C. (2004) *Buyways: Billboards, Automobiles, and the American Landscape* (New York and London: Routledge).

Gunter, P. A. Y. (2004) 'Review Essay: New Bergsons', *Continental Philosophy Review*, 37, 263–270.

Gurevitch, L. (2008) *The Cinemas of Transactions* (unpublished PhD thesis, Lancaster University UK).

Haas, S. (2000) 'Visual Discourse and the Metropolis: Mental Models of Cities and the Emergence of Commercial Advertising' in C. Wischermann and E. Shore (eds) *Advertising and the European City: Historical Perspectives* (Aldershot: Ashgate).

Habermas, J. (1991 [1962]) *The Structural Transformation of the Public Sphere: An Inquiry into a Category of Bourgeois Society* (Cambridge, MA: MIT Press).

Hackbarth, D. P., D. Schnopp-Wyatt, D. Katz, J. Williams, B. Silvestri and M. Pfleger (2001) 'Collaborative Research and Action to Control the Geographic Placement of Outdoor Advertising of Alcohol and Tobacco Products in Chicago', *Public Health Reports*, 116 (Nov–Dec), 558–567.

Hackbarth, D. P., B. Silvestri and W. Cosper (1995) 'Tobacco and Alcohol Billboards in 50 Chicago Neighborhoods: Market Segmentation to Sell Dangerous Products to the Poor', *Journal of Public Health Policy*, 16(2), 213–230.

Hackley, C. (2001) *Marketing and Social Construction: Exploring the Rhetorics of Managed Consumption* (London and New York: Routledge).

Hall, T. and P. Hubbard (eds) (1998) *The Entrepreneurial City: Geographies of Politics, Regime and Representation* (Chichester and New York: John Wiley and Sons).

Hannigan, J. (1998) *Fantasy City: Pleasure and Profit in the Postmodern Metropolis* (London: Routledge).

Haraway, D. (1997) *Modest_Witness@Second_Millennium.FemaleMan©_Meets_ OncoMouse™* (London and New York: Routledge).

Harold, C. (2009) 'Pranking Rhetoric: "Culture Jamming" as Media Activism' in J. Turow and M. P. McCallister (eds) *The Advertising and Consumer Culture Reader* (New and London: Routledge).

Hartley, J. (ed.) (2005) *Creative Industries* (Malden, MA and Oxford: Blackwell).

Hartley, J. (1996) *Popular Reality: Journalism, Modernity, Popular Culture* (London and New York: Arnold).

Harvey, D. (2001) *Spaces of Capital: Towards a Critical Geography* (Edinburgh: Edinburgh University Press).

Harvey, D. (1989) 'From Managerialism to Entrepreneurialism: the Transformation in Urban Governance in Late Capitalism', *Geografiska Annaler*, 71B, 3–17.

Harvey, D. (1985) *Consciousness and the Urban Experience* (Oxford: Blackwell).

Heon, L. S., P. Diggs and L. Dorin (1999) 'Thirty Years of Art on the Road: The Billboard Retrospective' in L. S. Heon, P. Diggs and J. Thompson (eds) *Billboard: Art on the Road* (Cambridge, MA: MIT Press).

Henkin, D. M. (1998) *City Reading: Written Words and Public Spaces in Antebellum New York* (New York: Columbia University Press).

Herd, D. and T. Patterson (2002) 'Poor Manchester: Old Problems and New Deals' in J. Peck and K. Ward (eds) *City of Revolution: Restructuring Manchester* (Manchester and New York: Manchester University Press).

Herron, J. (1993) *After Culture: Detroit and the Humiliation of History* (Detroit: Wayne State University Press).

Highmore, B. (2005) *Cityscapes: Cultural Readings in the Material and Symbolic City* (Basingstoke and New York: Palgrave Macmillan).

Holden, A. (2002) 'Bomb Sites: The Politics of Opportunity' in J. Peck and K. Ward (eds) *City of Revolution: Restructuring Manchester* (Manchester and New York: Manchester University Press).

Houssay-Holzschuch, M. and A. Teppo (2009) 'A Mall for All? Race and Public Space in Post-apartheid Cape Town', *Cultural Geographies*, 16(3), 351–379.

Hubbard, P. and K. Lilley (2004) 'Pacemaking the Modern City: the Urban Politics of Speed and Slowness', *Environment and Planning D: Society and Space*, 22(2), 273–294.

Hunt, S. (2009) 'Citizenship's Place: The State's Creation of Public Space and Street Vendors' Culture of Informality in Bogotá, Colombia', *Environment and Planning D*, 27(2), 331–351.

Iveson, K. (2007) *Publics and The City* (Malden, MA, Oxford and Carleton: Blackwell).

Jackson, J. L. Jr (2003) 'Abandoning Advertisements Over *Edificial Ekphrases*', *Journal of Visual Culture*, 2(3), 341–352.

Jacobs, J. (1972 [1961]) *The Death and Life of Great American Cities: The Failure of Town Planning* (Harmondsworth: Penguin).

Jhally, S. (2009) 'Advertising at the Edge of the Apocalypse' in J. Turow and M. P. McAllister (eds) *The Advertising and Consumer Culture Reader* (New York and London: Routledge).

Joyce, P. (2003) *The Rule of Freedom: Liberalism and the Modern City* (London and New York: Verso).

Judd, D. R. and S. S. Fainstein (eds) (1999) *The Tourist City* (New Haven: Yale University Press).

Julier, G. (2005) 'Urban Designscapes and the Production of Aesthetic Consent', *Urban Studies*, 42(5/6), 869–887.

Kayden, J. S. (2000) *Privately Owned Public Space: The New York Experience* (New York: John Wiley and Sons).

Kearns, G. and C. Philo (eds) (1993) *Selling Places: The City as Cultural Capital, Past and Present* (Oxford: Pergamon Press).

Kilian, T. (1998) 'Public and Private, Power and Space' in A. Light and J. M. Smith (eds) *The Production of Public Space* (Lanham, Boulder, New York and Oxford: Rowman and Littlefield).

Klein, N. (2000) *No Logo: Taking Aim at the Brand Bullies* (London: Flamingo).

Klingmann, A. (2007) *Brandscapes: Architecture in the Experience Economy* (Cambridge, MA and London: MIT Press).

Knorr Cetina, K. and U. Bruegger (2002a) 'Global Microstructures: the Virtual Societies of Financial Markets', *The American Journal of Sociology*, 107(4): 905–950.

Knorr Cetina, K. and U. Bruegger (2002b) 'Traders' Engagement with Markets: a Postsocial Relationship', *Theory, Culture and Society*, 19(5/6): 161–185.

Kopytoff, I. (1986) 'The Cultural Biography of Things: Commoditization as Process' in A Appadurai (ed.) *The Social Life of Things: Commodities in Cultural Perspective* (Cambridge: Cambridge University Press).

Kover, A. J. and S. M. Goldberg (1995) 'The Games Copywriters Play: Conflict, Quasi-control, a New Proposal', *Journal of Advertising Research*, 35(4), 52–62.

Kwate, N. O. A. and T. H. Lee (2006) 'Ghettoizing Outdoor Advertising: Disadvantage and Ad Panel Density in Black Neighborhoods', *Journal of Urban Health*, 84(1), 21–31.

Lacey, A. R. (1989) *Bergson* (London and New York: Routledge).

Laird, P. W. (1998) *Advertising Progress: American Business and the Rise of Consumer Marketing* (Baltimore and London: The Johns Hopkins University Press).

Lash, S. (2006) 'Life (Vitalism)', *Theory, Culture and Society*, 23(2–3), 323–349.

Lash, S. and J. Urry (1994) *Economies of Signs and Space* (London and Thousand Oaks, CA: Sage).

Lasn, K. (2000) *Culture Jam* (New York: HarperCollins).

Latham, A. and D. P. McCormack (2004) 'Moving Cities: Rethinking the Materialities of Urban Geographies', *Progress in Human Geography*, 28(6), 701–724.

Latour, B. (1993) *We Have Never Been Modern*, trans. C. Porter (Hemel Hempstead: Prentice Hall/Harvester Wheatsheaf).

Latour, B. and E. Hermant (1998) *Paris, Ville Invisible* (Paris: La Découverte).

Laurier, E. (2005) 'Doing Office Work on the Motorway' in M. Featherstone, N. Thrift and J. Urry (eds) *Automobilities* (London: Sage).

Law, J. (1994) *Organizing Modernity* (Oxford: Blackwell).

Leach, N. (2002) 'Introduction' in N. Leach (ed.) *The Hieroglyphics of Space: Reading and Experiencing the Modern Metropolis* (London and New York: Routledge).

Leach, W. (1996) Introductory essay, in W.R. Taylor (ed.) *Inventing Times Square: Commerce and Culture at the Crossroads of the World* (Baltimore and London: The Johns Hopkins University Press).

Leadbetter, C. (1999) *Living on Thin Air: The New Economy* (London: Penguin).

Lears, J. (1994) *Fables of Abundance: A Cultural History of Advertising in America* (New York: Basic Books).

Lee, N. K. (2009) 'How is a Political Public Space Made? The Birth of Tiananmen Square and the May Fourth Movement', *Political Geography*, 28, 32–43.

Lefebvre, H. (1996) *Writings on Cities*, trans. and edited by E. Kofman and E. Lebas (Oxford: Blackwell).

Lefebvre, H. (1992) *Éléments de Rythmanalyse: Introduction à la Connaissance des Rythmes* (Paris: Syllepse).

Lefebvre, H. (1991) *The Production of Space*, trans. D. Nicholson-Smith (Oxford: Blackwell).

Leiss, W., S. Kline, S. Jhally and J. Botterill (2005) *Social Communication in Advertising: Consumption in the Mediated Marketplace* (New York and London: Routledge).

Leyshon, A., S. French, N. Thrift, L. Crewe and P. Webb (2005) 'Accounting for E-commerce: Abstractions, Virtualism and the Cultural Circuit of Capitalism', *Economy and Society*, 34(3), 428–450.

Liggett, H. (2003) *Urban Encounters* (Minneapolis and London: University of Minnesota Press).

LiPuma, E. and B. Lee (2004) *Financial Derivatives and the Globalization of Risk* (Durham and London: Duke University Press).

Loeb, L. A. (1994) *Consuming Angels: Advertising and Victorian Women* (Oxford: Oxford University Press).

Lorimer, H. (2005) 'Cultural Geography: the Busyness of Being "More-Than-Representational" ', *Progress in Human Geography*, 29(1), 83–94.

Loukaitou-Sideris, A. and R. Ehrenfeucht (2009) *Sidewalks: Conflict and Negotiation Over Public Space* (Cambridge, MA and London: MIT Press).

Lury, C. and A. Warde (1997) 'Investments in the Imaginary Consumer: Conjectures Regarding Power, Knowledge and Advertising' in M. Nava, A. Blake, I. MacRury and B. Richards (eds) *Buy This Book: Studies in Advertising and Consumption* (London: Routledge).

Lyon, D. (2002) 'Surveillance Studies: Understanding Visibility, Mobility and the Phenetic Fix', *Surveillance and Society*, 1(1), 1–7.

Lynch, K. (1972) *What Time is This Place?* (Cambridge, MA and London: MIT Press).

Lynch, K. (1960) *The Image of the City* (Cambridge, MA and London: MIT Press).

MacKenzie, D. (2007) 'The Material Production of Virtuality: Innovation, Cultural Geography and Facticity in Derivatives Markets', *Economy and Society*, 36(3): 355–376.

MacKenzie, D. (2006) *An Engine, Not a Camera: How Financial Models Shape Markets* (Cambridge, MA and London: MIT Press).

MacKenzie, D. and Y. Millo (2003) 'Constructing a Market, Performing Theory: the Historical Sociology of a Financial Derivatives Exchange', *American Journal of Sociology*, 109(1): 107–145.

MacKenzie, D., F. Muniesa and L. Siu (eds) (2007) *Do Economists Make Markets? On the Performativity of Economics* (Princeton, NJ: Princeton University Press).

Marrati, P. (2005) 'Time, Life, Concepts: The Newness of Bergson', *Modern Language Notes,* 120, 1099–1111.

Massey, D. (2005) *For Space* (London: Sage).

Massumi, B. (2002) *Parables for the Virtual* (Durham and London: Duke University Press).

Merleau-Ponty, M. (1962) *Phenomenology of Perception* (London: Routledge).

McCarthy, A. (2001) *Ambient Television: Visual Culture and Public Space* (Durham and London: Duke University Press).

McFall, L. (2000) 'A Mediating Institution?: Using an Historical Study of Advertising Practice to Rethink Culture and Economy', *Cultural Values*, 4(3), 314–338.

McGraw, B. (2007) 'Life in the Ruins of Detroit', *History Workshop Journal*, 63(1): 288–302.

McNeil, M. (2007) *Feminist Cultural Studies of Science and Technology* (London: Routledge).

Mellor, R. (2002) 'Hypocritical City: Cycles of Urban Exclusion' in J. Peck and K. Ward (eds) *City of Revolution: Restructuring Manchester* (Manchester and New York: Manchester University Press).

Miles, M. (2004) *Urban Avant-Gardes: Art, Architecture and Change* (London and New York: Routledge).

Miles, S. and M. Miles (2004) *Consuming Cities* (London: Palgrave Macmillan).

Miller, D. (1997) *Capitalism: An Ethnographic Approach* (Oxford: Berg).

Miller, P. (1994) 'Accounting and Objectivity: the Invention of Calculating Selves and Calculable Spaces' in A. Megill (ed.) *Rethinking Objectivity* (Durham and London: Duke University Press).

Mitchell, D. (2003) *The Right to the City: Social Justice and the Fight for Public Space* (New York and London: The Guilford Press).

Mitchell, O. and M. Greenberg (1991) 'Outdoor Advertising of Addictive Products', *New England Journal of Medicine*, 88(5), 331–333.

Monmonier, M. (2002) *Spying with Maps: Surveillance Technologies and the Future of Privacy* (Chicago and London: University of Chicago Press).

Moor, E. (2003) 'Branded Spaces: The Scope of "New Marketing"', *Journal of Consumer Culture*, 3(1), 39–60.

Mullarkey, J. (2007) 'Life, Movement and the Fabulation of the Event', *Theory, Culture & Society*, 24(6), 53–70.

Mullarkey, J. (1999a) *Bergson and Philosophy* (Notre Dame, Indiana: University of Notre Dame Press).

Mullarkey, J. (1999b) '*La Philosophie Nouvelle*, or Change in Philosophy' in J. Mullarkey (ed.) *The New Bergson* (Manchester and New York: Manchester University Press).

Mullarkey, J. (1994) 'Duplicity in the Flesh: Bergson and Current Philosophy of the Body', *Philosophy Today*, 38(4), 339–355.

Mumford, L. (1945 [1938]) *The Culture of Cities* (London: Secker and Warburg).

Németh, J. (2009) 'Defining a Public: The Management of Privately Owned Public Space', *Urban Studies*, 46(11), 2463–2490.

Nevett, T. R. (1982) *Advertising in Britain: A History* (London: Heinemann).

Nixon, S. (2003) *Advertising Cultures: Gender, Commerce, Creativity* (London: Sage).

O'Connor, E. (2000) *Raw Material: Producing Pathology in Victorian Culture* (Durham and London: Duke University Press).

Odih, P. and D. Knights (2000) 'Just in Time? The Prevalence of Representational Time and Space to Marketing Discourses of Consumer Buyer Behaviour' in J. R. Bryson, P. W. Daniels, N. Henry and J. Pollard (eds) *Knowledge_Space_Economy* (London and New York: Routledge).

Ogilvy, D. (1983) *Ogilvy on Advertising* (London: Pan Books).

Ogilvy, D. (1964) *Confessions of an Advertising Man* (London: Longmans, Green and Co. Ltd.).

Olkowski, D. (2002) 'Flesh to Desire: Merleau-Ponty, Bergson, Deleuze', *Strategies*, 15(1), 11–24.

Osborne, T. and N. Rose (1999) 'Governing Cities: Notes on the Spatialisation of Virtue', *Environment and Planning D: Society and Space*, 17, 737–760.

Park, R. E., E. W. Burgess and R. D. McKenzie (1968 [1925]) *The City* (Chicago and London: University of Chicago Press).

Peck, J. and K. Ward (2002) 'Placing Manchester' in J. Peck and K. Ward (eds) *City of Revolution: Restructuring Manchester* (Manchester and New York: Manchester University Press).

Perec, G. (1999) *Species of Spaces and Other Pieces* (London: Penguin).

Perez, O. and G. Daskalakis (2001) 'Projecting Detroit' in G. Daskalakis, C. Waldheim and J. Young (eds) *Stalking Detroit* (Barcelona: Actar).

Pile, S. (2005) *Real Cities* (London: Sage).

Pope, D. (1983) *The Making of Modern Advertising* (New York: Basic Books).

Quilley, S. (2002) 'Entrepreneurial Turns: Municipal Socialism and After' in J. Peck and K. Ward (eds) *City of Revolution: Restructuring Manchester* (Manchester and New York: Manchester University Press).

Rabinbach, A. (1992) *The Human Motor: Energy, Fatigue, and the Origins of Modernity* (Berkeley: University of California Press).

Rice, C. (2001) 'Images at the Edge of the Built', *Architectural Design*, 71(3), 24–29.

Richards, T. (1990) *The Commodity Culture of Victorian England: Advertising and Spectacle 1851–1914* (London: Verso).

Rivlin, L. G. (2007) 'Found Spaces: Freedom of Choice in Public Life' in K. A. Franck and Q. Stevens (eds) *Loose Space: Possibility and Diversity in Urban Life* (London and New York: Routledge).

Robertson, S. (2007) 'Visions of Urban Mobility: the Westway, London, England', *Cultural Geographies*, 14, 74–91.

Robson, B. (2002) 'Mancunian Ways: Politics of Regeneration' in J. Peck and K. Ward (eds) *City of Revolution: Restructuring Manchester* (Manchester and New York: Manchester University Press).

Rodaway, P. (1994) *Sensuous Geographies: Body, Sense, and Place* (London and New York: Routledge).

Rose, N. (1999) *Powers of Freedom: Reframing Political Thought* (Cambridge: Cambridge University Press).

Rosewarne, L. (2007) 'Pin-ups in Public Space: Sexist Outdoor Advertising as Sexual Harassment', *Women's Studies International Forum*, 30, 313–325.

Sassen, S. (2006) *Cities in a World Economy* (Thousand Oaks, CA and London: Pine Forge Press).

Sassen, S. (2001) *The Global City: New York, London, Tokyo* (Princeton, NJ: Princeton University Press).

Schivelbusch, W. (1988) *Disenchanted Night: The Industrialization of Light in the Nineteenth Century* (Berkeley: University of California Press).

Schivelbusch, W. (1980) *The Railway Journey: Trains and Travel in the 19th Century*, trans. A. Hollo (Oxford: Blackwell).

Schudson, M. (1993) *Advertising, the Uneasy Persuasion: Its Dubious Impact on American Society* (London and New York: Routledge).

Scott, A. J. (2000) *The Cultural Economy of Cities: Essays on the Geography of Image-Producing Industries* (London: Sage).

Scott, K. (2004) 'The Waddesdon Manor Trade Cards: More Than One History', *Journal of Design History*, 17(1), 91–104.

Segal, A. J. (2000) 'Commercial Immanence: the Poster and Urban Territory in Nineteenth-century France' in C. Wischermann and E. Shore (eds) *Advertising and the European City: Historical Perspectives* (Aldershot: Ashgate).

Seltzer, M. (1992) *Bodies and Machines* (London and New York: Routledge).

Senie, H. (1999) 'Disturbances in the Fields of Mammon: Towards a History of Artists' Billboards' in L. S. Heon, P. Diggs and J. Thompson (eds) *Billboard: Art on the Road* (Cambridge, MA: MIT Press).

Sennett, R. (2002 [1974]) *The Fall of Public Man* (London: Penguin).

Sennett R. (1994) *Flesh and Stone: The Body and the City in Western Civilization* (New York and London: W.W. Norton and Company).

Sennett, R. (1992) *The Conscience of the Eye: The Design and Social Life of Cities* (New York and London: W.W. Norton).

Sheller, M. (2005) 'Automotive Emotions: Feeling the Car' in M. Featherstone, N. Thrift and J. Urry (eds) *Automobilities* (London: Sage).

Sheller, M. and J. Urry (2006) 'The New Mobilities Paradigm', *Environment and Planning A*, 38, 207–226.

Sheller, M. and J. Urry (2000) 'The City and the Car', *International Journal of Urban and Regional Research*, 24(4), 737–757.

Shukin, N. (2006) 'The Mimetics of Mobile Capital' in S. Böhm, C. Jones, C. Land and M. Paterson (eds) *Against Automobility* (Oxford: Blackwell).

Simmel, G. (1997 [1903]) 'The Sociology of Space' in D. Frisby and M. Featherstone (eds) *Simmel on Culture* (London: Sage).

Simmel, G. (1995) 'The Metropolis and Mental Life' in P. Kasinitz (ed.) *Metropolis: Centre and Symbol of our Times* (Basingstoke: Macmillan).

Simmel, G. (1991) 'Money in Modern Culture', *Theory, Culture and Society*, 8, 17–31.

Slater, D. (2002a) 'Capturing Markets from the Economists' in P. Du Gay and M. Pryke (eds) *Cultural Economy* (London: Sage).

Slater, D. (2002b) 'From Calculation to Alienation: Disentangling Economic Abstractions', *Economy and Society*, 31(2), 234–249.

Slater, D. (1989) 'Corridors of Power' in J. F. Gubrium and D. Silverman (eds) *The Politics of Field Research: Sociology Beyond Enlightenment* (London: Sage).

Slater, D. and F. Tonkiss (2001) *Market Society: Markets and Modern Social Theory* (Cambridge: Polity).

Smith, A. and T. Fox (2007) 'From "Event-Led" to "Event-Themed" Regeneration: The 2002 Commonwealth Games Legacy Programme', *Urban Studies*, 44(4/5), 1125–1143.

Sperb, J. (2008) 'Islands of Detroit: Affect, Nostalgia and Whiteness', *Culture, Theory and Critique*, 49(2), 183–201.

Steinmetz, G. (2008) 'Harrowed Landscapes: White Ruingazers in Namibia and Detroit and the Cultivation of Memory', *Visual Studies*, 23(3), 211–237.

Steinmetz, G. (2006) 'Drive-by Shooting: Making a Documentary About Detroit', *Michigan Quarterly Review*, 45(3), 491–513.

Stevenson, D. (2003) *Cities and Urban Cultures* (Maidenhead: Open University Press).

Stoker, V. (2003) 'Drawing the Line: Hasidic Jews, Eruvim, and the Public Space of Outremont, Quebec', *History of Religions*, 43(1), 18–49.

Sugrue, T. J. (1996) *The Origins of the Urban Crisis: Race and Inequality in Postwar Detroit* (Princeton, NJ: Princeton University Press).

Thomas, J. M. (1997) *Redevelopment and Race: Planning a Finer City in Postwar Detroit* (Baltimore and London: The Johns Hopkins University Press).

Thompson, H. A. (2001) *Whose Detroit? Politics, Labor, and Race in a Modern American City* (Ithaca and London: Cornell University Press).

Thrift, N. (2008) *Non-Representational Theory: Space, Politics, Affect* (Abingdon and New York: Routledge).

Thrift, N. (2006) 'Space', *Theory, Culture and Society*, 23(2–3), 139–155.

Thrift, N. (2005) *Knowing Capitalism* (London: Sage).

Thrift, N. (2004a) 'Driving in the City', *Theory, Culture and Society*, 21(4–5), 41–59.

Thrift, N. (2004b) 'Movement-space: the Changing Domain of Thinking Resulting From the Development of New Kinds of Spatial Awareness', *Economy and Society*, 33(4), 582–604.

Thrift, N. J. (2000) 'With Child to See Any Strange Thing: Everyday Life in the City' in G. Bridge and S. Watson (eds) *A Companion to the City* (Oxford: Blackwell).

Thrift, N. (1998) 'Virtual Capitalism: the Globalisation of Reflexive Business Knowledge' in J. Carrier and D. Miller (eds) *Virtualism: A New Political Economy* (Oxford: Berg).

Tunstall, J. (1964) *The Advertising Man in London Advertising Agencies* (London: Chapman and Hall Ltd.).

Turner, E. S. (1965) *The Shocking History of Advertising* (Harmondsworth: Penguin).

Urry, J. (2006) 'Inhabiting the Car' in S. Böhm, C. Jones, C. Land and M. Paterson (eds) *Against Automobility* (Oxford: Blackwell).

Urry, J. (2002) *The Tourist Gaze* (London, Thousand Oaks, CA, New Delhi: Sage).

Urry, J. (2000a) 'City life and the senses' in G. Bridge and S. Watson (eds) *A Companion to the City* (Oxford: Blackwell).

Urry, J. (2000b) *Sociology Beyond Societies: Mobilities for the Twenty-First Century* (London and New York: Routledge).

Venturi R., D. Scott Brown and S. Izenour (1972) *Learning From Las Vegas: The Forgotten Symbolism of Architectural Form* (Cambridge, MA and London: MIT Press).

Virilio, P. (1991) *The Lost Dimension*, trans. D. Moshenberg (New York: Semiotext(e)).

Vogel, S. (2005) 'Surviving to Create' in K. Park (ed.) *Urban Ecology: Detroit and Beyond* (Hong Kong: Map Book Publishers).

Weber, M. (1967) *From Max Weber: Essays in Sociology*, trans. and edited by H. H. Gerth and C. Wright Mills (London: Routledge and Kegan Paul).

Warner, M. (2002) *Publics and Counterpublics* (New York: Zone Books).

Wernick, A. (1991) *Promotional Culture: Advertising, Ideology and Symbolic Expression* (London: Sage).

Whatmore, S. (2006) 'Materialist Returns: Practising Cultural Geography in and for a More-Than-Human World', *Cultural Geographies*, 13, 600–609.

Watson, S. (2006) *City Publics: the (Dis)enchantments of Urban Encounters* (London: Routledge).

Williams, R. (2003) *Television* (New York and London: Routledge).

Williams, R. (1980) *Problems in Materialism and Culture* (London: NLB).

Williams, R. J. (2004) *The Anxious City: English Urbanism in the Late Twentieth Century* (London and New York: Routledge).

Williamson, J. (2000 [1978]) *Decoding Advertisements: Ideology and Meaning in Advertising* (London and New York: Marion Boyars).

Wilson, W. H. (1987) 'The Billboard: Bane of the City Beautiful', *Journal of Urban History*, 13(4), 394–425.

Winship, J. (2000) 'Women Outdoors: Advertising, Controversy and Disputing Feminism in the 1990s', *International Journal of Cultural Studies*, 3(1), 27–55.

Wirth, L. (1964) *On Cities and Social Life* (Chicago and London: University of Chicago Press).

Wischermann, C. and E. Shore (eds) (2000) *Advertising and the European City: Historical Perspectives* (Aldershot: Ashgate).

Wodiczko, K. (2000) 'Open Transmission' in A. Read (ed.) *Architecturally Speaking* (London and New York: Routledge).

Young, I. M. (2000) *Inclusion and Democracy* (Oxford and New York: Oxford University Press).

Zukin, S. (1996) 'Space and Symbols in an Age of Decline' in A. D. King (ed.) *Re-Presenting the City: Ethnicity, Capital and Culture in the 21st-Century Metropolis* (Basingstoke: Macmillan).

Zukin, S. (1995) *The Cultures of Cities* (Malden, Oxford and Carleton: Blackwell).

Zukin, S. (1991) *Landscapes of Power: From Detroit to Disney World* (Berkeley: University of California Press).

Index